BEHAVIOR MODIFICATION APPROACHES TO PARENTING

Behavior Modification Approaches to Parenting

Banff International Conference on Behavior Modification, 6th, 1974.

Edited by

ERIC J. MASH, Ph.D.
Associate Professor of Psychology
The University of Calgary, Alberta, Canada

LEE C. HANDY, Ph.D.
Associate Professor of Educational Psychology
The University of Calgary, Alberta, Canada

and

LEO A. HAMERLYNCK, Ed.D.
Coordinator, Mental Health/Mental Retardation
State of Montana, Helena

BRUNNER/MAZEL, *Publishers* • New York

Library of Congress Cataloging in Publication Data

Banff International Conference on Behavior Modification, 6th, 1974.
  Behavior modification.

  Includes bibliographies.
  1. Behavior modification—Congresses. 2. Child psychology—Congresses. 3.
Parent and child—Congresses. I. Mash, Eric J., 1943- II. Handy, Lee C., 1939-
III. Hamerlynck, Leo A., 1929- IV. Title. [DNLM: 1. Behavior therapy—
Congresses. 2. Family therapy—Congresses. 3. Parent-child relations—Con-
gresses. W3 BA203 1974ba / WM420 B215 1974ba]
BF637.B4B34   1974a   618.9'28'915   75-37993

ISBN 0-87630-119-7

Published by BRUNNER/MAZEL, INC.
64 University Place, New York, N. Y. 10003

PREFACE

This is one in a continuing series of publications sponsored by the Banff International Conferences on Behavior Modification. The conferences are held each spring in Banff, Alberta, Canada, and serve the purpose of bringing together outstanding behavioral scientists to discuss and present data related to emergent issues and topics in the field of what is now termed "Behavior Modification." Thus, the International Conferences as a continuing event have served as an expressive "early indicator" of the developing nature and composition of behavioristic science and scientific application.

The papers presented at the Sixth Banff Conference have given rise to two volumes in the area of families and parenting. The first, *Behavior Modification and Families* (edited by Eric J. Mash, Leo A. Hamerlynck, and Lee C. Handy, New York: Brunner/Mazel, 1975), is concerned primarily with theoretical and conceptual developments. The current volume focuses primarily on the applications of behavioral approaches to the area of parenting and provides a number of explicit descriptions of programs for parent training.

Many people have donated their energies and talents to the Conferences. Foremost, certainly, must be the conference participants who develop, present, and discuss the topics found in this volume.

Secondly, it should be gratefully noted that the material support and technical guidance of The University of Calgary's Division of Continuing Education have again been of a typically high order. Ms. Donna Fraser has been the person responsible for making this extraordinary service an everyday occurrence. Continuing a tradition from last year, Dr. David Leighton and the staff of the Banff Centre insured that the physical environment for the conference was enjoyable and facilitative. Dr. W. R. N. Blair again contributed his support and enthusiasm for the concept of the conferences.

Other members of the editorial board and conference planning committee deserve to be singled out for their substantial help and guidance. They are: Dr. Frank Clark, Social Work, The University of Calgary; Dr. Richard Stuart, Psychiatry, and Dr. Park O. Davidson, Psychology, The University of British Columbia.

Finally, we would like to conclude our acknowledgments by thanking our colleagues and conference participants, who guide our efforts by their feedback, and our families, who have continually refreshed our efforts.

ERIC J. MASH
LEE C. HANDY
LEO A. HAMERLYNCK

The University of Calgary, Alberta, Canada

CONTENTS

INTRODUCTION

In the conduct of any therapeutic program of family intervention, there are two distinct yet interrelated sets of issues. The first is concerned with the appropriateness of a particular set of procedures, particularly in relation to a description of the goals towards which they are directed. The second set of issues relates more to the feasibility and efficiency of procedures in achieving behavior change. The papers in this volume are predominantly concerned with the latter—the applicability and efficacy of behavioral change programs within the family system; that is, the development and elaboration of effective programs for bringing about change within the family. For some of the broader conceptual and ethical issues concerning the application of behavior modification approaches to the family, the reader is referred to other sources (Mash et al., 1975; Wood, 1975).

The papers in this collection cover a wide range of applications of behavioral technology for families. They reflect the high level of sophistication which has developed in the modification of family and parenting behaviors, as well as the many persistent problems which still plague behavioral practitioners and researchers working with families. This volume provides a clear description of some of the currently available programs for behavior change in the family, an indication of some newer emergent strategies and procedures, and a statement of areas in which further work is needed.

Almost ten years ago, Bachrach and Quigley (1966), in discussing behavioral treatment approaches, described a life cycle believed to be characteristic of most treatment techniques. This life cycle consisted of successive stages of development, involving an initial period in which *case studies* describing the use of a particular method with certain results appeared with increasing frequency. The increase in case reports was followed by a period in which a particular method was *compared* with other methods in terms of its clinical effectiveness. The next stage examined the long-term results of the intervention efforts, characterized by an increasing number of *follow-up* studies. Finally, there was a reevaluative phase in which the *mode of action* of the method was investigated.

In retrospect, these statements by Bachrach and Quigley appear prophetic in describing the later development of behavioral intervention strategies, generally, and of behavioral programs for parenting, specifically. Initially, behavior modification procedures for parenting were predominantly characterized by simple demonstrations showing that parents, or other agents in the natural family environment (Tharp and Wetzel, 1969), could serve as mediators in bringing about changes in simple, but troublesome, behaviors exhibited by their children (e.g., Williams, 1959). These important case study demonstrations have continued to appear with increasing frequency (e.g., Mathis, 1971; Napolitan and Peterson, 1972) and have shown that a diverse range of parent programs are effective across an increasingly wider range of problems, populations, situations, and systems. A recent and growing area of development has been the demonstration of the effectiveness of parenting programs for "normal" family systems (e.g., Clark and Risley, 1975; Risley et al., 1975), with an emphasis on prevention.

Concomitant with the voluminous number of case reports describing the applicability and effectiveness of parent programs (see Berkowitz and Graziano, 1972; Cone and Sloop, 1973; Johnson and Katz, 1973; O'Dell, 1974, for reviews) there have been an increasing number of studies which reflect later stages of development in the life cycle. Specifically, recent studies have attempted to compare different types of behavioral programs (e.g., Eyberg and Matarazzo, 1975; Kovitz, 1975, see this volume; Mash et al., 1973; Nay, 1975) and behavioral parenting programs with approaches based upon alternative models (Tavormina, 1975).

In addition, there has been an increasing concern with the generality of treatment effectiveness (e.g., Conway and Bucher, 1975) as reflected in follow-up studies (Patterson, 1974a, 1974b) and in studies examining effects on untreated family members (Arnold et al., 1974; Lavigueur et al., 1973) and untreated situations (Johnson et al., 1975). This growing concern is also reflected in the increasing number of studies using multiple outcome measures for evaluating program effectiveness (Eyberg and Johnson, 1974; Patterson, 1974c, 1975; White and Erickson, 1974), in contrast to previous case studies which have employed singular behavioral indices for measuring outcome.

Intermixed with these developments has been a concern for the mode of action of parenting programs reflected in controlled outcome studies (e.g., Mash and Terdal, 1973; Walter and Gilmore, 1973; Wiltz and Patterson, 1974), attempts at systematic replication (Ferber et al., 1974), and studies examining the stimulus controlling properties in family systems as related to behavior change efforts (e.g., Patterson, 1973).

Taken together, the developments described above serve to indicate that behavior modification approaches to parenting, while continuing to rely upon the strength of the single-subject case study design in order to establish the replicability of procedures across a diverse range of problem areas and situations, have also advanced beyond this point. While the development of such behavior modification approaches to parenting has not necessarily been sequential with respect to the comparative, follow-up, and mode-of-action phases described by Bachrach and Quigley, it is apparent that there has been an emerging interest in and concern for the particular problems inherent in each of the stages.

In connection with the papers in this volume, the question arises as to whether or not behavioral applications to parenting represent a unitary approach. Certainly, as shall be discussed, there is much diversity of procedures and conceptualizations represented in this collection of papers and in behavioral parenting programs generally; at the same time, however, there is a fair degree of consistency in an adherence to a more or less equivalent general strategy and underlying set of assumptions. These strategies and assumptions are synonymous with those that characterize behavior modification in general, including a reliance on experimentally established findings in the design of programs and an overriding concern for the development and systematic evaluation of procedures which are objective, replicable, and efficient.

At a descriptive level, behavior modification approaches to parenting have been characterized by heterogeneity of application. First, the range of individuals who have provided behavioral advice to parents has been as great as the number of social systems and agencies which are in one way or another concerned with the family. Practitioners in this area have included psychologists, social workers, nurses, teachers, probation officers, psychiatrists, general medical practitioners, family counselors, pastoral counselors, speech therapists, occupational therapists, physical therapists, relatives, neighbors, and others. It is perhaps a measure of the usefulness of behavioral approaches to parenting that they have received such widespread adoption across such disparate helping professions. At the same time, this widespread use by individuals with a

wide range of backgrounds and interests has probably made it quite
difficult to specify with accuracy the exact nature of many behavioral
parenting programs. This latter point reflects the high likelihood that
behavioral parenting programs have included not only dimensions
specific to behavior modification (Baer et al., 1968), but also the particular idiosyncrasies, information, and language base characteristic of
the particular discipline or population developing and applying the
procedures.

Equally diverse as the range of individuals applying behavioral parenting programs has been the range of people who have served as recipients of such efforts. While perhaps overemphasizing intervention in the
intact family system, programs have been developed for parents of
children exhibiting a wide range of problematic behavior. More recently,
parenting programs have been extended to take into account what
might be characterized as "special" family situations. For example, such
extensions would include programs for single-parent families (Blechman
and Depenbrock, 1975), families in which the child is deaf (see Rossett
and Eachus, this volume), or families in which the parent is blind
(Hunsaker et al., 1974).

Behavioral parenting programs have been carried out in multiple
settings, although a major emphasis has been on the provision of parenting information in the home setting in order to maximize the likelihood
of generalization. However, most parenting programs have involved
some agency contact in which at least part of the training has taken
place outside the home. Typically, such programs also involve home
assignments which permit the parents to practice skills in the natural
environment. These programs have included parent groups (see Tams
and Eyberg, this volume), parent training "labs," the provision of written materials (see Green et al., this volume), and special programs in
which the child is involved in a particular agency or hospital intervention which is supported by contingencies in the home environment (see
Blackmore et al., this volume).

Behavior modification parenting programs have also varied greatly
in terms of the content being presented, the manner in which this content is conveyed, and the context for presenting information. There has
been some agreement regarding what should be taught in a behavioral
parenting program. Usually, the parent is given information about the
contingent use of reinforcement and some of the related ramifications.
Standard behavioral parenting guides such as Becker (1971), Patterson
and Gullion (1968), and Smith and Smith (1964) cover the basic content

areas. However, a persistent problem has been the question of whether parents should be taught specific behavioral intervention skills or general principles and concepts of behavioral analysis. Most programs have attempted to include both in varying proportions, depending on the capabilities of parents involved in the program. This has, however, made it difficult to assess the relative importance of each in contributing to overall change.

Parenting programs have varied with regard to how the content is presented. A range of procedures including didactic presentations, discussion groups, reading materials, reinforced training and practice, modeling and role playing, videotape presentation and playback, etc., have all been employed. In addition, these procedures have been applied in a number of contexts including individual sessions and group training, both involving varying numbers of sessions. Motivational systems which attempt to maintain the behavior of parents in the program have also been used. For example, some programs have required parents to give a money deposit which is returned if the parents comply with the terms of the initial client-therapist contract, e.g., attendance at group meetings. The papers in this volume provide a wide sampling and elaboration of a number of specific contents, procedures, and contexts for behavioral parenting programs.

Foremost among the general points to be considered with respect to these papers is the question of program evaluation. The selection of adequate outcome measures for evaluating program effectiveness has been a persistent problem. Should such measures involve direct observation of targeted behavior, verbal reports concerning these behaviors, or subjective statements regarding whether or not individuals in the program "feel better" following intervention (Mash and Terdal, 1976)? More and more, all of these outcomes are being considered important and this is reflected in the consistent use of multiple outcome measures in almost all the programs presented in this collection.

Another aspect of program evaluation is relative effectiveness when compared with alternate approaches, in terms of the extent of change, program costs, and generalization of effects across time, situations, behaviors, and persons. If behavioral parenting programs are effective, then it will also be important to establish the reasons for their success. At one level, single-subject and control-group studies have established, and are likely to continue to establish, the efficacy of a variety of parenting programs. However, these studies have thus far failed to isolate the specific components of parenting programs which are the salient ingredients in producing change. Almost without exception, parenting programs have involved "a little bit of everything," and as such the information currently available refers only to the effectiveness of a complex set of procedures. Unless the components of such complex programs are examined, behavioral practitioners are in danger of perpetuating a large number of costly procedures which may not be at all necessary for achieving desired outcomes.

Finally, it is crucial that any behavioral parenting program be considered in relation to the broader goals towards which the program is being directed. What are the terminal behaviors that we want to teach? This question has been difficult, but manageable, within the context of programs that serve to reduce behaviors that are clearly deviant or self-destructive. If a child is damaging himself or others, there would likely be a high degree of consensus with respect to the goal of eliminating this behavior, in spite of the fact that there would probably be some disagreement regarding methods. However, as behavioral parenting programs concern themselves more and more with constructive and preventive aims, these issues become even more central and apparent. The papers in this volume point out some of the possibilities for bringing about change. The issues concerning how these programs are to be used and for what purpose are still unresolved.

REFERENCES

ARNOLD, L., LEVINE, A., and PATTERSON, G. R.: Changes in sibling behavior following family intervention. Unpublished manuscript, Oregon Research Institute, Eugene, Ore., 1974.

BACHRACH, A. J. and QUIGLEY, W. A.: Direct methods of treatment. In: I. A. Berg and L. A. Pennington (Eds.), *Introduction to Clinical Psychology*, Third Edition. New York: Ronald Press, 1966.

BAER, D. M., WOLF, M. M., and RISLEY, T. R.: Some current dimensions of applied behavior analysis. *J. Appl. Behav. Anal.*, 1, 91-97, 1968.

BECKER, W. C.: *Parents Are Teachers: A Child Management Program*. Champaign, Ill.: Research Press, 1971.

BERKOWITZ, B. P., and GRAZIANO, A. M.: Training parents as behavior therapists: A review. *Behav. Res. and Ther.*, 10, 297-317, 1972.

BLECHMAN, E. A., and DEPENBROCK, M.: A reward-cost analysis of the single-parent family. In: E. J. Mash, L. A. Hamerlynck, and L. C. Handy (Eds.), *Behavior Modification and Families*. New York: Brunner/Mazel, 1976.

CLARK, H. B., and RISLEY, T. R.: A system of family advice: Experimentally specifying and effectively disseminating normal child rearing procedures. Unpublished manuscript, 1975.

CONE, J. D., and SLOOP, E. W.: Parents as agents of change. In: A. Jacobs and W. Spradlin (Eds.), *The Group as Agent of Change*. New York: Behavior Publications, 1973.

CONWAY, J. B., and BUCHER, B. D.: Transfer and maintenance of behavior change in children: A review and suggestions. In: E. J. Mash, L. A. Hamerlynck, and L. C. Handy (Eds.), *Behavior Modification and Families*. New York: Brunner/Mazel, 1976.

EYBERG, S. M., and JOHNSON, S. M.: Multiple assessment of behavior modification with families: Effects of contingency contracting and order of treated problems. *J. Consult. and Clin. Psychol.*, 42, 594-606, 1974.

EYBERG, S., and MATARAZZO, R. G.: Efficiency in teaching child management skills: Individual parent-child interaction training versus parent group didactic training, Paper presented at the annual meeting of the Western Psychological Association, Sacramento, Cal., 1975.

FERBER, H., KEELEY, S. M., and SHEMBERG, K. M.: Training parents in behavior modification: Outcome of and problems encountered in a program after Patterson's work. *Behav. Ther.*, 5, 415-419, 1974.

HUNSAKER, L., BRANON, S., and STAGGS, B.: Implementation of behavioral management program by blind parents. Paper presented at the annual meeting of the Southeastern Psychological Association, May 1974.

JOHNSON, C. A., and KATZ, R. C.: Using parents as change agents for their children: A review. *J. Child Psychol. and Psychiat.*, 14, 181-200, 1973.

JOHNSON, S. M., BOLSTAD, O. D., and LOBITZ, G. K.: Generalization and contrast phenomena in behavior modification with children. In: E. J. Mash, L. A. Hamerlynck, and L. C. Handy (Eds.), *Behavior Modification and Families*. New York: Brunner/Mazel, 1976.

LAVIGUEUR, H., PETERSON, R. F., SHEESE, J. G., and PETERSON, L. W.: Behavioral treatment in the home: Effects on an untreated sibling and long-term follow-up. *Behav. Ther.*, 4, 431-441, 1973.

MASH, E. J., HAMERLYNCK, L. A., and HANDY, L. C. (Eds.): *Behavior Modification and Families*. New York: Brunner/Mazel, 1976.

MASH, E. J., LAZERE, R., TERDAL, L., and GARNER, A. M.: Modification of mother-child interactions: A modeling approach for groups. *Child Study J.*, 3, 131-143, 1973.

MASH, E. J., and TERDAL, L.: Modification of mother-child interactions: Playing with children. *Mental Retardation*, 11, 44-49, 1973.

MASH, E. J., and TERDAL, L. (Eds.): *Behavior-Therapy Assessment: Diagnosis, Design and Evaluation*. New York: Springer, 1976.

MATHIS, H. I.: Training a "disturbed" boy using the mother as therapist: A case study. *Behav. Ther.*, 2, 233-239, 1971.

NAPOLITAN, J. T., and PETERSON, R. A.: Treatment of a child with multiple stereotypes. Paper presented at the annual meeting of the Association for the Advancement of Behavior Therapy, New York, October 1972.

NAY, W. R.: A systematic comparison of instructional techniques for parents. *Behav. Ther.*, 6, 14-21, 1975.

O'DELL, S.: Training parents in behavior modification: A review. *Psychol. Bull.*, 81, 418-433, 1974.

PATTERSON, G. R.: Changes in status of family members as controlling stimuli: A basis for describing treatment process. In: L. A. Hamerlynck, L. C. Handy, and E. J. Mash (Eds.), *Behavior Change: Methodology, Concepts and Practice*. Champaign, Ill.: Research Press, 1973. Pp. 169-191.

PATTERSON. G. R.: Retraining of aggressive boys by their parents: Review of recent literature and follow-up evaluation. In: F. Lowy (Ed.), Symposium on the seriously disturbed pre-school child. *Canadian Psychiat. Assn. J.*, 19, 142-155, 1974 (a).

PATTERSON, G. R.: Interventions for boys with conduct problems: Multiple settings, treatments, and criteria. *J. Consult. and Clin. Psychol.*, 42, 471-481, 1974 (b).

PATTERSON, G. R.: Multiple evaluations of a parent training program. In: T. Thompson (Ed.), *Proceedings of the First International Symposium on Behavior Modification*. New York: Appleton-Century-Crofts, 1974 (c).

PATTERSON, G. R.: The aggressive child: Victim and architect of a coercive system. In: E. J. Mash, L. A. Hamerlynck, and L. C. Handy (Eds.), *Behavior Modification and Families*. New York: Brunner/Mazel, 1976.

PATTERSON, G. R., and GULLION, M. E.: *Living with Children: New Methods for Parents and Teachers*. Champaign, Ill.: Research Press, 1968.

RISLEY, T. R., CLARK, H. B., and CATALDO, M. F.: Behavioral technology for the normal middle-class family. In: E. J. Mash, L. A. Hamerlynck, and L. C. Handy (Eds.), *Behavior Modification and Families*. New York: Brunner/Mazel, 1976.

SMITH, J. M., and SMITH, D. E. P.: *Child Management: A Program for Parents and Teachers*. Ann Arbor, Mich.: Ann Arbor Publishers, 1964.

TAVORMINA, J. B.: Relative effectiveness of behavioral and reflective group counseling with parents of mentally retarded children. *J. Consult. and Clin. Psychol.*, 43, 22-31, 1975.

THARP, R. G., and WETZEL, R.: *Behavior Modification in the Natural Environment*. New York: Academic Press, 1969.

WALTER, H. I., and GILMORE, S. K.: Placebo versus social learning effects in parent training procedures designed to alter the behavior of aggressive boys. *Behav. Ther.*, 4, 361-377, 1973.

WHITE, G. D., and ERICKSON, M.: Multiple evaluation of a behavior modification parent training program. Unpublished manuscript, U. of Oregon, Eugene, Ore., 1975.

WILLIAMS, C. D.: The elimination of tantrum behavior by extinction procedures. *J. Abnorm. and Soc. Psychol.*, 59, 269, 1959.

WILTZ, N. A., and PATTERSON, G. R.: An evaluation of parent training procedures designed to alter inappropriate aggressive behavior of boys. *Behav. Ther.*, 5, 215-222, 1974.

WOOD, W. S.: *Issues in Evaluating Behavior Modification: Proceedings of the First Drake Conference on Professional Issues in Behavior Analysis, 1974*. Champaign, Ill.: Research Press, 1975.

CONTRIBUTORS

JAMES D. BARNARD
University of Kansas

JOHN BIRKIMER
University of Louisville

MERIHELEN, BLACKMORE
*Jefferson County Mental Health
Center, Colorado*

BARBARA STEPHENS BROCKWAY
University of Wisconsin

JOE H. BROWN
University of Louisville

ROBERT BROWN
University of Louisville

KAREN BUDD
University of Kansas

EDWARD R. CHRISTOPHERSEN
*University of Kansas Medical
Center*

TOD EACHUS
University of Massachusetts

SHEILA EYBERG
*University of Oregon Medical
School*

DENNIS FORD
University of Kansas

A. M. GAMBOA, JR.
University of Louisville

W. DOYLE GENTRY
Duke University Medical Center

BUELL E. GOOCHER
Edgefield Lodge, Oregon

DONALD R. GREEN
University of Kansas

DAVID N. GROVE
Teaching Research, Oregon

MOSES JOHNSON
Notre Dame University

KAREN KOVITZ
University of Calgary

SARAH LANG
University of Kansas

BARCLAY MARTIN
University of North Carolina

PETER D. MCCLEAN
University of British Columbia

WALLACE L. MEALIEA, JR.
University of Florida (Gainesville)

ZETTA MEANS
*Jefferson County Mental Health
Center, Colorado*

MIKE NALLY
*Jefferson County Mental Health
Center, Colorado*

TERRY L. PAULSON
Assertion Training Institute
North Hollywood, California

ELSIE PINKSTON
University of Chicago

NANCY RICH
Jefferson County Mental Health
Center, Colorado

ALLISON ROSSETT
Herbert H. Lehman College
New York

SARA RUDD
Northeast Missouri State
University

MARTIN SHOEMAKER
Assertion Training Institute
North Hollywood, California

DAVID STEWARD
Pacific School of Religion

MARGARET STEWARD
University of California, Davis

VIRGINIA TAMS
University of Nebraska, Lincoln

CRAIG TWENTYMAN
University of Wisconsin

W. WESTON WILLIAMS
University of Wisconsin

MONTROSE M. WOLF
University of Kansas

Section I

PROGRAMS FOR TRAINING PARENTS

1

Training Parents to Modify Problem Child Behaviors

DONALD R. GREEN, KAREN BUDD,
MOSES JOHNSON, SARAH LANG,
ELSIE PINKSTON, and SARA RUDD

Research findings within the area of applied behavior analysis have demonstrated the efficacy of behavior modification procedures for remediating a variety of severe, long-standing behavior problems in children (e.g., Bandura, 1969; Ulrich et al., 1970). Many of these behavior modification studies have relied quite heavily upon the training of persons who are a part of the child's natural environment, e.g., teachers, peers, and parents. The training of parents in systematic behavior management techniques to alter deviant behaviors in their own children has emerged as an active area of interest and an important challenge to behavioral scientists.

In the interest of selecting crucial members of a child's environment for training in behavior modification procedures, parents are an obvious choice because of the great amount of time children spend with their parents in their first few years of life and the cultural role of parents as the main dispensers of reinforcers and punishers for their children (Patterson et al., 1968). A convincing body of research has demonstrated that parents can apply treatment procedures in clinical settings (e.g., Pinkston and Herbert, 1971; Wahler et al., 1965), school classrooms (e.g., Patterson, 1969), and homes (e.g., Christopherson et al., 1972; Hawkins

This research is supported in part by a grant from the U.S. Public Health Service, National Institute of Mental Health (1 RO1 MH20410).

et al., 1966; Herbert and Baer, 1972; Wahler, 1969a; Zeilberger et al., 1968) to modify their own children's behavior problems.

To date, the optimal location for training parents has not been systematically analyzed. In view of the practical consideration of a professional personnel shortage and the scientific concern for experimental analysis, a controlled clinical setting may be the most desirable training base (Reisinger and Ora, 1972). However, several investigators have noted that, because of the very nature of behavior control by environmental consequences, behavior changes in both subjects and treatment agents frequently do not generalize to new settings (e.g., Baer et al., 1968; Kale et al., 1968; Wahler, 1969b; Walker and Buckley, 1972). Therefore, some investigators have suggested that parent training programs should occur in the situation where the problem naturally exists (e.g., Nordquist and Wahler, 1973; Patterson et al., 1967; Peterson, 1967). Little research has been conducted concerning the occurrence or non-occurrence of parents' generalization of treatment application across settings, and few procedures for programming generalization beyond the training site have been tested. Such research is crucial both for determining in which setting (s) parent training should take place and for ensuring that training and remediation will be of enduring value in natural environments.

In one of the few systematic investigations of generalization of parent training procedures across settings, Wagner (1971) reported that four sets of parents generalized their increased use of differential attention for cooperative child behavior and decreased attention to oppositional child behavior from the clinic (where training occurred) to the home (where parent-child interactions were simply observed); cooperative child behavior increased while oppositional responses decreased in both settings.

The parent training project described below constitutes a continuing effort to further evaluate training techniques and to maximize generality and maintenance of training effects across settings, behaviors, and parent-child subjects. This project is a component of an overall research program designed to study a two-environment (home and classroom) modification of problem child behaviors. The aims of the parent training project are:

1. To examine a variety of parent training techniques, beginning with those that could be used with practicality by other professionals and paraprofessionals for training parents in other settings, so as to identify the necessary and/or sufficient conditions for the modification of parent attention to child behavior.

2. To examine the durability of desired changes in parent and child behaviors after effective training techniques are identified.

3. To examine the generality of desired changes in parent and child behaviors from one activity to another (e.g., from a teaching to a play situation), or from one setting to another setting (e.g., from the training lab to the home and/or classroom setting).

4. To evaluate the relative effectiveness of those parent training techniques identified as effective in producing significant, durable, and generalized behaviors.

GENERAL METHODOLOGY

Subjects

The subjects for the project consist of children who exhibit maladaptive behaviors and their parents. Referrals of children to the program have come from local internists, pediatricians, private and university-supported preschools, Head Start, University of Kansas Medical Center, etc. The children selected are those (1) who exhibit a variety of behavioral deficits and/or excesses, (2) who are unacceptable for or have been rejected from other locally available programs (e.g., private preschools, remedial education projects), and (3) whose parents plan to live in this area for at least two years. An effort is made to locate children in the three- to four-year-old age group; however, these children are often not identified until they contact the public school system. Thus, the program typically includes elementary-school and older children. Because the research calls for the intensive treatment and analysis of individual subjects' behaviors, a large N is not required or sought. However, subjects of both sexes are selected to represent a wide range of behavior problems, learning disabilities, physical handicaps, ethnic backgrounds, and socioeconomic levels.

Settings

The parent training studies are typically conducted in two different settings—training lab and home, or training lab and classroom, or home and classroom. In a few cases, studies have been conducted in one setting exclusively. The selection of setting(s) is based upon the nature of the behavior problem, the environment in which the problem is most typically exhibited, convenience of the parents, etc. For example, if a parent has trouble managing the aggressive behaviors of the child at home and other places, then the parent might receive training in both the home and the training lab. On the other hand, if the parent's problems with the child are only observed in the home environment, then parent training is limited to the home.

Basic Data-Collection Techniques

The primary data for the parent training studies are collected by human observers time-sampling in 10-second intervals, according to specified definitions of parent and child behaviors (Cooper et al., 1970). Using this technique, an observer watches parent-child interactions, looking for the occurrence of the defined behaviors under study. The occurrence or nonoccurrence of each type of behavior is recorded once per 10-second interval. Following this procedure, the observer does not need to know when a behavior started or stopped, but only that it occurred or did not occur within the interval. The fact that a score (+ or —) is entered every 10 seconds allows for the calculation of rate-like measures, usually by expressing the number of intervals the subject was observed. Thus, observation spans of somewhat uneven lengths become comparable when the behaviors are expressed as percentages.

The definition of behaviors constitutes an important step in the research. Definitions are phrased in plain English, emphasizing the physical makeup of the behaviors under study. In cases where the physical makeup of the behavior cannot be anticipated, as with compliance-with-instructions, definitions are phrased so as to minimize interpretations. However, the adequacy of a behavioral definition is determined by the interobserver reliability it allows. Using a 10-second interval recording system, two observers' records are compared interval by interval for agreements and disagreements. The total number of agreements is divided by the number of agreements plus disagreements to yield a reliability index of a percent of agreement. Interobserver agreements of 85% or higher are considered acceptable reliability; behavioral definitions yielding such reliability are considered adequate and are used for the parent training research. Formal data collection is not begun until all definitions demonstrate acceptable reliabilities.

Basic Research Designs

The parent training studies rely very heavily upon single-subject research designs. Such designs are particularly suited for the intensive study of behaviors over long spans of time, with a small number of subjects. Typically, the parent training project works intensively with six or seven families at any one time. Single-subject designs stem from the research logic described in Sidman's *Tactics of Scientific Research* (1960). Research over the past 15 years has produced two generic designs of wide usefulness which are used for the purpose of evaluating parent training studies; these are the reversal and the multiple baseline designs. The nature and utility of these designs have been clearly explicated in previous publication (e.g., Baer et al., 1968).

General Procedures

The "typical case" will be used to explain the general procedures employed by the parent training project. When a referral is made (or a parent contacts the project), an initial observation session is arranged. During the first part of this initial contact, the parent (s) meets with a staff member to specify the nature of the problems experienced with managing child problem behaviors. In the case of multiple parent-child problems, the parent (s) ranks problems in terms of severity and concern, with the assistance of the staff person. During the second part of the initial contact (or at a subsequent time), arrangements are made to observe problem parent-child interactions. At this time, at least two observers are present to take observations on the listed problems and the frequency of their occurrence. These observations, together with the parent (s) specifications, are then formulated into behavioral definitions of parent and child behaviors. Subsequently, arrangements are made with the parent (s) to schedule observation sessions four or five times per week for approximately 30 minutes each. During these sessions, formal observations are taken by observers, definitions are referred to, and a behavioral observation-recording system (code) is developed.

Once the definitions and recording procedures demonstrate acceptable reliability, formal data collection is begun. Observers study parent-child interactions in at least two settings, typically beginning with experimental operations in one of these settings only, while inspecting interactions in the second for possible generalization. In addition, at least two classes of parent-child interactions are usually observed in one or both settings, again with procedures limited at first to one class, while the other is checked for possible generalization. The first setting is usually our laboratory, and the second is the child's home; similarly, the first behavior class is either a work session in which the parent attempts to teach the child some useful skills, or a play session in which the two interact freely and with little structure. More recently, some studies have examined adult-child interaction in a classroom setting and the home, while others were conducted exclusively in the home. The parent training studies to be presented below will provide specific details of methodology regarding definitions, observations, settings, etc.

STUDY I

TRAINING VIA INSTRUCTIONS

Subjects

The subjects for this study consisted of a mother and her four-year-old son. The mother expressed concern over her inability to manage a number of disturbing problems with her son. The child's behavior problems included tantrums, aggression, opposition, destructiveness, cursing, playing with matches, attacking the dog, stealing, sleepwalking, and urinating on his older brother. The family had been involved in two previous child and/or family therapy programs. In addition, the family pediatrician had prescribed Thorazine to decrease the child's "hyperactive" behavior. The mother exhibited a high rate of undifferentiated attention to the child's behaviors. She was highly inconsistent across time, failed to praise the few desirable child behaviors, and relied very heavily on such means as threatening, scolding, and nagging.

Method

This study was conducted in two settings—the parent training lab and the family's home. Sessions were conducted four days per week, with each session lasting approximately 30 minutes. Home sessions were conducted immediately following lab sessions. The lab setting consisted of a small workroom in which the mother and child worked together on tasks such as puzzles, geometric insets, and number and shape sorters. In the home setting, the child and parent were not restricted in movement or activity (the barring of TV watching during observations being the only exception).

Using the 10-second recording system, observers defined a class of child behaviors for measurement. Deviant behaviors consisted of any negative verbal and/or physical response that opposed parental requirements, such as aggression, tantrums, cursing, and spitting at his mother. Parent attention to child behaviors was also measured; it consisted of any physical and/or verbal action by the parent that occurred simultaneously with or immediately following the child's behaviors.

To evaluate the effectiveness of the training procedure, a multiple baseline across settings (lab versus home) was used. The training procedure consisted of providing the mother with a set of explicit written and verbal instructions on how to implement a "time-out" technique for deviant child behaviors. For example, the mother was instructed to firmly and immediately take the child to a time-out room whenever he emitted one of the defined deviant behaviors.

Results

Several reliabilities were taken throughout the study, with at least one determination in each condition. The mean reliability for deviant child behaviors was 89%, while the reliability for parent attention to child behavior was 85%.

Figure 1 shows the mean occurrence of behaviors for the child and parent before training, during training, and during follow-up observations.

Before training, the child's deviant behaviors averaged 27% of the total 10-second intervals observed, with the mother attending 21% of the total intervals. During training, deviant child behaviors and parent attention to them declined to 4% and 2%, respectively. Follow-up observation, taken in the training lab 139 days after the termination, revealed that the child's deviant behaviors occurred only 2% of the time, with the parent attending only 1% of the intervals. The bottom half of Figure 1 shows that similar results were obtained in the home setting.

STUDY II

TRAINING VIA INSTRUCTIONS AND CUES

Subjects

The subjects for this study consisted of a five-year-old girl and her mother. The mother reported concerns about the extreme difficulty she had in getting her daughter to "mind," and her daughter's delayed speech and language development, frequent tantrums, aggression, and hyperactivity. The mother's behaviors were similar to those described in Study I.

Method

This study was conducted exclusively in the parent training lab, in the same room as in Study I, and using materials similar to those de-

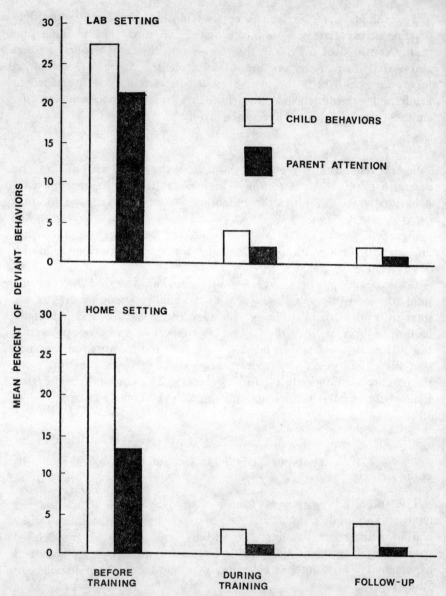

FIGURE 1. Mean percent of deviant child behaviors and parent attention to these behaviors in the lab and home settings before training, during training and at follow-up observations.

scribed there. Sessions were conducted four days per week, with each lasting approximately 25 minutes.

In this study, two classes of child behaviors and parent attention to each were defined for measurement, using the previously described 10-second interval recording system. Inappropriate child behavior was defined as an action, such as leaving the room, lying down, throwing task materials, scooting the chair more than an arm's length from the table, and pounding on materials, that interfered with the execution and/or completion of a designated response or task. Deviant child behaviors included any behaviors that were in opposition to parental requirements, such as refusing to comply with instructions, aggression, tantrums, and self-stimulation. Parent attention to these classes of child behaviors consisted of any physical and/or verbal parent behavior that occurred simultaneously with or immediately following the child's behavior, such as hugging, kissing, and saying "good" or "stop that."

The experimental design for this study was the multiple baseline across two behaviors with the same subjects and in the same setting. The steps in the parent training consisted of (1) providing the mother with written-verbal instructions on when and how to ignore deviant behaviors, (2) instructions on when and how to time-out deviant behavior, (3) an auditory cue that signaled when to time-out deviant behaviors, and (4) instructions to time-out inappropriate behaviors.

Results

Figure 2 presents the results of this study for both child behaviors and parent attention to child behaviors. Baseline measures before training indicate that the child displayed deviant behaviors an average of 9% of the time, with the mother attending 8% of the observed time. During the ignore deviant condition, child behaviors averaged 8%, with the mother reducing her attention to 3%. When the mother was instructed to use time-out and then subsequently given cues to apply time-outs, child deviant behaviors decreased to a mean of 1%, and parent attention also averaged 1%. When the parent was instructed to apply time-out for inappropriate behavior, child behaviors decreased from an average of 24% before training to 6% during treatment, with parent attention correspondingly dropping from a mean of 16% to 5% (see the bottom graph of Figure 2). Follow-up observations taken six months after the study revealed that both deviant and inappropriate behaviors occurred at a frequency of less than 1%.

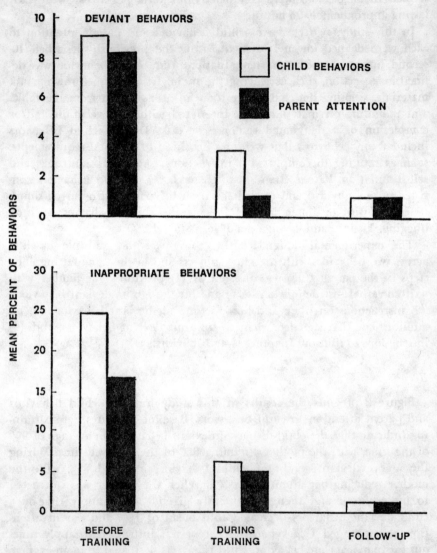

FIGURE 2. Mean percent deviant and inappropriate child behaviors and parent attention to these behaviors before training, during training and at follow-up.

STUDY III

MODELING AS A PARENT TRAINING TECHNIQUE

Subjects

The subjects for this study consisted of both parents and their five-year-old daughter. The child exhibited a variety of hyperactive and bizarre behaviors, in addition to general verbal and motor retardation. The parents were very concerned about her academic and social development.

Method

Both parents worked with their child in the training lab. The setting and data observation procedures were the same as described in the previous studies. Both parents worked with their daughter on pre-academic tasks that included lotto, shape sorters, color-matching, and number sorters. The child worked with each parent separately in approximately 20-minute sessions, four days per week.

For both mother-child and father-child dyads, two classes of behaviors were specified for study. Inappropriate child behaviors consisted of any behavior related to the misuse of task materials or actions incompatible with performing the designated task while sitting. Deviant child behaviors consisted of such behaviors as attacks on the parent, gross disruptive acts, and throwing materials. Observations of parent attention to child behaviors were also recorded. The multiple baseline design was used to evaluate the effectiveness of modeling as a parent training technique. For each parent-child dyad, a multiple baseline design was employed across deviant and inappropriate child behaviors.

Both parents in this study were trained to control deviant and inappropriate child behaviors by observing a person modeling expected parent behaviors. The experimenter modeled a treatment package for each parent separately, using the parents' own child, while the parent observed from a sound-equipped observation room. The treatment package included modeling (1) how to praise and give food reinforcers for appropriate behaviors, (2) how to ignore deviant and/or inappropriate behavior, depending upon which behavior was currently under treatment, and (3) how to implement a 3-minute time-out for deviant and/or inappropriate behaviors. Each parent watched the experimenter model the treatment for three or four consecutive sessions.

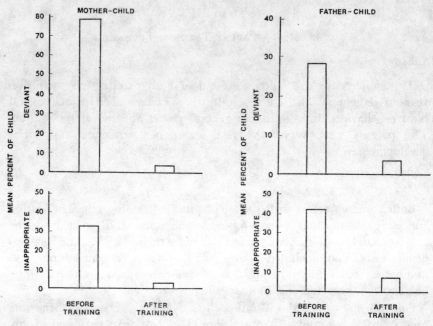

FIGURE 3. Mean percent deviant and inappropriate child behaviors with the mother and the father before and after training.

Results

Figure 3 shows deviant and inappropriate child behaviors with the mother as a percentage of total 10-second intervals, before and after modeling. Before modeling, child deviant behaviors with the mother averaged 78% and inappropriate behaviors averaged 32%. After the mother observed the model and resumed working with her child, deviant behaviors averaged 3% and inappropriate behaviors averaged 3%. The graphs on the right side of Figure 3 depict deviant and inappropriate child behaviors exhibited with the father. It can be seen that before the modeling training sessions for the father, deviant behavior averaged 27% and inappropriate behavior averaged 42%. After modeling sessions for the father, deviant and inappropriate behaviors were maintained at 8% and 7%, respectively.

DISCUSSION

The studies described above provided examples of three techniques that have been used to train parents to modify problem child behavior—

written and verbal instructions, instructions and cues, and modeling. All three techniques were found to be effective in changing both parent and child behaviors.

After comparing the three techniques on the basis of the amount of professional time involved, the written-verbal instructions, as used in Study I, would appear to be the recommended training technique. This procedure simply requires the trainer to write a set of instructions detailing for the parent what behavior (s) to look for and what consequences to provide following the behavior (s). In spite of its apparent simplicity, however, giving instructions alone has been found to be an unreliable parent training technique. This observation has been made in at least three other studies conducted in the project. Perhaps the success observed in Study I is attributable to the fact that the mother, who was a professional nurse, probably had a long history of being under written and verbal instructional control. Thus, one needs to consider the history of the parent in deciding among various parent training techniques. This is a point worthy of future investigation. The contrasting findings (Study I versus II), in terms of the necessary training procedures (cues versus no cues), of these two parent-child pairs are currently leading us to an examination of some of the variables that would appear to control parents' receptivity to instructions. Determining these variables would certainly be valuable in making reasonable judgments about which training methods are most functional for different parents.

In Study II, written and verbal instructions alone did not initially prove to be effective. Thus, instructions had to be supplemented by cueing the mother to indicate when and how to behave. Once cues were added, the mother increased her efficiency in applying time-out. Moreover, it was observed that once the mother had been trained to time-out deviant child behavior (using cues), she was able to treat a new class of inappropriate behavior without being cued. The mother was simply instructed to apply the time-out procedure to inappropriate behavior, and she did with success. Apparently, for this mother, the cues served an important teaching-learning function. This learning probably occurred by way of a negative reinforcing process; the mother frequently hurried to implement the time-out before the experimenter delivered the cue—perhaps a type of avoidance or escape response.

In terms of professional time, cueing is perhaps the most expensive training technique. This technique requires that a staff person be present in the training session for the purpose of watching for specified behavior and providing auditory or visual cues to the parent. Clearly, if there is a choice between cueing and other equally effective training techniques, it is advisable to avoid cueing.

The third study investigated modeling as a technique for training a mother and father to remediate the deviant and inappropriate behaviors in their child. This technique appears to be a training procedure that produces very rapid and dramatic changes in both parent and child behaviors. However, this study did not provide conclusive evidence to indicate whether the improvement in child behaviors was due to the effect the model had on the child, improved parent behavior after observing the model, or a combination of both possible influences. A study currently in progress was designed to investigate whether the experimenter-applied treatment implicit in modeling for the mother will result in remediation of problem child behaviors in the mother's presence, independent of her later imitation of that treatment procedure. To test this possibility, the experimenter implemented the treatment procedures, in the mother's absence, in a multiple baseline design across the two target child behaviors. The sessions with the experimenter were conducted on the same days as sessions with the mother, before the experimenter modeled the treatment procedures for the mother. Our initial findings indicate that, when the experimenter applied the treatment procedures for out-of-seat behavior in the mother's absence, the overall percentage of out-of-seat behavior in sessions with the mother decreased to some extent from the prior baseline level; however, the rate of this behavior remained much higher than was desirable. This study, with additional data, should provide clear indications of the respective roles that models and parents play in observed improvements in child behaviors.

In addition, our experience with modeling as a training technique suggests that there are probably several other parameters of modeling that need further investigation. Our studies, so far, have used the parent's own child to model treatment procedures. There are reasons to believe that the use of a different child with similar behavior problems might lead to increased efficiency with which a parent will imitate and practice a modeled treatment procedure. First, the parent would avoid the social embarrassment associated with watching her (or his) own child misbehave with another adult. Second, without these obvious social concerns, a parent would probably focus greater attention on the details of the treatment procedure being modeled. Some of our future studies will be designed to investigate these dimensions of modeling.

REFERENCES

BAER, D. M., WOLF, M. M., and RISLEY, T. R.: Some current dimensions of applied behavior analysis. *J. Appl. Behav. Anal.*, 1, 91-97, 1968.

BANDURA, A.: *Principles of Behavior Modification.* New York: Holt, Rinehart and Winston, 1969.

CHRISTOPHERSON, E. R., ARNOLD, C. M., HILL, D. W., and QUILITCH, H. R.: The home point system: Token reinforcement procedures for application by parents of children with behavior problems. *J. Appl. Behav. Anal.*, 5, 485-497, 1972.

COOPER, M. L., THOMPSON, C. L., and BAER, D. M.: The experimental modification of teacher attending behavior. *J. Appl. Behav. Anal.*, 3, 153-157, 1970.

HAWKINS, R. P., PETERSON, R. F., SCHWEID, E. I., and BIJOU, S. W.: Behavior therapy in the home: Amelioration of problem parent-child relations with the parent in a therapeutic role. *J. Exper. Child. Psychol.*, 4, 99-107, 1966.

HERBERT, E. W., and BAER, D. M.: Training parents as behavior modifiers: Self-recording of contingent attention. *J. Appl. Behav. Anal.*, 5, 139-149, 1972.

KALE, R. J., KAYE, J. H., WHELAN, P. A., and HOPKINS, B. L.: The effects of reinforcement on the modification, maintenance, and generalization of social responses of mental patients. *J. Appl. Behav. Anal.*, 1, 307-314, 1968.

NORDQUIST, V. M., and WAHLER, R. G.: Naturalistic treatment of an autistic child. *J. Appl. Behav. Anal.*, 6, 79-87, 1973.

PATTERSON, G. R.: Teaching parents to be behavior modifiers in the classroom. In: J. D. Kromboltz and C. E. Thoresen (Eds.), *Behavioral Counseling: Case and Techniques.* New York: Holt, Rinehart and Winston, 1969. Pp. 155-161.

PATTERSON, G. R., McNEAL, S., HAWKINS, N., and PHELPS, R.: Reprogramming the social environment. *J. Child Psychol. and Psychiat.*, 8, 181-195, 1967.

PATTERSON, G. R., RAY, R. F., and SHAW, B. A.: Direct intervention in families of deviant children. Oregon Research Institute Bull., 8, 1968.

PETERSON, R. F.: Expanding the behavior laboratory: From clinic to home. Paper presented in a symposium on The Application of Behavior Modification Techniques in Expanding Behavioral Laboratories, at the 75th Annual Convention of the American Psychological Association, Washington, D. C., September 1967.

PINKSTON, E. M., and HERBERT, E. W.: Modification of irrelevant and bizarre verbal behavior using mother as therapist. Paper presented at the 79th Annual Convention of the American Psychological Association, Washington, D. C., September 1971.

REISINGER, J. J., and ORA, J. P.: Parents as change agents for their children: A review. Unpublished manuscript, George Peabody College, 1972.

SIDMAN, M.: *Tactics of Scientific Research: Evaluating Experimental Data in Psychology.* New York: Basic Books, 1960.

ULRICH, R., STACHNIK, T., and MABRY, J.: *Control of Human Behavior: From Cure to Prevention,* Vol. 2. Glenview, Ill.: Scott, Foresman, 1970.

WAGNER, L. I.: Generalization of parents' behavior from the clinic to the home during oppositional child training. Unpublished manuscript, George Peabody College, 1971.

WAHLER, R. G.: Oppositional children: A quest for parental reinforcement control. *J. Appl. Behav. Anal.*, 2, 159-170, 1969. (a)

WAHLER, R. G.: Setting generality: Some specific and general effects of child behavior therapy. *J. Appl. Behav. Anal.*, 2, 239-246, 1969. (b)

WAHLER, R. G., WINKEL, G. H., PETERSON. R. F., and MORRISON, D. C.: Mothers as behavior therapists for their own children. *Behav. Res. and Ther.*, 3, 113-124, 1965.

WALKER, H. M., and BUCKLEY, N. K.: Programming generalization and maintenance of treatment effects across time and across settings. *J. Appl. Behav. Anal.*, 5, 209-224, 1972.

ZEILBERGER, J., SAMPEN, S. E., and SLOANE, H. N., JR.: Modification of a child's problem behaviors in the home with a mother as therapist. *J. Appl. Behav. Anal.*, 1, 47-53, 1968.

2

Training in Child Management: A Prevention-Oriented Model

BARBARA STEPHENS BROCKWAY

and

W. WESTON WILLIAMS

Training parents in the use of behavior modification techniques has generally focused on procedures which achieve positive outcomes with specific current problems of children, e.g., aggression, temper tantrums, social withdrawal (Wahler, 1969; Bernal et al., 1968; Gardner et al., 1968; Zeilberger et al., 1968; Russo, 1964; Wolf et al., 1964; Hall et al., 1972; Johnson and Brown, 1969). Typically, parents are taught specific behavior management techniques (e.g., ignoring, praising, consistency) and more general programs for a presenting behavior problem. The programs are usually both designed by and implemented under the close supervision of professionals (Patterson et al., 1973).

An underlying assumption of the programs appears to be that parents who know management principles and have had some successful practice modifying behaviors such as temper tantrums will, without professional supervision, be able to design an effective program to modify future troublesome behaviors with different topographies, e.g., social withdrawal. However, there is a paucity of data to support this assumption. Little attention has been given to teaching parents to utilize behavior management principles to effectively design and implement behavior management programs for a wide range of current and potential behavior management problems. Training of this kind would constitute a prevention-oriented model and would stress training parents to respond effectively to a variety of child management problems, whether or not they have already occurred. The model would not focus

19

on a particular population of children nor specific behavior management problems, but on general behavior programs and behavior management strategies. Through such a model, the parents would become adept at managing specific presenting behavior problems and learn strategies that would enable them to respond effectively to potential problems.

COMPONENTS OF A PREVENTION-ORIENTED MODEL

A prevention-oriented training model should consist of a series of behavioral strategies (i.e., systematic approaches to problem solving) in at least four areas—problem detection, program design, program implementation, and program evaluation. These are common steps in any behavioral treatment. However, as applied in a prevention-oriented model, the "problem" is a much broader range of behavior and the "program" is therefore necessarily more complex. A prevention-oriented model should incorporate training in a variety of responses which, taken together, define the range of skills necessary to modify problematic behavior of the *class* the training was designed to prevent. For example, a prevention-oriented model of assertive training might incorporate training in verbalizing positive affective statements ("I like the way you did that." "I love you."), negative affective statements ("I don't like the way you did that." "I dislike it when you . . ."), suggestion-giving responses ("In my opinion . . ."), and refusal responses ("I don't have time to serve on the committee."). In other words, training would focus on the range of responses commonly placed under the label "assertive." The model would also assess and teach those responses across different situations (in school, at home, on the job) and across different human environments (peers, authority figures, friends, enemies). Providing the trainee with strategies to function well in *any* potential assertive situation would define the model as prevention-oriented.

The same holds true for a parent training model in which the behavioral skills are in the area of child management. Parents learn strategies for the management of three-year-olds, but they also learn what to do when the three-year-olds grow into their teens. The training model described here incorporates specific strategies in each of the four prerequisite areas necessary for the prevention-oriented model:

1. *Problem Detection.* Trainees learn strategies which include such skills as analyzing the environment functionally, recognizing potentially inappropriate behaviors, and defining behaviors operationally.

2. *Program Design.* Trainees learn procedures for monitoring and measuring behavior, and learn to match treatment with problems (e.g., when and when not to use a response cost system or a time-out).

3. *Program Implementation.* Training focuses on the skills needed to teach behavior effectively, e.g., limit-setting, consistency, shaping. The skills are taught to all family members to facilitate generalization and maintenance of change.

4. *Program Evaluation.* Objective evaluation which measures change in all child management skills across time and environments is an integral part of the model. Trainees learn to make program changes based upon such evaluations.

PURPOSE

The following study was conducted as a pilot to facilitate the refinement and articulation of a prevention-oriented parenting training model which could be implemented on a broader scale. One family with several intense behavioral problems was arbitrarily selected as the pilot family. Criteria for selection of the pilot family were not important at this stage. It was felt that further investigations would have to be conducted across a range of families if the pilot proved successful. A variety of training devices have been used in parent training; these include: bug-in-the-ear (Welsh, 1966), programmed texts (Patterson et al., 1967), modeling and role play plus feedback (Patterson and Brodsky, 1966; Rose, 1969), and videotape (Bernal, 1969). The model under study incorporated many of these training tactics. Through didactic instruction, role playing, behavior rehearsal, videotapes, printed handouts, written and verbal exercises, and weekly quizzes, the model was planned to teach the family specific behavior management and program implementation tactics, plus systematic approaches to problem solving. The specific behavior management and program implementation tactics included: verbal reinforcement, physical reinforcement, limit-setting, consistency, time-out, ignoring, repeat to success, stop-the-world, extended isolation, shaping, modeling, behavior rehearsal, cueing, graphing, operationally defining behavior, data analysis, and program evaluation.

The purpose of the study was to teach the family to utilize the behavior management tactics and problem-solving strategies on selected presenting behavior problems in a supervised situation, and then to assess their ability to utilize them on different behavior problems while unsupervised. The unsupervised condition was intended to be a measure of whether or not the family had learned how to implement behavior management programs for potential behavior problems. In other words, it assessed whether they had merely learned a *tactic* to manage a specific behavior or had learned a *strategy* which was potentially useful across behavior problems.

A CASE STUDY

Procedure

Subjects. The family selected for training had participated in a variety of therapeutic interventions for over one year at a midwestern state institution for emotionally disturbed children. The family's eight-year-old son Ted has been a residential patient, but at the time of this study was in a day care program at the institution. A year of traditional therapy with the parents, which included suggestions for and advice on child management, as well as a highly structured school program, had produced some improvement in Ted's school behavior, but no improvement at home. Ted's problem behaviors included high frequency fidgeting, a short attention span, noncompliance, making "funny" noises at inappropriate times, "darting," temper tantrums, bossiness, touching and breaking other people's possessions, cluttering the house, and performing dangerous acts (e.g., turning the boiler up to capacity, pouring gasoline over himself). Compared to those in his peer group, he exhibited poor gross and fine motor skills, as well as poor social skills. Academically he averaged first-grade work and scored a full scale I.Q. of 94 (WISC). There were a total of six family members: mother, father, two brothers— George, age 16, Joe, age 13—and a sister Geri, age 19. Because of work commitments, Geri did not participate in formal training and father attended irregularly.

Pre-treatment Assessment. Three different procedures were used to assess the parents' child management skills and to identify the stimuli controlling Ted's problem behaviors:

a. *Home Observation.* A series of three two-hour home visits were made by experienced child care workers and professional trainees. Observation techniques were modifications of those used by Patterson et al. (1973). An analysis was made of the family's interaction patterns, e.g., type of reinforcement used, method of teaching discipline, affection giving and receiving, antecedent and consequent conditions of inappropriate behaviors.

b. *Activity Videotape.* A one-hour videotape was made of the family's interactions during a semistructured situation, viz., playing a game like Chutes and Ladders. Ted's behavior was analyzed with different combinations of family members (mother alone, mother and brothers, brothers alone). The mother's child management skills were also analyzed. The tapes were shown to the family to facilitate defining Ted's inappropriate behaviors.

c. *Child Management Skill Level.* Mother's responses to five role-played child management problem situations were videotaped. Treatment staff took the part of children, and mother was asked to "handle the situations the best way you can." Some of Ted's problem behaviors were incorporated into the role-played vignettes, as well as other behavior which might occur in the family, e.g., sibling fights over which TV program to watch. Inappropriate management practices, e.g., repeated prodding to perform tasks, were noted by staff and given special emphasis during training. These vignettes served as pre-data for an assessment of the "quality" of child management skill. Post-data were taken and evaluated following training. The same treatment staff and situations were used in the post-tape, allowing pre- and post-tapes to be paired for comparison.

Treatment

Family Training. A series of ten two-hour training sessions were held at the institution. Each session, co-led by three staff members, followed the same format—didactic instruction, written exercises, role play, behavior rehearsal, and test and program evaluation (Brockway, 1974). The following principles and procedures were taught and evaluated: positive and negative reinforcement; punishment; defining, counting, and graphing behavior; techniques of delivering social praise; how to ignore, set limits, and be consistent; shaping; behavior rehearsal; and token economy. Segments of the activity videotape were shown to the family during the training to demonstrate responses which probably maintained Ted's behavior and which therefore needed modification. As the sessions progressed, the family rehearsed responses to a variety of role-played child behavior problems. The role plays were designed to become progressively more difficult in terms of management, e.g., verbal fights which developed into physical melees. Both staff and family critiqued the performance of the "parent." Often the "parent" was one of the children who either was assigned a role play by staff or designed one. Training began with a heavy emphasis on didactic instruction and

ended with a heavy emphasis on practice. At the end of the instruction-
practice portion of the training, a 10- to 15-item objective exam was
given encompassing the subject matter covered in the sessions. The tests
were immediately graded and discussed. The final two sessions were a
series of live child-management vignettes performed by staff to which
the family responded in turn. Feedback was given after each role play.

The second portion of each session (30-45 minutes) involved evaluation
of the home management program designed to modify Ted's behaviors.
The home program fell into two phases. In Phase I, treatment staff
designed the programs, and mother carried them out. In Phase II, mother
designed and carried out her own programs on previously untreated
behaviors. Staff periodically phoned mother between training sessions to
resolve problems and give positive reinforcement for program implementation.

Samples from Training Sessions

Exercises: Praise practice (Responses given verbally). John is ten.
He's a messy eater, and you want him to develop better table manners.
The vegetables are all over the table, and there are pieces of meat on
the floor. He has a salad bowl in front of him. No salad has dropped
on the floor or table even though he's taken some to eat. (You are Dad
and you say . . . .)

What's Wrong with the Program? (Responses are written or verbal).
Jane and Mary, ages 11 and 12, fight every night over TV. Mom decided
to set up a behavior program to change this. Mom defined her target
behavior as "no more verbal or physical fights." She decided to give
them each 25 cents if they did not fight for two days. What's wrong
with the program?

1. . . . .
. . . .

2. . . . .
. . . .

3. . . . .
. . . .

Home Management Program

Phase I. The following behaviors were defined and treated during Phase I of the home management program:

1. a. *Darting.* Leaving an area assigned to him by parent without asking for permission or after permission was refused.

   b. *Asking to go.* Asking permission to leave an assigned area and only going to a place designated by parent.

2. a. *Leaving room messy.* Leaving a room or specified area more cluttered or dirtier than it was before he entered it.

   b. *Leaving room clean.* Leaving a room or specified area as clean as it was before he entered it.

3. a. *Touching other people's possessions.* Touching objects not belonging to him or specified out-of-bounds without asking permission.

4. a. *Interrupting.* Making imperative statement in a loud harsh voice.

   b. *Polite requests.* Using the terms "may I," "could I," "would you" in a soft voice and waiting for a verbal or physical response without asking again.

A modified ABA design and a variation of a multiple baseline design (Baer et al., 1968) were used in treatment. All Phase I treatment procedures were identical except that new target behaviors were added to the contingencies. Ted's time at home was divided into half-hour blocks. Tangible reinforcement could be earned at the end of each half-hour block, with social praise earned for appropriate behavior within time blocks. Treatment for each behavior was as follows:

1. *Darting versus Asking to Go.* Baseline I was taken during the first week of training. The method of recording was demonstrated to mother, who took data. For each complete half-hour block during which Ted did not dart, a plus mark (+) was recorded on a chart. Each time he darted a minus mark (—) was tallied. Treatment staff role played a series of situations which involved darting versus asking to go. From the simulated situation, mother coded data which were checked for reliability with staff coding. Mother was told to treat the behaviors at home "as usual."

Treatment (Training Week 2). Ted received a gold star on a chart for each plus he earned. Mother designed the chart, which she kept in view in the kitchen. Each star was worth five minutes of "late night," i.e., five minutes extended beyond his usual bedtime. If Ted "darted," he was sent to his room for the remainder of the time block. Ted's room was stripped of all high-interest activities during the treatment.

Baseline II (Training Week 3). Mother was told to treat the darting versus asking-to-go behaviors "as usual . . . any way she wanted," except that she could not use the established contingencies of the program, viz., stars, late nights or sending Ted to his room. No specific suggestions were given to mother for controlling the behavior other than those techniques she had learned during training sessions.

2. *Messy versus Clean.* Baseline I (Treatment Week 1). With staff help, mother defined the targeted behaviors. At home she counted the incidents of "messy" (M) and "clean" (C). Ted earned a C for each half-hour time block during which he made no "messes."

Baseline II (Treatment Week 2). Mother was told she could treat the behavior any way she wanted but could not use stars, late nights or room time.

3. *Touching Others' Possessions.* Baseline I (Week 3). Mother defined the behavior and recorded data. Each time Ted touched an out-of-bounds item a (0) was recorded on the chart. Mother was instructed to "treat the behavior as usual." Treatment, which began during week 4, was identical to the treatment for darting versus asking to go, except that touching was added to the contingency. Now if Ted darted *or* touched, he was sent to his room. If he asked to go *and* kept the area clean, he earned a star.

Baseline II began during Week 7 of training. Instructions to mother were the same as mentioned above under this condition.

4. *Polite versus Interrupt.* Baseline I (Week 5), Treatment (Week 7), and Baseline II (Week 9) conditions were identical to those for behaviors 1-3, except that polite and interrupt were the target behaviors. Target behaviors 1, 2, and 3 were in the Baseline II phase when treatment was implemented on polite versus interrupt.

Phase II. The following behaviors were treated during Phase II of the home management program:

a. *Temper tantrums:* Stamping feet, running into a room and slamming the door hard after command had been given by parent, and/or yelling in response to a command or request.

b. *Compliance.* Performing a behavior in time limit specified by command without exhibiting temper tantrum behaviors.

Baseline and treatment were conducted during Weeks 8 and 9 of training. Mother designed and implemented every step in the program, from problem definition to graphing data. During treatment, Ted got a five-minute time-out (Patterson and Gullion, 1968) for each tantrum and earned a penny and praise for each compliance. Staff did not supervise this program or make program suggestions; they only collected data from mother each week.

Criteria of Evaluation

Four criteria were used to assess the success of parent training:

1. *Knowledge of behavior principles and child management techniques.* This was measured through written exams given at the end of each session. The exams included items covered during the session as well as review items from earlier sessions. The tests were objective, viz., fill in the blank, circle the correct answer.

Sample:

> If mom gives Tom 25¢ to stop him from screaming in the store, mom has (positively) (negatively) reinforced Tom's screaming behavior.

> If a program fails, name two possible reasons.
> 1. . . . .
> 2. . . . .

2. *Maintenance of behavior change at pre-established criteria levels.* Maintaining a level over 80% for "asking to go," "leaving room clean," polite approaches, and less than one "touch per hour" were established as success levels. Mother counted the behaviors at home and reported data to staff weekly.

3. *Change in the "quality" of child management skills.* Change was assessed through rating pre- and post-videotapes of mother responding to simulated child management problem situations. A six-point Likert-type scale was developed to rate gains in child management skills (Brockway, 1973). Two independent, reliable observers rated the pre- and post-tapes. On the next page is a partial protocol rating one skill, viz., verbal reinforcement:

	N.A.	Never	Seldom	Usually	Often	Always
Praises appropriate behavior	0	1	2	3	4	5
Gives praise frequently	0	1	2	3	4	5
Gives praise immediately	0	1	2	3	4	5
Speaks in warm tone	0	1	2	3	4	5
Speaks enthusiastically	0	1	2	3	4	5
Uses different phrases/words	0	1	2	3	4	5
Facially animated when speaking	0	1	2	3	4	5
Makes praise statements without mixing punishing statements	0	1	2	3	4	5

Ratings were taken on mother's performance in the following areas: verbal reinforcement, physical reinforcement, limit-setting, consistency, giving a time-out, ignoring, and repeat to success.

4. *Positive behavior change in parent-designed program.* In the final phases of training, mother designed a program to modify a behavior which was not treated during the training period. She was responsible for all phases of program development and implementation. Mother counted behaviors at home and reported to staff weekly.

Interjudge Agreement

Interjudge Agreement on written tests was obtained by having two staff members grade the exam papers. Since the tests were objective, percent agreement was 100.

Two independent raters were trained to use the child management assessment scale. They discussed behavioral definitions and coded parenting skills from role-played situations similar to those on the pre- and post-videotapes. Agreement on definitions and coding was obtained prior to tape viewing. The rating code was divided into three categories: Not applicable (N.A.), Never and Seldom, and Usually, Often, and Always. The interjudge agreement was calculated by dividing the total number of agreements within categories by the total number of agreements plus disagreements. The agreement percentage was 91.0.

No interjudge agreement checks were made on mother's recording behaviors in the home. Prior to treatment of any Phase I behavior, however, staff role played and discussed a variety of situations involving the targeted behavior which might occur. For example, Ted speaks in harsh tone, but says, "Please, may I?"; Ted leaves the room clean but briefly runs into an undesignated area to get a new toy. Mother coded each situation. Practice coding continued until staff and mother achieved perfect agreement—100%.

Results

Test Results. The post-instruction objective tests were given to assess the amount of information the family members learned each session. Test scores of mother and George, age 16, averaged 89 and 81 respectively. Ted and Joe, age 13, averaged 50 and 66. If test results are taken as the only criteria, these indicate that Ted and Joe did not learn as much during training as mother and George.

Child Management Assessment (Table 1). Since the data were on an

TABLE 1

	N	Fewer Signs	Significance
Verbal Reinforcement	7	0	P. .008
Physical Reinforcement	7	0	P. .008
Limit Setting	6	0	P. .016
Consistency	7	0	P. .008
Time-Out	7	0	P. .008
Ignore	7	0	P. .008
Rehearse to Success	7	0	P. .008

Child Management Rating Test Results: Statistical significance of changes in mother's parenting skills on pre- and post-treatment role plays of potential problem behaviors.

TABLE 2

	Baseline I	Treatment	Baseline II
Phase I:			
% Ask to go	41%	89%	96%
% Rooms left clean	60%		96%
# of Touches per hour	1.2	0.01	0.01
% Polite approaches	60%	92%	100%

Mean of Target Response Per Treatment Phase: Changes in, and maintenance of, Ted's behavior across treatment phases assessed in relation to predetermined success criterion levels.

ordinal scale within pairs and the samples were related (the S served as her own control pre and post), the Sign Test (nonparametric) was utilized (Siegel, 1956). Interest was only in change in one direction (behavior improvement), and a one-tailed test was employed. The "quality" of parenting skills within techniques changed significantly in the direction of "good" to "excellent" (a score of 4 or 5 on the scale) between pre- and post-role-played videotapes.

Home Management Program (Table 2). Phase I (Figure 1). All Phase I behaviors showed a change in the desired direction between Baseline I and treatment (the predetermined success levels were met and maintained). There were no changes in the direction of Baseline I during Baseline II. Using procedures she had learned in training, the mother

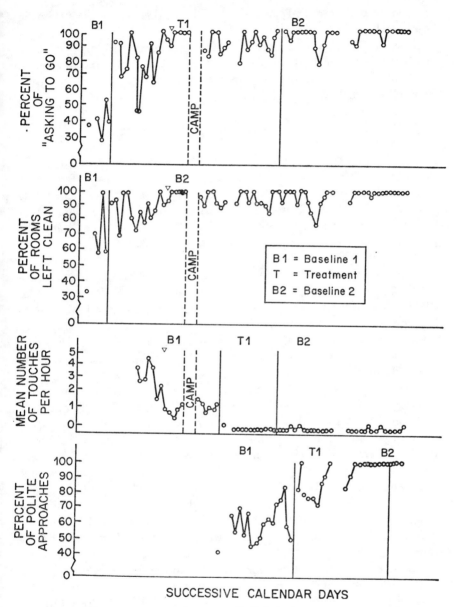

FIGURE 1. Changes in and maintenance of Ted's behavior across treatment phases.

was able to maintain Ted's behaviors at the success criteria levels during Baseline II.

Phase II. There was a change in the percentage of time Ted complied without tantrums between baseline ($\bar{x} = 79\%$) and treatment ($\bar{x} = 85\%$). This indicates that mother had learned general strategies for modifying behavior.

Discussion

Experimental control in Phase I (Figure 1) was demonstrated within the multiple baseline design. The change in behavior from Baseline I levels to Baseline II supports the effectiveness of increased parenting skills in maintaining behaviors at desired levels. In the Baseline II condition, mother was to respond to the behaviors "as usual," and the program contingencies were lifted. Since she had been exposed to training, however, her "usual" parenting skills had changed. If future research in this area incorporates both a reversal (ABAB) design and a Baseline II condition, it would delineate more clearly the amount of change in treatment conditions due to program contingencies rather than increases in parenting skills. The success of Phase II and Baseline II indicates that mother learned not only specific management techniques, but general strategies as well, enhancing the credibility of a prevention-oriented model.

This study has several limitations: (1) It did not delineate what training variables or parent management skills were effective; one only knew in a gross sense that something worked. This suggests that future research in parent training should focus on a component analysis of the effectiveness of specific training devices. For instance, can role-play and behavior rehearsal alone produce as much positive change as role-play rehearsal plus didactic instruction? (2) It would have been advantageous to have had the parents carry out more than one self-designed treatment. (3) Follow-up data on the child's behavior and other programs implemented by the parents would greatly enhance the significance of the study.

Parent training focused primarily on developing mother's management skills, although other family members attended the sessions and participated in the discussions and role plays. The ability of Ted's brothers to use behavior modification tactics was not systematically measured. While test results do indicate that the younger boys learned some principles, the discussions and exams were primarily geared to mother. Protocols for teaching younger siblings to understand and perform behavior modification need development. Sibling training within a prevention-oriented model would enhance the maintenance of desired behavior over time and environment, since siblings often spend at least as much time with a problem child as the parents do.

Paternal involvement in this training program was minimal. The father's job kept him out of town for several days at a time. The program data may indicate the necessity for training both parents in two-parent families. Note the triangles in Figure 1. The data following the triangle become more stable and change in the desired direction. Review of the data indicated extreme differences in behavior away from the desired direction when father was in town versus out of town. The parents were interviewed separately and the data difference noted. The father admitted he did not understand the program, and in front of Ted he would often disagree with his wife on her management decisions. Mother confirmed this behavior. Treatment staff explained the program and discussed the necessity for the tight contingencies on Ted. Father signed a contract with staff and his wife which stipulated both his and mother's behaviors in relation to the program. The triangle denotes the day father signed the contract. Although a number of variables were not controlled, the data suggest the possible need for parental agreement in operating behavior programs. Further research is needed to demonstrate the efficiency of parent training with one rather than both parents, as well as training individual families or groups of families.

The results of the pre- and post-training videotapes and the written exams demonstrate mother's ability to intellectualize and perform behavior modification. Her ability to design and carry out her own programs demonstrates the efficiency of parent training in maintaining and generalizing desirable behavior change in mother and child across time and environments while minimizing treatment staff time.

Although there were staff-parent interjudge agreement checks on simulated program behavior prior to treatment conditions, no reliability ratings were attempted in the home. This could be done with periodic staff visits or neighbors serving as confederates. However, the authors argue that interjudge agreement rating done in the clinic setting involved the observation of more salient behaviors, and in that way was more valid. Often parents report that in short-term (1-2 hour) home observations the child "was not really as bad as usual." Discussion with staff at the residential institution who had observed children in their home and residential setting supports this fact. Therefore, parent-staff agreement on a wide range of potential behavior of similar topography may constitute a more valid observation. Inferences of agreement across settings could be reasonably made even if home observation reliability is sacrificed. This type of agreement rating may prove more useful for a broad range of social behaviors. Of course, both types of agreement could be obtained (clinic and home), which would resolve the methodological difficulties. However, even if in-home agreement checks were more valid than clinic settings, this type of data collection is not feasible to a majority of clinicians; they are limited by staff numbers and staff time.

For any training model to function as a prevention model, the setting from which the training was delivered should be examined. In order to actually prevent severe behavior problems in families, training should be offered through premarital and pediatric clinics, as part of premarital counseling, and/or as a component of family-life curriculum in high schools. Through research, the field is developing effective intervention strategies. A prevention model can be described as an effective intervention model delivered through "natural environments" or prevention settings, i.e., pre-problem settings. Since the training model of this setting was delivered through a problem setting, viz., a residential treatment center, it lacks one essential component of a prevention model.

Ultimately a prevention-oriented parent training model should evolve into a self-generating system; i.e., there should be minimal direct mental health professional involvement in implementation and supervision of the model. Parents, pediatric clinics, premarital counselors, and high school faculty who have been trained should become the parent trainers and program implementers.

In summary, as a method of achieving positive behavior changes in children, parent training has emerged as a powerful intervention technique (Berkowitz and Graziano, 1972). As a treatment approach it involves limited professional involvement in terms of the gains achieved, and enhances maintenance and generalization of desirable behavior since the programs can be carried out in the natural environment. A prevention-oriented model needs to incorporate training in problem-solving strategies and in a broad range of possible behavior problems of children. It should not be limited to the successful modification of a presenting problem. This study incorporated these procedures and can be considered a prevention-oriented model that needs further research on a wider client population.

REFERENCES

BAER, D. M., WOLF, M. M., and RISLEY, T. R.: Some current dimensions of applied behavior analysis. *J. Appl. Behav. Anal.*, 1, 91-97, 1968.

BERKOWITZ, B., and GRAZIANO, A.: Training parents as behavior therapists: A review *Behav. Res. and Ther.*, 10, 297-317, 1972.

BERNAL, M.: Behavioral feedback in the modification of brat behavior. *J. Nerv. Ment. Dis.*, 148, 375-385, 1969.

BERNAL, M., DURYEE, J. S., PRUETT, H. L., and BURNS, B. J.: Behavior modification and the brat syndrome. *J. Consult. Clin. Psychol.*, 32, 447-455, 1968.

BROCKWAY, B.: *Parent Training in Child Management.* Dubuque, Iowa: Kendall-Hunt, 1974.

BROCKWAY, B.: *Child Management Technique Assessment Scale.* U. of Wisconsin, Madison, Wis. (mimeographed), 1973.

GARDNER, J. E., PEARSON, D. T., BERCOVITI, A. N., and BRICKER, D. E.: *Measurement, Evaluation and modification of selected social interactions between a schizophrenic child, his parents and his therapist. J. Consult. Clin. Psychol.*, 32, 537-542, 1968.

HALL, R. V., AXELROD, S., TYLER, L., GRIEF, E.. JONES, F. C., and ROBERTSON, R.: Modification of behavior problems in the home with a parent as observer and experimenter. *J. Appl. Behav. Anal.*, 5, 53-64, 1972. (Tyler, Grief, Jones, Robertson—parents)

JOHNSON, S. M., and BROWN, R. A.: Producing behavior change in parents of disturbed children. *J. Child Psychol. Psychiat.*, 10, 107-121, 1969.

PATTERSON, G. R., COBB, J. A., and RAY, R. S.: A social engineering technology for retraining aggressive boys. In: H. Adams and L. Unikel (Eds.), *Georgia Symposium in Experimental Clinical Psychology,* Vol. II. Oxford: Pergamon Press, 1973.

PATTERSON, G. R., and BRODSKY, G.: A behavior modification program for a child with multiple problem behaviors. *J. Child Psychol. Psychiat.*, 7, 277-295, 1966.

PATTERSON, G. R., and GULLION, M. E.: *Living with Children: New Methods for Parents and Teachers.* Champaign, Ill.: Research Press, 1968.

PATTERSON, G. R., McNEAL, S., HAWKINS, N., and PHELPS, R.: Reprogramming the social environment. *J. Child Psychol. Psychiat.*, 8, 181-195, 1967.

ROSE, S.: A behavioral approach to the group treatment of parents. *Social Work*, 14, 21-29, 1969.

RUSSO, S.: Adaptations in behavior therapy with children. *Behav. Res. and Ther.*, 2, 43-47, 1964.

SIEGEL, S.: *Nonparametric Statistics for the Behavioral Sciences.* New York: McGraw-Hill, 1956.

WAHLER, R. G.: Oppositional children: A quest for parental reinforcement control. *J. Appl. Behav. Anal.*, 2, 159-170, 1969.

WALDER, L. O., COHEN, S. I., DASTON, P. G., BREITER, D. E., and HIRSCH, I. S.: Behavior therapy of children through their parents. Revision of a paper presented at the meetings of the American Psychological Association, Washington, D. C., 1967.

WELSH, R. S.: A highly efficient method of parent counseling. Paper presented at the meetings of the Rocky Mountain Psychological Association, 1966.

WOLF, M. M., RISLEY, T., and MEES, H.: Application of operant conditioning procedures to the behavior problems of an autistic child. *Behav. Res. and Ther.*, 1, 305-312, 1964.

ZEILBERGER, J., SAMPEN, S., and SLOANE, H.: Modification of a child's problem behaviors in the home with the mother as therapist. *J. Appl. Behav. Anal.*, 1, 47-53, 1968.

3

The Family Training Program: Improving Parent-Child Interaction Patterns

EDWARD R. CHRISTOPHERSEN,
JAMES D. BARNARD, DENNIS FORD,
and MONTROSE M. WOLF

Within the past decade, numerous attempts to develop behavioral programs to treat child behavior problems have been reported (Christophersen, 1973). Results of many of these efforts have suggested the efficacy of training parents to assume responsibility for implementing these treatment programs (e.g., Bernal, 1969; Stuart, 1971; Patterson et al., 1973).

A Family Training Program has recently been developed to extend and refine this technology for intervening with parents and children in their homes. A complete description of these procedures has previously been reported (Christophersen et al., 1973).

The purposes of this research program were: (1) to compare, using random assignment, an intensive in-home family training program with conventional outpatient treatment, (2) to train parents to treat behavior problems in community settings, and (3) to improve parent-child interaction patterns by increasing the number of positive interactions.

This research was partially supported by a grant (HD 03144) from the National Institute of Child Health and Human Development to the Bureau of Child Research, University of Kansas.

A Comparison of the Family Training Program with Conventional Outpatient Treatment

An evaluation of clinical services has been initiated and has compared treatment in the Family Training Program with treatment in conventional psychological intervention strategies. Children referred to a child guidance clinic for psychological treatment were placed in a "therapy pool"; that is, the folders of these children (including their medical and social histories, and any psychological tests) were made available to each of the psychotherapists at the clinic, as well as to the Family Training Program staff.

Each of the therapists who had an opening for referral was asked to review the case history of each child placed in this therapy pool. A judgment was made as to whether the therapist thought that the referred child could profit from his or her treatment program and whether the therapist was able to take the child into treatment. This procedure was used to safeguard against a therapist being assigned a child who was not appropriate for his or her therapy program.

The criteria used by the Family Training Program staff for excluding children were: (1) problems that were primarily organic (e.g., a hemiplegic following a stroke), (2) I.Q. less than 70, (3) geographical location too distant for home visits, and (4) no parent mediator in the home a sufficient amount of time for training in the Family Training Program. The criteria for selection or rejection by the child guidance clinic psychotherapists were not specified.

When both a clinic psychotherapist and the Family Training Program staff found a child acceptable for their respective programs, the child was randomly assigned (with a coin toss) to one of the programs.

Treatment Techniques

A child assigned to a therapist at the guidance clinic received whatever form of treatment the clinic deemed appropriate. All children assigned to the Family Training Program were exposed to a common set of treatment procedures.

The home intervention can be best conceptualized in terms of three general phases. During the first and most intensive phase, the therapist actively intervened with the children (in the presence of the parents), established initial control with the children, and modeled correct application of the intervention techniques. In the second phase, the therapist involvement was altered to the extent that the natural parents assumed responsibility for implementing the techniques in the presence of the therapist. The therapist's role in this phase was that of monitoring ongoing behavior and providing the parents and children with feedback about the adequacy of their performance (cf. Bernal, 1969). The third and final phase consisted of making infrequent contacts with parents to assure maintenance of behavioral change or to assess new problems which may have been confronted. During this final phase, it was not uncommon for parents to describe not only the problems with which they had been confronted, but also the techniques they had utilized to deal with them.

The three treatment programs to be described (Toddler, Preschool, and School-Age) each contained multiple components. None of these components have been assessed for their individual contribution in effecting the desired behavioral changes. While specific treatment techniques often varied as a function of such variables as the nature of the referring problem and the age of the referred child, all programs were designed to provide the children with a maximum amount of instruction, feedback, and consequences for their behavior.

Each of the programs was implemented in the child's natural home environment (cf. Hawkins et al., 1966; Wahler, 1969) and trained parents to systematically strengthen or weaken specific behaviors by programming positive or negative consequences contingent upon their occurrence. Consequences ranged from simple "hugs" for younger children to large token or point awards for older children.

Each program made extensive use of behavioral rehearsal or "practicing" (cf. Ford et al., 1974). Parents and children were encouraged to model or practice engaging in those behaviors which the family and the therapist agreed were important to the individual child or the entire family (e.g., accepting criticism). It was felt that such practicing was a necessary first step in having family members gradually acquire, and later naturally exhibit, behaviors which fostered appropriate parent-child interaction in the home.

A brief review of the content of typical home visits, along with descriptions of the three treatment programs, will be presented here to familiarize the reader with important procedures of the intervention. The first contact with the family took place in the office. During that meeting, a standard intake interview was conducted, parental complaints (child behaviors considered inappropriate) were listed, and the Family Training Program was described. Parents were requested to construct lists of appropriate behaviors (behaviors they were interested in maintaining or teaching), inappropriate behaviors (behaviors they were interested in decreasing or eliminating), and items or activities which they thought might be used as reinforcers or rewards). The Family Training Program Manual (Christophersen et al., 1973) was given to the parents, and they were requested to read prescribed sections. A strong emphasis was placed on the importance of carefully following the instructions and procedures described in the Family Training Program Manual. Parents were cautioned that the program would probably not be successful if they did not strictly adhere to these instructions (cf. Wright, 1973). All subsequent contacts with the family were made at their home.

The first home visit was usually made in the evening, when all family members were likely to be present. Details of implementing the program were described by the therapist. Both specific behaviors and more general interaction patterns were modeled by the therapist and practiced by the parents and children. Examples of child behaviors which were practiced included performing simple household chores, responding to criticisms from parents, and interacting appropriately with siblings. Examples of parent behaviors practiced included giving praise and attention for appropriate child behavior, and pleasantly providing feedback to the child about inappropriate behavior. When a token system was implemented, time was devoted to reviewing behaviors which would earn or lose points, items and/or privileges to be exchanged for points, household jobs to be completed regularly (and by whom), and other rules and procedures important in the operation of a home token economy (Christophersen et al., 1972).

During this first visit, questions were frequently raised by family members about specific problem situations or behaviors of concern to them. For example, parents might have asked how to handle back talking, while children often asked how they might voice disagreement without being accused of back talking. Therapists addressed these questions and practiced or rehearsed these situations when possible. An important but unanalyzed component of the program was that the home visits were made as positive as possible to all family members. Therapists often played with the children and conversed informally with the parents about topics unrelated to the treatment program. The first home visit was usually a lengthy one, sometimes lasting three hours.

Over the course of treatment (30 hours for the average family) appropriate interactions were modeled less by the therapist, while feedback to individual family members about their behavior was increased. Throughout treatment, families were routinely encouraged to telephone the therapist as problems were encountered. (It is estimated that a mean of one and one-half hours were spent on the telephone with each family.) Equally important, the therapist frequently programmed home visits at times when problems were known to occur, e.g., at night for bedtime problems or at suppertime for problems with eating. Parents were assured that the therapists would visit the home whenever it seemed indicated.

Description of the Toddler Program *(Ages One to Three)*

A premise stated to parents of "toddlers" was that their children were capable of learning appropriate ways of behaving. From the information provided by the parents during the intake interview, rules and consequences were specified for use in increasing their child's appropriate behavior and decreasing the inappropriate behavior (e.g., fight with brothers and sisters, leave toys out). During the home visits, the therapist modeled and practiced the proper method of administering these rules (cf. Engeln et al., 1968). The following five points were stressed during home visits with toddlers:

1. Be consistent with each rule and procedure.
2. Be as pleasant and calm as possible.
3. Avoid hugging, picking up, or physically loving the child when he misbehaves, or immediately after disciplining him.
4. Give abundant attention, love, and praise throughout the day, especially when the child is behaving appropriately.
5. Spend time teaching and having the child practice new ways of behaving.
6. Use "time-outs" as demonstrated for the child's inappropriate behaviors.

Again, parents were cautioned that ignoring these procedures or giving in to the child when a rule was violated would only be confusing and make learning more difficult for the child.

Description of the Preschool-Age Program *(Ages Three to Six)*

A token economy using poker chips was established. Behaviors that were to be rewarded or punished were enumerated based on information supplied by the parents and the children. The parents were instructed to reward the children with chips each time they engaged in appropriate behaviors and punish the children by taking away chips each time they misbehaved. The chips were "backed up" by making access to desired privileges contingent upon having a specified number of chips. To buy a privilege, a child needed both the predetermined number of chips and parental consent. The parents were instructed to give their consent unless the privilege interfered with normal activities (e.g., the child could not buy a snack too near mealtime).

Parents were told that there might be times when, for various reasons, the child would not stop behaving inappropriately when chips were taken away. In that event, a brief "time-out" was to be used. The therapist practiced time-out with the child and the child earned chips for practicing. The first few time-outs were practiced when the child had been behaving appropriately and neither the parent nor the child was upset. In this way, parent and child were able to learn how to initiate and complete a time-out under fairly pleasant, nonstressful conditions. Various areas in the home were used for time-out periods (e.g., kitchen chair or living room sofa). The only restriction was that time-out be conducted in an area where the child could not engage in privileges like social interaction or watching TV. Areas such as darkened closets or pantries, however, were excluded. The duration of time-out was usually set for five minutes or less. If the child spoke or had a tantrum during time-out, the period was re-initiated. If the child left the chair before the interval had expired, he or she was given *one* hard spank and placed back on the chair (cf. Bernal, 1969). When time-outs were completed the child could immediately begin re-earning chips by practicing behaviors incompatible with those that required placement in time-out.

Description of the School-Age Program (Ages Seven to Twelve)

The primary component of the program for school-age children consisted of a token reinforcement system (using points) to teach and maintain appropriate behaviors and to discourage inappropriate behaviors. The Family Training Program motivational systems have been patterned closely after those used in Achievement Place group homes (cf. Phillips et al., 1973).

A token economy was constructed from lists of appropriate and inappropriate behaviors and privileges provided by the parents and children during the intake interview. Points were given by the parents contingent upon appropriate behaviors specified by the family's lists, and taken away for specified inappropriate behaviors. These points were, in turn, redeemable for various privileges such as having friends over and going to movies. This system differed from that of the preschoolers in that more household activities were included as tasks that could earn points, and a greater variety of privileges were available for purchase by children.

This program emphasized teaching appropriate social behaviors. Children could earn a large number of points by exhibiting good conversational skills, accepting and giving criticism tactfully, and interacting pleasantly with family and significant others. Children were also given points for maintaining good personal hygiene, assisting with household responsibilities, and performing satisfactorily at school.

The three treatment programs described each contained multiple components. Although specific treatment techniques often varied as a function of the referring problem and the age of the referred child, all programs were designed to provide the children with a maximum amount of instruction, feedback, and consequences. These programs were primarily designed to improve parent-child interaction patterns. Parents were instructed in more effective methods of dealing with those inappropriate behaviors which led to their children's referral. In addition, parents received instruction in methods of teaching their children new and more acceptable ways of behaving in their home, school, and community. The degree to which these objectives have been realized are described in the following sections on program evaluation.

EVALUATION MEASURES OF FAMILY TRAINING PROGRAM AND CHILD GUIDANCE CLINIC PROGRAMS

The two treatment programs have been analyzed in terms of (1) the parameters describing the degree to which treatment was implemented and (2) the outcome, or effects produced by the treatment. Descriptive parameters of treatment included the number of in-person contacts (home visits in the case of the Family Training Program) needed to implement the treatment regimen and the total duration of such contacts. Data were also gathered on the number and duration of therapist visits to schools for the purpose of ameliorating school-related problems for Family Training Program referrals.

Parent Evaluation Measure

Parents were requested to list as many as 15 behaviors exhibited by the referred child which they viewed as problem behaviors. Illustrative and

BEHAVIOR	SUN.		MON.		TUES.		WEDS.	
	TRUE	FALSE	TRUE	FALSE	TRUE	FALSE	TRUE	FALSE
Backtalk	X		X		X			X
Non-Compliance	X		X		X		X	
Fighting		X		X	X		X	

FIGURE 1. A representation of a parent evaluation sheet.

frequently listed complaints have included "back talking" and "does not follow instructions." Once these problems were isolated, defined, and recorded by the parents on a standardized parent-evaluation sheet, the parents were requested to take the list home and evaluate the child each day for one week's time. Parents were instructed to check a "True" for each complaint on any given day if the problem behavior was observed to occur one or more times. If the problem behavior was not observed, the parents were instructed to check a "False" for that behavior. The percent of reported problems that occurred was calculated for each day by summing the number of problems checked "True" and dividing by the number of problems evaluated. When the sheet was completed (at least five consecutive days) it was returned by mail in a self-addressed envelope. All families treated by the Family Training Program were given parent evaluations before treatment and following treatment. We are greatly indebted to Gerald Patterson (1973) for recommending this dependent variable measure. In addition to the parent-evaluation measures, the Walker Problem Behavior Identification Checklist was also administered to all families on a pre- and post-treatment basis.

RANDOM FAMILY TRAINING PROGRAM REFERRALS: CHARACTERISTICS

Table 1 presents the demographic characteristics of the families randomly referred to both the Family Training Program and the child guidance clinic. To date, 25 families have been randomly assigned to either of these two programs. Data are now available on 19 children, 10 of whom were randomly assigned to the Family Training Program. In these 10 families, there were a total of 27 children, ranging in age from

TABLE 1

	Family Training Program (N = 10)	Child Guidance Clinic (N = 9)
Total Number of Children in Families	27	19
Age Range—All Children	3 mos.-17 yrs.	NA
Average Age of Prime Referrals	5 yrs.	6 yrs.
Average Number of Children per Family	2.7	2.1
Percent of Two-Parent Households	90	78
Mothers' Average Age	29 yrs.	30 yrs.
Mothers' Average Education	13 yrs.	12 yrs.
Fathers' Average Age	32 yrs.	33 yrs.
Fathers' Average Education	13 yrs.	13 yrs.
Average Annual Per Capita Income	$3,358	$2,463

3 months to 17 years. The mean chronological age of the prime referrals was 5 years. The mean number of children per family was 2.7.

Ninety percent of these households were two-parent families. The mothers' mean age was 29 years, and their average education was 13 years. The fathers' mean age was 32, and their average level of education was 13 years. Mean per capita annual income was $3,358.00.

Figure 2 shows the referring complaints of families assigned at random to the Family Training Program. One hundred percent of the families reported noncompliance (for example, failure to follow instructions or back talking) to be a major complaint. Tantrums, hyperactivity, and school-related problems ranked as the second, third, and fourth most frequently occurring complaints.

RANDOM REFERRALS TO THE CHILD GUIDANCE CLINIC: CHARACTERISTICS

Data are also available on 9 families randomly referred for treatment to the child guidance clinic. These 9 families had a total number of 19 children. Their average age was 6 years. The mean number of children per family was 2.1.

Seventy-eight percent of these households were two-parent families. The mothers' mean age was 30, and their average formal education was 12 years. The mean age of the fathers was 33 years, and their mean number of years of formal schooling was 13. Annual per capita income for these families averaged $2,463.00.

Figure 2 summarizes the prime referring complaints of families as-

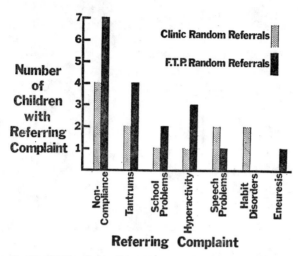

FIGURE 2. Number of randomly assigned children with each referring complaint.

signed at random to the child guidance clinic treatment program. Of these nine families, 57% reported noncompliance to be a problem. Tantrums, speech problems (no speech), and habit disorders were reported with equal frequency as the second most common complaint. School-related problems and hyperactivity were the third most frequently reported complaints in these families.

FAMILY TRAINING PROGRAM RANDOM REFERRALS: TREATMENT OUTCOME

The average number of home visits made for the referred children was 19, and the average duration of treatment hours was 30. An average of 1.2 hours was spent during office visits with the families. A mean of 3 hours was required for visits to the school to extend the treatment program to that setting.

Figure 3 presents the parent evaluation data collected on all referrals randomly assigned to the two treatment programs. For the children in the Family Training Program, the seven days of pretreatment baseline showed a mean of 61% of referring problems present. Following termination from the Family Training Program, the parents reported that an average of 20% of the behavior problems were present.

Pre- and post-test data on Family Training Program random referrals

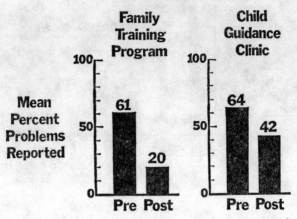

FIGURE 3. Mean percent of problem behaviors reported by parents of randomly assigned children.

using the Walker Problem Behavior Identification Checklist are presented. Pre-tests were available on all 10 children, while to date, post-tests have become available on 8 children. Pre- and post-test comparisons for the 8 children showed a significant reduction in problem behaviors. The mean total score for these referrals before treatment was 31, ten points above the norm of 21 (the dotted line). Following treatment, this group of children showed a reduction of 14 units to a post-treatment score of 17 (well below the norm of 21).

CHILD GUIDANCE CLINIC RANDOM REFERRALS TREATMENT OUTCOME

Records of treatment contacts kept by the child guidance clinic were reviewed, and data were gathered on such contacts. The number of hours (clinic visits) needed to implement treatment averaged 25.

Parent evaluation data are presented in Figure 3. Pre-test data have been obtained on seven of the nine referred children. As can be seen in Figure 3, the seven days of pretreatment baseline data showed a mean of 64% of reported problems to be present. Post-treatment parent evaluations of the seven children on whom such data are available showed a reduction in reported problems to a mean level of 42%.

Pre- and post-treatment measures were gathered on nine referrals

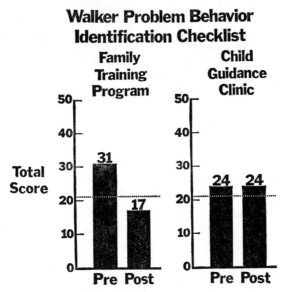

FIGURE 4. Walker pre- and post-test scores on randomly assigned children.

utilizing the Walker Problem Behavior Identification Checklist. The comparison data are presented in Figure 4. Results showed a pattern dissimilar to that documented in the comparison with random Family Training Program referrals. The mean pretreatment score for the child guidance clinic random referrals was 24, and the mean post-treatment score was 24. Both scores were above the norm score of 21.

To document the degree to which parents could be instructed in methods of teaching their children more appropriate ways of behaving (thereby improving parent-child interaction patterns) and to extend these procedures for use in out-of-home settings, an in-depth study of child behavior in community settings was undertaken.

TRAINING PARENTS TO MANAGE BEHAVIOR IN SETTINGS OUTSIDE THE NATURAL HOME*

A complaint frequently voiced by mothers of children referred to the Family Training Program was that they experienced difficulty controlling their children's behavior in settings outside of the home. Mothers

---

* A more complete description of this research is available in Barnard, Christophersen and Wolf, 1974.

of younger children often cited the supermarket as one such problem setting. To validate the authenticity of these complaints, a questionnaire was administered to 43 mothers and 25 supermarket managers. Virtually all respondents felt it important for children to stay with their parents while shopping, and most considered it inappropriate for children to pick up or handle store items without permission to do so. Both groups of respondents reported that they frequently observed children misbehaving while in the supermarket.

Problems in obtaining reliable estimates of parent and child behaviors in naturalistic settings have frequently been reported by parent trainers. Patterson et al. (1973) reported a methodology for in-home observation; however, extensive training (80 hours or more) was required for observers to reliably utilize the procedures. Bernal (1969) has made use of the video-taping studio to obtain samples of child behavior. While obtaining much reliable, analyzable data, she has reported problems in obtaining sufficiently representative samples of deviant child behavior in such a controlled, but artificial, setting.

The purposes of the following study were (1) to assess the feasibility of making observations of parent and child behavior in the supermarket setting and (2) to develop techniques for significantly improving two child behaviors identified by parents and store personnel as "problem behaviors."

METHOD

Participants

Three male elementary-school-age children and their mothers participated in this study. The children had been referred to the Family Training Program as a result of behavior problems at home and in the community, and families had received treatment through a parent-mediated, home point system for approximately six weeks prior to the study.

All mothers cited the supermarket as being one setting in which they had difficulty controlling their children's behavior.

Behaviors

Two child behaviors chosen for analysis were (a) proximity to the parent while in the store and (b) product handling or disturbances. Proximity was defined in terms of the child's being within reaching or touching distance of the parent while shopping. Product disturbances were defined as the child's responses to purchasable store items which resulted in observable movement of the product. Estimates of the levels of both behaviors were obtained by having an observer accompany the mother and child throughout the supermarket and score the occurrence or nonoccurrence of each behavior during specified time intervals. Percent measures of the occurrence of proximity behavior and nonoccurrence of (or absence of) product disturbance behavior were computed. The measures were assessed for their reliability by having a second observer periodically accompany the regular participant to the store and independently record the results of his or her observations in a fashion identical to that of the regular observer. Roughly one hour was required to train a naive observer in the use of the observation procedure.

Parent Satisfaction

Two measures of mother satisfaction with child behavior in the store were obtained. Parent evaluation of the presence or absence of inappropriate child behavior was obtained at the conclusion of each shopping trip. Four or five objectionable behaviors (e.g., "does not stay with me") had been specified by the mother and listed on a parent evaluation form. The mother rated each behavior as being "true" if she observed the behavior to have occurred during the store visit. If the objectionable behavior was not observed, it was rated false. A percent measure of the occurrence of "behavioral complaints" could thus be computed.

A subjective measure was also obtained at the end of each store visit by having the mother rate the child's overall behavior on a 5-point scale (5—excellent, 4—good, 3—satisfactory, 2—poor, 1—intolerable). A numerical rating thus became available which reflected the mother's general satisfaction with the child's behavior during each store visit.

Parent-Child Interactions

All store visits for one mother-child pair were tape-recorded and later analyzed for mother's verbal attention to appropriate and inappropriate child behavior during specified time-sampling intervals. During each interval, instances of general praise for appropriate behavior were noted, and the quality of the mother's verbal attention was scored as being positive, neutral, or negative.

Design and Treatment

A multiple baseline analysis was performed across the two child behaviors. During baseline, mothers were requested to shop as they nor-
mally would. Following baseline, the training package was sequentially
introduced to each of the two behaviors.

Prior to visiting the store on training days, appropriate and inappropriate behaviors (staying within reach of the mother versus leaving the
mother) were described to and modeled for the children at home. The
children were given the opportunity to "practice" engaging in the
appropriate behavior and received praise and verbal feedback about their
performance (Ford et al., 1974). Once taken to the store, token reinforcement and response-cost procedures were employed. Mothers periodically awarded points (exchangeable for goods and privileges in the
child's home) for proximity and subtracted points for each instance of
nonproximity. In addition to levying point consequences for appropriate
and inappropriate behavior, mothers were encouraged to provide their
children with descriptive verbal feedback about their ongoing behavior
during store visits. An identical sequence of procedures was employed
in the subsequent condition for product disturbance behavior. The
children earned and lost points for the absence or presence of inappropriate product disturbances.

RESULTS

For purposes of brevity, data will be presented for only one of the
three children who participated. Results obtained for this child were
representative of those obtained for the other two children. Reliability
of the measures of child behavior was assessed on five different occasions
(at least one assessment for each measure, in each condition). Occurrence
agreement between observers averaged 91% (range 73%-100%) for the
proximity measure and 96% (range 93%-100%) for the product disturbance measure.

Child Behavior

Figure 5 summarizes the changes in child behavior achieved with
training. During baseline, Dicky remained within reach of his mother
(upper portion of the figure) during an average of 51% of all sampling
intervals (range 36%-78%). With the introduction of the training package, his proximity behavior increased to a mean level of 95% (range
88%-100%).

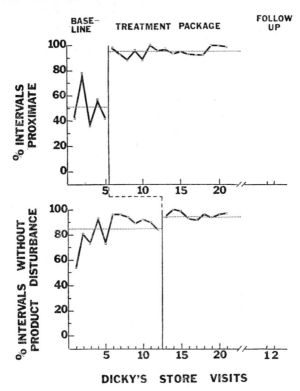

FIGURE 5. Percent of intervals with appropriate store behaviors over consecutive store visits for Dicky.

During baseline, Dicky refrained from disturbing products during an average of 84% (range 54%-96%) of sampling intervals (lower portion of the graph). When training was introduced, this mean level increased to 96% (range 92%-100%). Follow-up data indicated that the behavioral changes were maintained 13 weeks after the termination of training.

Parent Satisfaction

Figure 6 (upper portion) presents the results of the parent evaluation measure (percent of problems reported to occur) and of the overall evaluations of child behavior (lower portion).

Prior to treatment, Dicky's mother reported an average of 78% of her complaints about his shopping behavior to have been present. Her average, overall evaluation of his behavior was "poor." During treat-

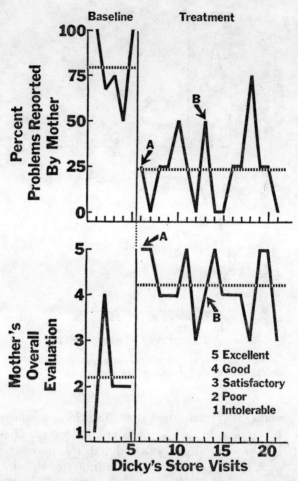

FIGURE 6. Percent of problem behaviors reported by the mother and the mother's overall evaluation of the child's behavior during store visits. A—the introduction of the treatment package for the child's proximity behavior; B—the introduction of the treatment package for the child's product disturbance behavior.

ment, the mother's complaints were reduced to a mean level of 23%, and her subjective evaluation improved to an average of "good."

Parent-Child Interaction

Preliminary results of analysis of audiotapes of parent-child interactions for Dicky's mother indicated that most of her pretreatment attention was devoted to inappropriate behavior. Few statements of praise were noted, and the quality of her verbal attention was consistently rated neutral or negative. With training, significant changes were noted in the mother's verbal behavior. More attention was devoted to appropriate behavior, and less to inappropriate behavior. The number of general praise statements increased, as did the number of verbalizations which were scored as being positive. The number of verbalizations scored as being negative decreased to zero levels.

DISCUSSION

The results of the questionnaire survey suggested that both parents and store personnel had significant concerns about the behavior exhibited by children in the community supermarket setting. Store managers consistently reported that they observed children behaving inappropriately and that such misbehavior resulted in increased effort and cost for their companies. In addition, they reported that a large number of parents might well benefit from training in techniques of more effective child management.

The study demonstrated the feasibility of utilizing the naturally occurring supermarket setting to objectively analyze patterns of parent and child behavior. The observational methodology used in this analysis seemed practical, as naive observers could be trained in its reliable use with only about one hour of training. Problems with obtaining sufficiently deviant samples of child behavior, as reported by Bernal (1969), were not encountered in the public supermarket setting. Parents and children appeared to adapt readily to the presence of an observer.

The package of training procedures produced significant improvement in both child behaviors for all three children, and the changes appeared durable over time. Parent satisfaction with changes in child behavior increased, and significant change was noted in the quality of one mother's verbal interaction with her child. The procedures utilized seemed both simple and practical. It would seem likely that, with a minimum of professional advice, many "troubled" parent/shoppers could be taught to utilize these or similar procedures to teach their children more acceptable ways of behaving in community settings.

SUMMARY AND GENERAL DISCUSSION

The Family Training Program, an intensive in-home behavior management program for working with families whose children exhibit behavior problems, supports and extends the family intervention model proposed by Gerald Patterson, Martha Bernal, Richard Stuart, and others. According to the Family Training Program Model, all intervention took place in the families' homes. At first, the therapist actively intervened with the children (in the presence of the parents), established initial control with the children, and modeled correct application of the intervention techniques. As treatment progressed, the parents assumed increasingly more responsibility for implementing the techniques, while the therapist provided parents and children with feedback about their performance and/or behavior.

The three treatment programs described (Toddler, Preschool, and School-Age) each contained multiple components. While specific treatment techniques often varied as a function of the nature of the referring problems and the age of the referred child, all programs were designed to provide the child with a maximum amount of instructions, feedback, and consequences.

Treatment in the Family Training Program was compared with treatment in other, more conventional, intervention strategies. Families referred to a child guidance clinic for psychological treatment were randomly assigned to either that clinic or the Family Training Program. Descriptive data gathered on families (for example, ages of parents and children, common types of referring complaints) indicated that both samples seemed to be drawn from essentially the same population.

Preliminary results indicated that the Family Training Program was more effective than the conventional intervention strategies employed by the participating child guidance clinic. Pre- and post-test comparisons were obtained using the Walker Problem Behavior Identification Checklist. Children referred to the Family Training Program showed a 45% decrease in problem behaviors as measured by this instrument, whereas children referred to the child guidance clinic showed no decreases in problem behaviors. Daily parent evaluations showed an average decrease in problem behaviors of 67% for Family Training Program referrals, but only a 34% decrease for child guidance clinic referrals.

The Family Training Program required more time for implementation. An analysis of the time required to implement the treatment programs indicated that the Family Training Program required an average of 30 hours of home visits (not including approximately 13 hours travel time). In contrast, psychologists at the child guidance clinic spent an average of 25 hours implementing their treatment programs. Thus, although the Family Training Program appeared to be more effective than outpatient procedures, it was also somewhat more expensive to implement.

In addition to training parents to deal with behavior problems occurring in the home, the Family Training Program has developed and analyzed procedures for improving child behavior in out-of-home settings. One such study analyzed child behavior in the supermarket setting. Data were presented for one of three mothers who trained her child to stay with her and refrain from handling store products during community shopping trips. The mother reported increased satisfaction with her child's improved shopping behavior. In addition, improvements were noted in the way the mother interacted verbally with her child.

Conclusions about the Family Training Program's effectiveness, practicality, or suitability for wide-scale dissemination must remain somewhat guarded at this early juncture. The Family Training Program has been implemented with a relatively small number of children. Preliminary results using two outcome measures suggested that children treated by the Family Training Program showed more improvement than did children treated by more conventional treatment strategies implemented at a child guidance clinic.

REFERENCES

BARNARD, J. D., CHRISTOPHERSEN, E. R., and WOLF, M. M.: The management of problem behaviors in a community setting. Paper presented at the annual convention of the American Psychological Association, New Orleans, La., Division 25 (informal), 1974.

BERNAL, M. E., DURYEE, J. S., PRUETT, H. L., and BURNS, B. J.: Behavior modification and the brat syndrome. *J. Consult. and Clin. Psychol.*, 32, 447-455, 1968.

BERNAL, M. E.: Behavioral feedback in the modification of brat behavior. *J. Nerv. and Ment. Dis.*, 148, 375-385, 1969.

CHRISTOPHERSEN, E. R.: Behavior modification in the family. In D. P. Hymovich and M. U. Barnard (Eds.), *Family Health Care.* New York: McGraw-Hill, 1973.

CHRISTOPHERSEN, E. R., ARNOLD, C. M., HILL, D. W., and QUILITCH, H. R.: The home point system: Token reinforcement procedures for application by parents of children with behavior problems. *J. Appl. Behav. Anal.*, 5, 485-497, 1972.

CHRISTOPHERSEN, E. R., RAINEY, S. K., and BARNARD, J. D.: *The Family Training Program Manual.* Lawrence, Kans.: University Printing Service, 1973.

ENGELN, R., KNUTSON, J., LAUGHY, L., and GARLINGTON, W.: Behavior modification techniques applied to a family unit—A case study. *J. Child Psychol. and Psychiat.*, 245-252, 1968.

FORD, D., FORD, M. E., CHRISTOPHERSEN, E. R., PHILLIPS, E. L., FIXSEN, D. L., and WOLF, M. M.: The effects of the social interaction components of a token economy. Paper presented at the meeting of the American Psychological Association, New Orleans, September 1974.

HAWKINS, R. P., PETERSON, R. F., SCHWEID, E., and BIJOU, S. W.: Behavior therapy in the home: Amelioration of problem parent-child relations with the parent in a therapeutic role. *J. Exper. Child Psychol.*, 4, 99-107, 1966.

PATTERSON, G. R.: Personal communication, 1973.

PATTERSON, G. R., RAY, R. S., SHAW, D. A., and COBB, J. A.: *Manual for Coding Family Interactions*, 1969, ASIS National Auxiliary Publication Service, CMM Information Services, Inc., 909 Third Avenue, New York, New York 10022, Document 01234.

PATTERSON, G. R., COBB, J. A., and RAY, R. S.: A social engineering technology for retraining aggressive boys. In: H. Adams and L. Unikel (Eds.), *Georgia Symposium in Experimental Clinical Psychology*, Vol. II. Springfield, Ill.: Charles C Thomas, 1973.

PHILLIPS, E. L., PHILLIPS, E. A., FIXSEN, D. L., and WOLF, M. M.: Achievement Place: Behavior shaping works for delinquents. *Psychol. Today*, June 1973.

STUART, R. B.: Behavioral contracting within the families of delinquents. *J. Behav. Ther. and Exper. Psychiat.*, 2, 1-11, 1971.

WAHLER, R. G.: Oppositional children: A quest for parental reinforcement control. *J. Appl. Behav. Anal.*, 2, 159-170, 1969.

WALKER, H. M.: *Walker Problem Behavior Identification Checklist*. Los Angeles: Western Psychological Services, 1970.

WRIGHT, L.: Handling the encopretic child. *Prof. Psychol.*, 137-144, 1973.

4

A Model for Training Parents to Manage Their Family Systems Using Multiple Data Sources as Measures of Parent Effectiveness

BUELL E. GOOCHER

and

DAVID N. GROVE

A major task of a child rehabilitation agency is the generalization of new behaviors acquired in the treatment setting to the child's natural environment. It is no longer reasonable to assume that children can be plucked from their environment, have their behavior modified in a clinician's office or other artificial setting, and subsequently be returned to their natural milieu with the expectation that they will maintain their newly acquired behaviors. Hence, the key to a successful treatment program lies in the ability of the behavior therapist to modify the environment (e.g., parent behaviors) which may have inadvertently encouraged and promoted, or may be maintaining, the child's maladaptive behaviors (Reid and Patterson, 1973). Since children's behaviors are viewed as a function of interactions with their present environment, significant persons such as parents must be trained to provide appropriate remedial experiences which will enhance the acquisition and maintenance of behaviors that are naturally rewarding both to the children and to their social environment (Tharp and Wetzel, 1969).

The Edgefield Lodge parent training model assumes that the following five components are critical for an effective program: (1) Adequate systems which facilitate the identification of problem areas to be modified

57

must be developed. These systems typically include subjective parental reports which are subsequently substantiated through objective sources such as third party observations and parental documentation. (2) Instructional methodologies which are individualized to meet the idiosyncratic needs of each family while concurrently providing basic information concerning effective child management skills must be developed. In addition, activities must be delineated so that the parents can practice and hence demonstrate the acquisition of effective child management skills. These demonstrations must eventually occur in the same environment in which the parent is expected to produce child remediation. (3) Methodologies must be established whereby the parents consolidate their practice skills to remediate the problems identified. (4) Systems which will allow for the gradual withdrawal of the parent training counselors while concurrently maintaining a high degree of parental effectiveness must be implemented. (5) Evaluation techniques must be sufficient to allow the parent training counselor to make continuous treatment-effectiveness decisions while collaterally providing a method of substantiating the ability of the parent to generalize training to untreated behaviors and environments. Each of these components will be discussed briefly, followed by family case data which will illustrate agency utilization of the methodology and implications of the overall effectiveness of this model for parent training.

1. *Identification of Problem Areas.* The identification process is an often overlooked area which has traditionally relied upon parental reports. It has become increasingly apparent, however, that untrained parents are poor observers not only of their own behavior, but also of their children's behavior.* The Edgefield identification system begins with an initial intake conference which attempts to pinpoint general areas of maladaptive behavior. These maladaptive behaviors may be child- and/or adult-focused. During this conference, the parents also complete the Walker Problem Behavior Identification Checklist (Walker, 1970). Parental responses to these standardized questions allow the examiner to establish a profile for all children in the family. The questionnaire is answered by all adult family members. The five scales (i.e., acting out, withdrawal, distractibility, disturbed peer relations, and immaturity) not only allow for comparisons between parents regarding specific children, but also act as a method through which discussions

---

* Parents can typically reliably report that a behavior occurs or does not occur but are unable to accurately report critical treatment variables concerning frequency, duration, and rate of problem behavior.

centered around problem identification can be generated. In addition, the checklist provides basic information about the attitudes the parents hold toward their child's behavior. Following the intake conference, three hours of on-site family observations are conducted by an Edgefield staff member who is independent of all present and proposed family treatment staff. This observation system, or Family Observation Record (FOR) (Edgefield Lodge, Inc., 1974), is utilized to delineate the daily functioning of an entire family constellation. The major behaviors observed are: (a) appropriate social interaction; (b) inappropriate social interaction; (c) commands and command/compliance; (d) positive interactions; (e) negative interactions; (f) violation of social norms (i.e., expectations specified by each family); and (g) self-directed behaviors.* The information from these three sources (i.e., intake, FOR, and checklist) is compiled to design an Initial Problem List (IPL) which specifies the precise parental and child behaviors to be remediated. It is subsequently agreed upon and signed by the treatment staff and parents. The final problem behavior substantiation is derived from baseline data, gathered during training by the parents, for each of the behaviors on the Initial Problem List.

2. *Instructional Methodologies and Activities.* After completion of the IPL, the parents are immediately enrolled in a series of ten individual weekly sessions which include presentations by the parent trainer, followed each week by skill development exercises which are part of an overall sequence. Some of the developed sequences are as follows:

A. Problem Behavior Management
 Phase I: Identify and define behaviors.
 Phase II: Record the occurrence of defined behaviors.
 Phase III: Identify potential child and parent consequences.
 Phase IV: Deliver selected consequences contingently and consistently.
 Phase V: Make decisions based upon accumulated data.
 Phase VI: Institute treatment-fading procedures.

B. Skill Development Behaviors
 Phase I: Identify and define skill to be acquired.
 Phase II: Task-analyze skill to be taught.

---

* Reliability checks between independent observers achieved a point-by-point reliability of 85% with a range of 82% to 90%. All FOR data reported in this report had a category by category reliability of at least 85%.

Phase III: Record the occurrence of the skill.

Phase IV: Identify potential child consequences.

Phase V: Deliver selected consequences contingently and consistently.

Phase VI: Make decisions based upon accumulated skill data.

Phase VII: Institute fading procedures.

Each of the above phases is broken down into steps ranging from those requiring staff supervision in a structured situation (i.e., requiring staff at-the-elbow supervision) to those requiring no support from the training staff. An example of some of the steps for Phase A-II, "Occurrence of defined behaviors," follows.

Phase A-II: Record the occurrence of defined behaviors.

Step 1. Observe and count hand raising in Edgefield classroom with concurrent observations being made by an Edgefield staff member. *Terminal criterion*: 95% point-by-point reliability.

Step 2. Observe and count out-of-seat behavior in an Edgefield classroom with concurrent observations being made by an Edgefield staff member. *Terminal criterion*: 90% point-by-point reliability.

Step 3. Observe and count talk-outs in an Edgefield classroom with concurrent observations being made by another parent. *Terminal criterion*: 85% point-by-point reliability.

Step 4. Observe and count swearing in home with another adult (i.e., parent or Edgefield staff). *Terminal criterion*: 85% point-by-point reliability.

Step 5. Observe and count mand compliance in the home. *Terminal criterion:* 1 week of data.

Step 6. Observe and count positive and negative statements emitted by another adult. *Terminal criterion*: 2 days of data.

Step 7. Observe and count one's own positive and negative statements. *Terminal criterion*: Edgefield FOR percentages of positive and negative statements compare within 10 percentage points of parent's data.

It must be emphasized that, if parents are able to successfully complete the terminal criterion at Step 7, they need not undergo training at the lower steps. In addition, program branching may occur within or between steps based upon the particular needs of each parent. Finally, the phases do not represent a developmental sequence and, consequently, parents can be working on several phases concurrently.

Some of the early activities within each phase are performed by the parents at Edgefield Lodge with the supervision of the staff. Later activities are performed at home and monitored through materials returned to the parent trainer. As parents demonstrate mastery of increasingly complex steps, they are required to move to the next step.

3. *Remediation of Problems.* After basic skills are demonstrated, the parents are required to conduct "treatment" programs for those behaviors listed on the Initial Problem List. In order to initiate treatment programs before all the necessary skills are acquired, the Agency uses portions of the Agency token system as a part of the treatment package until the parents acquire the necessary skills. This allows the Agency to begin treatment with each family within an average of 3.6 days after admission, even though the parents have not acquired all the child management skills.

For example, one of the criteria for movement of the child from Phase I to Phase II of the token economy is that the parents must collect daily data which are returned to the Agency with the child. The child receives Agency token points which are subsequently exchanged in the Agency economy. Thus, the major responsibility of the parents initially is to record rather than consequate behaviors. During the child's progression through Phase II of the token economy, which coincides with sessions 4, 5, 6, and 7 of parent training, the parents are instructed in additional steps of program design with the added contingency that program controls, e.g., positive and aversive consequences, must be dispensed in the home environment. Home programs are monitored by the Agency staff and during training sessions.

4. *Maintenance of Parental Behavior.* The gradual introduction of specific skills and the gradual withdrawal of Agency treatment support (i.e., token system) tend to facilitate long-term maintenance. In addition, increased responsibility of the parent for the child can be achieved by transferring the child from five-day residential to day treatment, to outpatient and, finally, to follow-up. If skills begin to extinguish during this process, the progression can be reversed. Final termination is not completed until a corresponding positive change has occurred in the par-

ent's responses on the Walker Checklist. It is believed that this instrument measures the influence of the parent's previous history (attitudes) regarding their children. Terminating involvement based upon improved performance of family members in the absence of a corresponding attitudinal change certainly reduces the likelihood of the family maintaining intervention gains.

5. *Evaluation.* The effectiveness of the parent training program is evaluated at several different levels. The FOR is taken not only upon intake, but also at discharges and follow-up. This instrument allows for a measure of generalization effect to a majority of behaviors that may not have been specifically treated. The Walker Problem Behavior Identification Checklist is readministered at discharge and follow-up, providing a comparison of pre- and post-treatment verbal reports. In addition, the daily individual data derived from behavior-specific programs conducted by the parents are monitored continuously. Finally, the number of skills acquired is also reported as the parents progress through the parent training sessions.

CASE STUDY

Family data presented here were obtained in the natural environment, in a setting where there were two natural parents and three children. The youngest child (19 months) was not involved in the data analysis. The other two children were 6 and 3 years of age. Dad was a student who also held a full-time job. Mother was a housewife. Both parents were involved in the parent training.

Table 1 contains data from a portion of the intake FOR on commands emitted, what the deposition of those commands were, and the percent of positive and negative consequences emitted by family members. The command data indicated that Mom emitted 22 commands—40% of the total number of commands given during the recorded observation period. Of these, 9, or 41%, were complied with by the person to whom the command was directed while 13, or 59%, terminated in noncompliance. At no time did Mom give a command and then proceed to complete the request herself (i.e., Do For, 0%). Dad gave slightly fewer commands (19) and received less compliance than Mom. Son, referred because of management problems, emitted 22% of all commands, 83% of which were complied with by other members of the family. During the intake conference, the parents had indicated that their son was "demanding" their time, and this is reflected in the high percentage of commands given by him.

TABLE 1

Number and their percent values of commands and
consequences emitted by family members at Intake.

Category	Mom		Dad		Family Members Son*		Daughter		Total	
	N	%	N	%	N	%	N	%	N	%
Commands Emitted	22	40	19	34	12	22	2	4	55	100
A. Compliance	9	41	7	37	10	83	1	50	27	-
B. Non Compliance	13	59	11	58	2	17	1	50	27	-
C. Do For	0	-	1	5	0	-	0	-	1	-
Total	22	100	19	100	12	100	2	100	55	-
Consequences Emitted	4	44	1	12	1	11	3	33	9	100
A. Positive	1	25	0	-	0	-	2	67	3	-
B. Negative	3	75	1	100	1	100	1	33	6	-
Total	4	100	1	100	1	100	3	100	9	-

*In this Table and all subsequent Tables, the son is the child who was subsequently
admitted to an Edgefield Treatment Program.

TABLE 2

Number and their percent values of commands and
consequences received by family members at Intake.

Category	Mom		Dad		Family Members Son		Daughter		Total	
	N	%	N	%	N	%	N	%	N	%
Commands Received	1	2	0	-	41	74	13	24	55	100
A. Compliance	1	100	0	-	15	37	11	85	27	-
B. Non Compliance	0	-	0	-	25	61	2	15	27	-
C. Do For	0	-	0	-	1	2	0	-	1	-
Total	1	100	0	-	41	100	13	100	55	-
Consequences Received	0	-	1	11	7	78	1	11	9	-
A. Positive	0	-	1	100	2	29	0	-	3	-
B. Negative	0	-	0	-	5	71	1	100	6	-
Total	0	-	1	100	9	100	1	100	9	-

TABLE 3

Number and their percent values of Inappropriate

Social Interactions by family members at Intake

Category	Family Members									
	Mom		Dad		Son		Daughter		Total	
	N	%	N	%	N	%	N	%	N	%
Inappropriate Social Interaction										
A. Emitted	0	0	2	13	12	74	2	13	16	100
B. Received	7	44	4	25	2	13	3	18	16	100

The Consequence Emitted data in Table 1 show that only 9 consequences were emitted during the three-hour observation, with Mom delivering 44% of the total consequences of which 25% and 75% were positive and negative, respectively. Of all the consequences emitted by Dad, 100% were negative.

Table 2 shows that Son received 74% of the total commands given, of which 61% resulted in noncompliance. This is in sharp contrast to Daughter who received 24% of the total requests and had 85% compliance. Of all the consequences received, Son was the recipient of 78%, of which 29% were positive and 71% were negative. Daughter maintained a high rate of compliance (i.e., 85%) although she received no positive consequence.

A review of data from Tables 1 and 2 tentatively suggests that (1) command compliance might be an important remediation area (i.e., only 41% of Mom's and 37% of Dad's requests were terminated with compliance); (2) few consequences were emitted by Mom and Dad, and of these only 25% were positive—a program to teach the parents to consequate is indicated; and (3) Dad commanded other members of the family but did not receive any commands in return, which might indicate a need to increase his involvement with the family.*

Additional information can be obtained from Table 3, which contains the data for inappropriate social interactions. These data suggest that Son emitted 12 inappropriate social behaviors (typically, physical aggression) and that Mom was the primary recipient of the inappropriate

* Editors' note: Since the data being presented represent, in many instances, infrequently occurring events, the previous statements should be regarded as potentially fruitful clinical hypotheses in need of further elaboration.

social interaction (i.e., 44%). These data tentatively suggest that Mom needs to receive training in how to deal with inappropriate social behavior.

Profiles from the Walker Problem Behavior Identification Checklist (Figures 1, 2, 3, and 4) indicated that Mom and Dad shared similar views of Son and Daughter, and also agreed that there were major differences between the behavior patterns of the children. These data, together with the observation data, suggested that Son should be the primary focus of any intervention program and alerted the family trainer that parental attitudes toward child management would need shaping in order to maximize long-range effects of behavior change programs. Data from the FOR, Walker, and intake interview were combined to form an Initial Problem List. Some of the areas identified were: (1) increase command compliance by Son; (2) reduce Son's inappropriate social behavior, which took the form of laughing, teasing, interrupting, pushing, physical aggression, and talking back; (3) teach the parents and have them demonstrate child management skills in the areas of (a) "I don't want to" behavior—both passive and active avoidance of chores; (b) self-indulgence—crying and temper tantrums; and (c) aggressive behaviors against both people and physical objects; and (4) increase parental communication.

Based upon priorities established by the parents and concurred with by the Agency, parental instruction was begun, and baseline data were collected on: (1) number of complaints to Father by Mother (related to 4 above); (2) number of inappropriate laughs by Son (related to 2 above); (3) number of demanding behaviors (related to 2 above); and (4) number of school assignments completed (related to 3a above).

After baseline data substantiated the occurrence (i.e., frequency, rate, and/or percentage) of the specified behaviors, intervention programs were initiated. It is interesting to note that programs were developed in the four areas for which baseline data were collected. Generally, token systems were utilized to expedite the behavioral changes in all behavior-specific intervention programs. Specifically, Son earned points which were exchangeable for a variety of home-oriented reinforcers. In the program established between the parents, Dad dispensed to Mom blue slips of paper for positive comments and pink slips of paper for negative comments. Each slip of blue paper had a cash-in value of 10 cents; each pink slip resulted in a 20-cent loss. The money was saved for a mutual activity specified by Mom. In addition, if Mom reached the goal established by the parent trainer (number of blue slips per

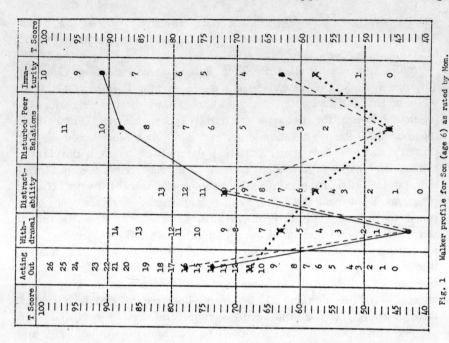

Fig. 1   Walker profile for Son (age 6) as rated by Mom.

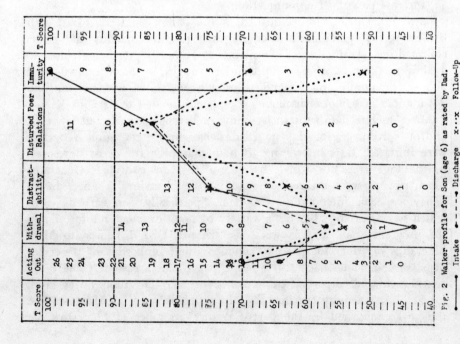

Fig. 2   Walker profile for Son (age 6) as rated by Dad.

●———● Intake   ●- - - -● Discharge   x·····x Follow-Up

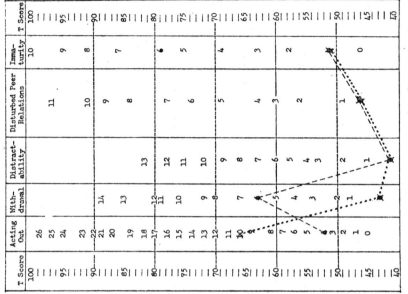

Fig. 3   Walker profile for Daughter (age 3) as rated by Mom.*

● Intake   ●‑‑‑‑● Discharge   x·····x Follow-up

*Intake profile was not obtained on Daughter.

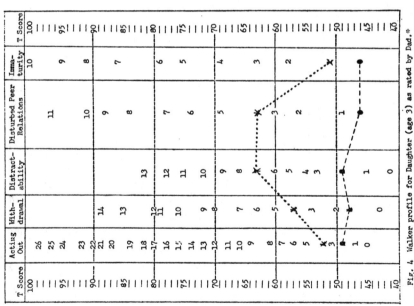

Fig. 4   Walker profile for Daughter (age 3) as rated by Dad.*

● Intake   ●‑‑‑‑●Discharge   x···x Follow-up

*Intake profile was not obtained on Daughter.

TABLE 4

Program

	# of complaints to father by mother/day	# of inappropriate laughs by son/day	# of inappropriate behaviors (teasing, interrupting, pushing, talking back by son/day	% of assignments completed by son/day
Baseline	2.3	2.7	15.5	50
Total number of Days	13	7	6	3
Treatment First 3 days	.33	.95	6.3	76
Last 3 days	.33	.19	3.3	100
Total number of treatment days	47	63	6	43

week), she received double the amount earned—up to $7.50 per week. Although continuous day systems were utilized, only summary data are presented in Table 4.

FOR data shown in Tables 5, 6, and 7 indicate the changes that had occurred in commands, consequences, and inappropriate social behaviors at the time of discharge five weeks after treatment intervention had begun. Comparing baseline FOR data from Tables 1, 2, and 3, Mom maintained approximately the same number of commands (22 during intake and 25 at discharge), while compliance to these commands increased from 41% to 88%. There was a slight reduction in the number of commands given by Dad and a concurrent increase in compliance from 37% to 72%. Son's number of commands (demanding) emitted dropped from 12 to 1 at discharge, and there was a reversal in compliance to those commands, i.e., 83% as compared to 20% at discharge,

TABLE 5

Number and their percent values of commands and
consequences emitted by family members at Discharge.

Category	Mom		Dad		Son		Daughter		Total	
	N	%	N	%	N	%	N	%	N	%
Commands Emitted	25	56	14	31	5	11	1	2	45	100
A. Compliance	22	88	10	72	1	20	0	-	33	-
B. Non Compliance	2	8	3	21	4	80	1	100	10	-
C. Do For	1	4	1	7	0	-	0	-	2	-
Total	25	100	14	100	5	100	1	100	45	-
Consequences Emitted	23	59	15	38	1	3	0	-	39	100
A. Positive	20	87	15	100	0	-	0	-	35	-
B. Negative	3	13	0	-	1	100	0	-	4	-
Total	23	100	15	100	1	100	0	-	39	-

TABLE 6

Number and their percent values of commands and
consequences received by family members at Discharge.

Category	Mom		Dad		Family Members Son		Daughter		Total	
	N	%	N	%	N	%	N	%	N	%
Commands Received	1	2	1	2	22	49	21	47	45	100
A. Compliance	1	100	0	-	18	82	14	67	33	-
B. Non Compliance	0	-	1	100	4	18	5	28	10	-
C. Do For	0	-	0	-	0	-	2	5	2	-
Total	1	100	1	100	22	100	21	100	45	-
Consequences Received	0	-	0	-	18	46	21	54	39	100
A. Positive	0	-	0	-	16	89	19	90	35	-
B. Negative	0	-	0	-	2	11	2	10	4	-
Total	0	-	0	-	18	100	21	100	39	-

Behavior Modification Approaches to Parenting

TABLE 7

Number and their percent values of Inappropriate
Social Interactions by family members at Discharge.

Category	Family Members									
	Mom		Dad		Son		Daughter		Total	
	N	%	N	%	N	%	N	%	N	%
Inappropriate Social Interaction										
A. Emitted	0	0	0	0	8	67	4	33	12	100
B. Received	5	42	5	42	2	16	0	0	12	100

The Consequences Emitted data in Table 5 show that the family increased the number of consequences, of which 97% were emitted by the parents during the three-hour observation. Approximately 87% of Mom's and 100% of Dad's consequences were positive. These data show a major shift in Mom's and Dad's ability to dispense positive reinforcers for command compliance and other appropriate social behaviors.

Table 6 shows that Son and Daughter share receipt of total commands given (49% and 47%, respectively) at time of discharge. Again, there has been a reversal in rate of compliance and noncompliance for Son, i.e., compliance increased from 37% to 82%, while noncompliance dropped from 61% to 18%. For Daughter, however, there was a slight increase in noncompliance to commands received. Furthermore, Son now receives only 46% of all consequences (down from 78% at baseline), and the percent of positive and negative consequences has reversed from 29% and 71%, respectively, to 89% and 11%, respectively. Daughter's rate of positive consequences received has increased to 90% whereas previously she was receiving no reinforcers for complying with commands and other social expectations.

Table 7 shows little change on the part of family members in their handling of inappropriate social interactions at the time of discharge. Son's rate of emitting these behaviors decreased slightly (57% from 74%) but, in general, there was a spreading effect on emitting and receiving inappropriate social interactions across parents.

A summary of data comparisons between Tables 1, 2, and 3 (baseline) and Tables 5, 6, and 7 (discharge) suggests that Mom was emitting more commands, and both she and Dad were receiving more compliance at discharge. There was a spreading of commands received between Son and Daughter and an increase in their compliance percentage. Both Son and Daughter received increased positive recognition for their appropriate behaviors but, more importantly, there appears to have been a shift from a crisis orientation in the family, in which positive reinforcers were used sparingly, to a higher incidence of reinforcement shared by Son and Daughter. For example, out of the total percentage of consequences she received, Daughter now received 90% positive reinforcement for command compliance whereas previously she was receiving no reinforcement.

Parent training on specific behavioral skills, such as assignments completed and reducing inappropriate demanding behaviors, appears not to have generalized to the handling of inappropriate social interactions, and these behaviors continued to occur at about the same rate as at baseline.

Parental attitudes toward Son (identified patient), as measured by the Walker Checklist, suggest that the parents were making more positive statements about him at discharge as his behavior became more appropriate and compliant (see Figures 1, 2). Both Mom and Dad reported a lessening of acting-out behaviors and a higher level of responsibility, although peer relations continued to be problematic. There was little difference between the profiles of parental attitudes toward Daughter.

Tables 8, 9, and 10 report FOR data five months after discharge, at which time the parents again requested help with their disturbed family relationships. These data, compared with discharge data in Tables 5, 6, and 7, show that Mom maintained the same number of commands, but her "percentage share" reduced because of a dramatic increase in the number emitted by Dad. Mom's compliance percentage dropped to 52% while Dad's increased from 72% to 84%. There was some drop in the number and percent of consequences emitted by both parents, although the distribution of consequences (positive and negative) remained about the same. Both Son and Daughter were getting more compliance for the commands they, too, emitted.

Dad continued to receive about the same percentage of commands, but Son was again beginning to receive more (63% as compared with 49% at discharge). Compliance and noncompliance percentages of commands received maintained the same pattern distribution as at discharge.

There was a slight increase in the percent of consequences received by Son (from 46% to 53%), although the number and distribution of

TABLE 8

Number and their percent values of commands and
consequences emitted by family members at Follow-Up.

Category	Mom		Dad		Son		Daughter		Total	
	N	%	N	%	N	%	N	%	N	%
Commands Emitted	25	32	37	47	11	14	6	7	79	100
A. Compliance	13	52	31	84	7	64	3	50	54	-
B. Non Compliance	9	36	6	16	3	27	3	50	21	-
C. Do For	3	12	0	-	1	9	0	-	4	-
Total	25	100	37	100	11	100	6	100	79	-
Consequences Emitted	14	44	9	28	2	6	7	22	32	100
A. Positive	13	93	8	89	2	100	7	100	30	-
B. Negative	1	7	1	11	0	-	0	-	2	-
Total	14	100	9	100	2	100	7	100	32	-

TABLE 9

Number and their percent values of commands and
consequences received by family members at Follow-Up.

Category	Mom		Dad		Family Members Son		Daughter		Total	
	N	%	N	%	N	%	N	%	N	%
Commands Received	0	-	2	3	50	63	27	34	79	100
A. Compliance	0	-	1	50	35	70	18	67	54	-
B. Non Compliance	0	-	1	50	15	30	5	18	21	-
C. Do For	0	-	0	-	0	-	4	15	4	-
Total	0	-	2	100	50	100	27	100	79	-
Consequences Received	2	7	2	7	19	59	9	33	32	100
A. Positive	2	100	2	100	17	89	7	78	28	-
B. Negative	0	-	0	-	2	11	2	22	4	-
Total	2	100	2	100	19	100	9	100	32	-

TABLE 10

Number and their percent values of Inappropriate

Social Interactions by family members at Follow-Up.

Category	Family Members									
	Mom		Dad		Son		Daughter		Total	
	N	%	N	%	N	%	N	%	N	%
Inappropriate Social Interaction										
A. Emitted	0	0	0	0	1	50	1	50	2	100
B. Received	0	0	0	0	1	50	1	50	2	100

these between positive and negative remained very close to the discharge rate. However, Daughter's number and percentage of consequences received dramatically decreased.

There was a remarkable reduction in the number of inappropriate social interactions. During discharge there were a total of 12, while at follow-up only 2 such responses occurred during the three-hour observation.

Parental attitudes toward Son were even more positive at follow-up as measured by the Walker Checklist.

In general, the children increased their compliance to commands through the discharge period. These changes held up at the time of follow-up. Similarly, they received more positive consequences for command compliance both at discharge and at follow-up. Mom and Dad emitted more commands and achieved more compliance through the periods of discharge and follow-up.

There was not much change in the percent of inappropriate social interaction either at discharge or follow-up. However, parental attitudes toward the children improved at discharge, and the parents continued to report more positive attitudes toward the children at the time of follow-up. These data, when evaluated with additional information from the FOR and parent reports, suggested to the counselor that the request for intervention was probably based on issues other than childrearing, e.g., marital disharmony. This hypothesis was confirmed by the parents, who were then referred to a mental health clinic for marital counseling.

CONCLUSION

The model presented in this paper attempts to train parents by utilizing a scope and sequence approach to skill development in the area of effective child management. These skills can be initially taught in a structured agency environment and, subsequently, skill development for each parent can be shaped through the sequence, depending upon previous training, susceptibility to training, and other idiosyncratic differences.

The model also assumes a responsibility to document through diverse data sources the impact of the training program on specific child problems, as well as on the total family unit. These data sources include direct family observations by independent observers and data submitted by parents concerning specifically delineated checklists. It is only through these data sources that effective treatment decisions can be made by the parent training and child treatment specialists.

REFERENCES

Edgefield Lodge, Inc.: *Family Observation Record.* Unpublished, 1974.
REID, J. B., and PATTERSON, G. R.: *The Modification of Aggression and Stealing Behavior of Boys in the Home Setting.* Paper presented at the Third International Symposium on Behavior Modification, Mexico City, Mexico, January 1973.
THARP, R. G., and WETZEL, R. J.: *Behavior Modification in the Natural Environment.* New York: Academic Press, 1969.
WALKER, H. M.: *Walker Problem Behavior Identification Checklist.* Los Angeles, Cal.: Western Psychological Services, 1970.

5

Summer Therapeutic Environment Program – STEP: A Hospital Alternative for Children

MERIHELEN BLACKMORE, NANCY RICH,
ZETTA MEANS, and MIKE NALLY

The purpose of this study was to evaluate the magnitude of positive behavioral change in chronic problem children that might be effected and maintained by combining two existing remedial approaches—namely, an environmental activity camping program and a home-based reinforcement system anchored to school activities and achievement.

The effectiveness of camping programs for youngsters has long been recognized. Over the years, numerous therapeutic residential camping experiences for troubled youth have been developed (McNeil, 1957, 1962; Meyers, 1961; Loughmiller, 1965; Rickard and Dinoff, 1965; Nelson et al., 1973). These environmental programs, using a residential camping model lasting anywhere from two weeks to year-round, have employed a variety of treatment approaches in dealing with all types of disturbances. The intent of these programs is to demonstrate to youngsters that problem behavior interferes with living. Each camping incident offers a learning opportunity to the youngster for coping more adequately with daily living experiences.

Without the support of the Arvada and Wheatridge-Golden Teams of the Jefferson County Mental Health Center, STEP could not have occurred. We wish to acknowledge the teams' contributions.

Special thanks to Sherrie Martin, Jim Schoemaker, Marianne Kunze, and Maura Mansfield for all of their help during STEP; and for collateral efforts, we wish to thank Cyndi Auten, Dr. Dean Baxter, Steve Chapman, Sandy Martin, and Pat Miller.

Last and certainly not least, "Thanks, Mother Nature, you did more than your share!"

The use of home-based reinforcement as a means for modifying mal-adaptive classroom behavior was discussed by Bailey et al. (1970). They demonstrated that a home-based reward system was effective in modifying classroom behavior. A similar home-based system of reinforcement was found to be appropriate for the purposes of the present study.

METHOD

The Summer Therapeutic Environment Program (STEP) was a hospital alternative treatment approach for children with chronic emotional and behavioral problems. STEP combined the two above-mentioned remedial techniques in an attempt to change a child's maladaptive behavior both at home and school. In addition, the intent of STEP was to (1) teach parents methods for modifying their children's school behavior, (2) counsel parents in increasing their effectiveness in child management, (3) arrange reward contingencies to enhance maximum generalization of adaptive behavior by the youngsters, and (4) evaluate all phases of the program's effectiveness in influencing behavior change and in maintaining the behavior change over time.

Subjects

All *S*s were drawn from the county served by the Jefferson County Mental Health Center and attended Jefferson County Public Schools. Experimenters established certain criteria for acceptance in STEP; these criteria were: (1) *S*s must have exhibited chronic maladaptive behavior both at home and school; (2) *S* or *S*'s parents must have been in prior treatment (e.g., mental health center, private counseling, another social agency) in an attempt to change *S*'s behavior; (3) prior treatment was considered unsuccessful or incomplete by the counselor or parent; and (4) parents had to be willing to carry out certain requirements. More specifically, parents agreed to complete all requested research, attend all parent-group sessions, assist in the establishment of home conditions, maintain *S*'s attendance in the school and mountain activities, and take a ten-day baseline count of *S*'s problem home behaviors prior to *S*'s involvement in STEP.

Potential parents for the program were referred by the public school system or mental health center to the *E*s in the two months prior to the starting date of STEP. *E*s explained the program and spelled out the requirements to the parents. Parents received no pressure to become involved in STEP; the decision to enter the program was left totally up to the parents. Parents who declined STEP were offered the regular resources of the mental health center.

Eight *S*s, all males between the ages of 8 and 11 years old, were placed in STEP. Four *S*s were in treatment at the mental health center, and four were in treatment through the school system. Six *S*s had both parents living at home; two *S*s had one-parent families. Six *S*s had two or more siblings; one *S* had one sibling; and one *S* had none. All parents had a high school education, and six of the parents had advanced training. Average family income was lower middle class to upper middle class.

Some of the problem behaviors were noncompliance, lack of personal responsibility, low self-esteem, inappropriate peer relationships, temper tantrums, encopresis, withdrawal, disruptiveness in structural settings, short attention span, and stealing.

Measurements Used

Several instruments and methods were used for data collection during the course of STEP. Changes related to academic performance were measured in three ways: (1) The Wide Range Achievement Test (WRAT) (Jastak and Jastak, 1965) was administered by mental health center staff before, immediately after, and six months following STEP to measure academic level and change. (2) The Manual for Coding Discrete Behaviors in School Settings (Cobb and Ray, 1971) was used to measure appropriate and inappropriate classroom behavior in *S*'s regular classroom prior to STEP, daily during the STEP school phase, and as a follow-up measure in *S*'s regular classroom in the fall (regular classroom observations also provided normative classroom behavior for each *S*). Observations were taken by three independent observers using a time-sampling technique. The observers recorded *S*'s behavior as well as responses by the teacher and peers within a six-second interval. (3) Daily during the school phase, teachers initialed 3″ x 5″ cards to record a single occurrence of inappropriate behavior and to subjectively judge whether *S* had engaged in appropriate behaviors. The teachers' cards corresponded to the observers' code but grouped several classes of behavior for condensation (Table 1). All of the *S*s' regular teachers continued recording in the fall.

Two measures were taken by an observer during the mountain-activities phase of STEP; *S*'s equipment was checked daily to determine what, if any, equipment had been lost, and *S*'s responses to time limits were noted.

TABLE 1

School Reporting Card

Name						Date						
Class		Math		Free time								
	Yes	No	Yes	No	Yes	No	Yes	No	Yes	No	Yes	No
Was student physically or verbally aggressive to others?												
Was student excessively noisy?												
Did student attend to his task during work periods?												
Did student complete expected amt. of work?												
Was student out of his seat w/o permission?												
Did student interact appropriately w/ peer?												
Was student generally cooperative?												
Teacher's initial												

During simulated classroom, only two class columns were used. The card was also used in *S*'s regular fall classroom and has enough spaces for six classes.

Before, during, and six months after the termination of STEP, parents kept frequency counts of (1) *S*'s identified problem behaviors, and (2) their own patterns of reinforcement.

The Louisville Behavior Checklist, Form E (Miller, 1967) was used to test maturity level and change during STEP. Parents completed this form before STEP, at termination, and six months after termination of STEP.

Program Overview

STEP was an intensive three-phase treatment program with follow-up. An overview of the various phases is given in Table 2. These phases included (1) six parent-group sessions aimed at helping parents set up behavior modification programs for *S*s in the home, (2) eighteen two-hour simulated classroom sessions, held in an area summer school, aimed

TABLE 2

STEP Schedule of Events and Therapy Conditions

Sunday	Monday	Tuesday	Wednesday	Thursday	Friday	Saturday
	Home Cond.1 School Cond.A	Home Cond.1 Field Trip Parent= Group	Home Cond.1 School Cond.A	Home Cond.1 Field Trip	Home Cond.1 School Cond. A	Home Cond.1
Home Cond.1	Backpack 4 miles	Backpack move camp 3 miles	Backpack same camp group hike 6 miles	Backpack walk out 7 miles	Home Cond.2 School Cond.B	Home Cond.2
Home Cond.2	Home Cond.2 School Cond.B	Home Cond.2 School Cond.B Parent-Group	National Holiday	Home Cond.2 School Cond.C	Home Cond.2 School Cond.C	Home Cond.2
Home Cond.2	Backpack Travel - Bus	Backpack move camp 5 miles	Backpack move camp 4 miles	Backpack same camp group mtn. climb 8 mi.	Backpack move camp 9 miles	Backpack walk out 5 miles
Backpack Travel - Bus	Home Cond.3 School Cond.C	Home Cond.3 School Cond.C Parent-Group	Home Cond.3 School Cond.C	Home Cond.3 School Cond.D	Home Cond.3 School Cond.D	Home Cond.3
Home Cond.3	Home Cond.3 School Cond.D	Home Cond.3 School Cond.E	Home Cond.3 School Cond.E	Home Cond.3 School Cond.E	Home Cond.3 School Cond.E	Home Cond.3
Home Cond.3	Backpack 3 miles	Backpack move camp 4 miles	Backpack move camp 4 miles	Backpack same camp group activities	Backpack move camp 5 miles	Backpack same camp cloud burst
Backpack walk out 5 miles	Follow-up Program Starts	Parent-Group				

at improving Ss' classroom behavior (the classroom was staffed by two teachers and three observers, all mental health center employees), (3) eighteen days of backpacking—one four-day backpack and two seven-day backpacks—and two preparatory day trips, all of which were conducted in wilderness areas of the Colorado Rocky Mountains (the mountain activities were staffed by two mental health center employees, one observer, and one graduate student), and (4) follow-up observation, testing, and consultation which were done in *S*'s regular fall classroom, at the mental health center, and over the telephone.

Contingency Systems

A variety of contingency systems were used throughout STEP. An other-environment reinforcement model (i.e., school behaviors were reinforced at home and on the backpacks, and home behaviors were reinforced on the backpacks) was used extensively during STEP to facilitate generalization. Reinforcement for specific behaviors was delayed anywhere from one hour to two weeks (e.g., *S* may be earning credit for provisions for a backpack trip two weeks away).

During the simulated school portion of the program, teachers initiated a school behavior reporting card after each class session. *S*s took these cards home daily and presented them to parents. Parents, on the receipt of the card, were responsible for delivering the appropriate contingency (i.e., lunch and/or monetary credit for backpack provisions, or neither). If *S* did not bring home the card, he received neither reinforcer and also lost an additional 50-cent monetary credit toward backpack provisions. If *S* did not earn lunch for more than two days, parents were contacted to learn whether, in fact, *S* was not getting lunch or the food was not an important reinforcer to S. Another reinforcer was substituted (e.g., play time with friends) if the lunch was not a powerful reinforcer.

S was reinforced for appropriate home behavior on the backpacks. Parents marked a home behavior chart daily which was presented to the mountain activities staff prior to each backpack trip. The staff, upon receipt of the charts, would provide that portion of the reinforcement (i.e., food) that *S* had earned.

Contingencies during the backpacking phase of STEP were natural and provided by the environment (e.g., loss of fork and spoon meant eating with fingers or sticks). In addition to experiencing the natural consequences of equipment loss, *S*s could replace the lost equipment if they so desired by performing special jobs for parents or staff in the interim between backpacks.

Parent Involvement

This phase of STEP consisted of (1) one pre-program meeting, (2) four parent-group meetings, two hours in length, spaced throughout

TABLE 3

Home Behavior Chart

Name_____	Total necessary for credit $ 10.20									
Behaviors Dates	Actual Total $_____									
Target Behavior 1 _____ $.35 daily credit										
Target Behavior 2 _____ $.35 daily credit										
Chore Behavior 3 _____ $.10 daily credit										
Chore Behavior 4 _____ $.05 daily credit										
School card $.25 daily credit										
Loss of school card - $.50										

STEP (see Table 2), (3) one follow-up group, two months after STEP, (4) individual contact with parents to monitor or modify S's behavioral program, and (5) crisis contact as needed.

The goals were to teach parents the principles and application of reinforcement and contingency management, and to teach parents how to influence change in inappropriate school behavior through contingency management.

The parent-group sessions were jointly staffed by the two teachers from the simulated classroom and one staff member of the mountain team. This combined staffing permitted information and input to the parents from other program phases.

A typical parent-group meeting consisted of:

1. Education or re-education in the principles of behavior modification;

2. Reports from the parents of Ss' home behavior charts;

3. Establishing new home conditions;

4. Evaluation of parents' reinforcement patterns;

5. Report by the teachers of Ss' behaviors in the simulated classroom;

6. Report by the mountain activities staff of Ss' behaviors on the last backpack trip;

7. Information about the upcoming backpack—locale, special equipment, etc.;

8. Aid with specific family problems.

There were three successive home conditions during STEP. Conditions were established by negotiation between Ss' parents and the STEP staff. Each condition was individualized to meet the needs of each S and his parents. Since each set of parents had identified the S's problem behavior in the home and had taken a frequency count of these behaviors prior to acceptance in STEP, changing these behaviors became the parents' goal in treatment. The home conditions were established to decrease to acceptable levels or eliminate S's inappropriate behaviors.

Condition One. At the first parent-group meeting two weeks prior to the start of the school activities, parents and staff established behavior charts for each S. The behavior charts served three purposes: (1) to earn food for the backpacks; (2) to monitor S's behavior changes; and (3) to help focus S's energies toward behavior change. The charts went into effect on the first school day and gave S seven days to earn $5.60 (the total necessary for all of the food on the first backpack). To assure at least limited success and to allow Ss and parents the opportunity to become acquainted with the charts, Condition One focused on improving chore behavior and improving a lesser behavior problem, rather than S's identified target behaviors. Each chore and behavior was given a monetary value; each day the chore was accomplished and the behavior improved, S earned food credit (see Table 3). Parents explained this procedure to S, and on the first day of school and the first mountain field trip, staff reiterated the procedure so S fully understood the negative and positive consequences of the charts. This chart had more flexibility under Condition One than during any other condition. S had to earn $5.60 to receive a full complement of food; however, if S completed every chore and decreased the problem behavior, he could earn $8.25. If S earned over the necessary amount, he was reinforced at home (e.g., movie, extra TV time, etc.).

Parents kept a frequency count of their own praise and criticism given to S and were asked to reinforce S each time he earned food credit.

Condition Two. Following the first backpack, a new behavior chart was implemented. The chart included the reduction of S's target behaviors based on baseline. For example, if S had seven tantrums daily during baseline, to earn part of his daily food credit for the upcoming backpack, he had to decrease the tantrums to three times a day or less. Other behaviors, school reports, and certain chores earned the rest of the daily food credit. Target behaviors and the school report received the highest monetary values. Condition Two was in effect until the next backpack (ten days), and S needed to earn $10.20 to earn a full complement of food. The chart had a limited amount of flexibility (i.e., the maximum a child could earn if he did everything correctly was $11.00).

Parents maintained a count of their own praise and criticism of S and were asked to increase praise and reduce the criticism.

Condition Three. This condition was in effect for 14 days (from backpack two to backpack three). Target behaviors were further reduced or eliminated to earn part of the daily food credit. Since the charts for Condition One and Two showed a great improvement in lesser behaviors, parents were given the option to keep the same lesser behaviors on the chart or add new behaviors for the rest of the food credit. The school report was given a lesser monetary value to enhance transfer to home reinforcement for good school behavior. The total necessary for food credit was $12.50. There was no leeway in this chart.

Upon reviewing the parents' praise and criticism count, parents were asked to either maintain or increase praise toward S.

After the last backpack, parents and staff established individualized follow-up programs for Ss. Since the backpacks were no longer a possible reinforcer for good behavior, other home activities were substituted.

School

There were three goals for this phase of the program; they were to teach Ss to (1) attend to and complete assigned work in a structured setting where work is done independently, (2) work in an unstructured, open setting where work is selected by the child and completed with the help of a peer, and (3) interact appropriately with peers and adults in a school setting.

Each class day consisted of a structured 45-minute math period, a 20-minute recess and snack period, and an unstructured 45-minute free choice time. During the math period, Ss were given several sheets of math problems taken from workbooks. When these sheets were completed by Ss, the work was checked for accuracy and completion, and Ss were presented with new papers. Teachers made no attempts to teach new academic skills, and all work was kept below Ss' academic levels. This was done so that the Es could determine whether or not the control of inappropriate school behavior would result in academic gains as measured through The Wide Range Achievement Test (Jastak and Jastak, 1965), administered before and after the program to Ss.

At the beginning of the free choice period, Ss could pick an educational game (e.g., Monopoly, card games, Scrabble) with the stipulation that they play with at least one peer. This was done to increase the rate of appropriate interactions among Ss.

During the school portion of STEP, there were five successive conditions and follow-up which imposed more stringent behavioral requirements on Ss.

Condition A: Baseline. A three-day baseline of Ss' on-task behavior was taken. Ss were instructed to complete their work, and no consequences were enforced for Ss' failure to do so. Teachers purposely gave attention to Ss inconsistently, often ignoring good behaviors and frequently nagging Ss for inappropriate behavior. This was done to limit the possibility of teachers becoming reinforcers which could possibly control Ss' behaviors. Parents gave no consequences for school behavior during baseline.

Condition B: Introduction of Cards. Once baseline was established, Ss were told that they could not fight, destroy property, or say anything that would hurt someone. They were given the 3" x 5" cards (see Table 1) and were responsible for having them initialed by the teacher at the end of each class period. Good behavior for the math period (as indicated on the card) earned lunch at home for that day. Good behavior during free choice earned 35 cents toward buying food for backpacking needed within the next week. Ss took the cards home where parents delivered reinforcement—lunch, if earned, and 35-cents credit for backpack food, if earned. Failure to have the card signed meant loss of reinforcement. Failure to deliver the cards to parents by Ss resulted in a 50-cent loss of credit for backpack food and loss of lunch. A new card was given each day of the three-day condition, and Ss were reminded to have the cards initialed. Teachers continued to be inconsistent in the delivery of praise and nagging, and remained behind their desks during most of the class period.

Condition C: Six out of Seven Behaviors. This condition was the same as Condition B except that Ss had to have six out of seven good marks on the cards, and one of the six behaviors had to be completion of work. Ss received no reminders about having their cards initialed. Parents continued to deliver reinforcement at home, using the cards as feedback. Teachers continued to reinforce Ss inconsistently.

Condition D: Return to Baseline. Teachers told the children and parents that the cards would not be sent home for the next three days. Ss received lunch and backpack credit regardless of behavior. This was done to determine whether the cards were controlling school behavior. Teachers remained inconsistent in giving reinforcement.

Condition E: All Behaviors Appropriate. Once it was determined that the cards were, in fact, controlling behavior, the cards were reinstated and Ss were required to have all behaviors appropriate in order to receive reinforcement. The time for the math period was extended to one hour. The money credit for backpack was decreased to 15 cents so that the backpack, as a reinforcer, could be faded and emphasis put on working for reinforcement delivered only at home. Again, Ss were not reminded to have the cards initialed.

At the resumption of regular fall classes, the Es contacted all of Ss' regular teachers. The teachers were shown the results of STEP—in particular, the increase in appropriate school behavior. The Es, teachers, and parents met at the individual Ss' schools and agreed to continue the use of the STEP school cards (see Table 1) to insure maintenance of appropriate behaviors. Consequences for Ss were changed to dinner or special privileges (e.g., TV time, day trips with parents). Es met with teachers at two-week intervals to assess Ss' maintenance levels. At present, Ss are being faded from use of the card to maintain appropriate behavior with less reinforcement (i.e., specific class times or days are not marked by the teachers).

Mountain Activities

The goals of the mountain activities were (1) to let Ss experience the full consequences of their behavior in a natural setting and (2) to reinforce appropriate behavior at home and school.

This phase of STEP included two one-day trips, one four-day backpack, and two seven-day backpacks. The two one-day trips prior to the first backpacking experience were used to assess the physical conditioning of Ss and to begin instruction in outdoor skills. The mountain trips were structured to enhance Ss' problem-solving abilities by successively increasing the physical and emotional challenges. Staff for the mountain activities related to Ss as instructors, mediators, models, and therapists.

Since all Ss had limited skills in backpacking and camping, Ss were instructed in:

1. Backpack weight distribution;
2. Walking with a backpack;
3. Sleeping bag care;
4. Outdoor bathing;
5. Latrine use and maintenance;
6. Map and compass orientation;
7. What to do when it rains or snows;
8. Duties related to food preparation and utensil care.

The primary social and work unit was the cook team. Each team was composed of two or three Ss whose behaviors indicated that they would probably be incompatible and nonproductive as a team (e.g., aggressive Ss paired; nonreaders paired). Cook team composition changed after each backpack. The cook team was responsible for all duties involved in food preparation and utensil care.

Cooking duties started with each team determining the locale of its cooking operation and building a small fire pit out of rocks designed to hold a backpack grill. Firewood was gathered for the meal and stored under protection. (Staff carried backpack stoves in case the wood was too wet for cooking.) Ss carried a share of the pots, food, and utensils. At mealtime the proper meal was selected, and the pots and utensils were assembled. Staff controlled all matches, and each team was given four matches to start the fire.

Backpack meals consisted of major brand freeze-dried and dehydrated foods. Each meal had at least two items that needed cooking. Each set of directions required careful reading and execution for a fully cooked, palatable meal.

Once the meal was eaten, the team put out the fire, cleaned the utensils, picked up the litter, and put away the equipment. The total time necessary for food preparation and cleanup was approximately two hours per meal if the team was working efficiently.

Inappropriate peer interaction and problem solving were left to the teams to resolve. Staff ignored quarreling and lack of productivity; however, if personal injury seemed imminent, staff would intercede. If a team requested assistance in problem solving, the staff would point out alternatives and let the team determine which choice seemed best. The natural environment provided a variety of aversive consequences for poor team efficiency or noncompliance. For example, if a team argued about who would get the wood for supper, Ss would eventually find it too dark to look for the wood, and no one would eat cooked food. Teams quickly developed a rotation of duties to assure completion of meals.

Ss missing credit for food checked in daily with one staff member. Lack of full food credit could be handled in one of three ways—Ss could (1) miss parts of meals, (2) miss a whole meal, or (3) earn essential food by hard, dirty work. The method selected was based on which choice would have the most impact on S, taking into account the high caloric intake necessary while backpacking. If missing a whole meal was selected, it would be the evening meal. The physical exertion for the day was over, and the evening meals were the most appealing to Ss. Two cups of soup replaced the meal.

Each S was responsible for all of his belongings. On backpacks this meant as many as 32 personal items. Ss also carried a share of the food and cooking equipment. If S left an item at the previous night's campsite, he could go back after it (once an 18-mile round trip) or do without. The staff spelled out this rule clearly and regularly when breaking camp. The consequences, then, for losing a tent would be taking a long walk or sleeping outside. If S lost one of the team's meals, S and his teammates would have no meal. No extra food was carried to replace a misplaced meal.

All other rules and expectations were carefully spelled out to Ss. Ss knew, for example, how far they had to walk, how much time was allotted for task completion, and where the free-time bounds were established. If there was no natural consequence for an improper action, the staff set a consequence. The most frequently used staff-imposed consequence was time-out (i.e., isolation from the group for five minutes).

Ss would receive assistance from staff if they requested it in an appropriate manner; inappropriate requests were ignored. Staff modeled responsibility for belongings and problem solving, and Ss learned to follow the staff example.

A daily activities schedule would be as such:

```
 7:00- 7:30 A.M.  Get up and start breakfast
 7:30- 9:30 A.M.  Eat, clean up, break camp
 9:30-11:30 A.M.  Walk (2 to 5 miles, depending on terrain)
11:30-12:30 P.M.  Lunch, rest
```

12:30- 3:30 P.M.	Walk (2 to 5 miles, depending on terrain or campsites)
3:30- 5.30 P.M.	Establish camp, bathe
5:30- 7:30 P.M.	Collect wood, dinner, clean up
7:30- 8:30 P.M.	Free time: laundry, pot lid frisbee, chess, fishing
8:30- 9:30 P.M.	Campfire, singing, group discussion, role playing
9:30 P.M.	Bed

Staff assigned Ss to share a tube tent. After instruction, they were responsible for location, setup, maintenance, and keeping the area clean. Occasionally, the assignment process produced a negative pairing of Ss, and staff did not interfere unless requested. Each successive backpack placed more responsibility on Ss. On the first backpack, staff monitored interaction, took responsibility for trail finding, and gave physical assistance if needed. By the last backpack, Ss scouted trails, found stragglers, established free-time bounds, and physically assisted each other (and assisted staff as well).

Individual contact was kept with each S. This was done while doing such things as walking along the trail, sitting by the fire, or waiting for the fish to bite. Basically, this was a supportive contact, checking out how S was feeling, reinforcing good problem solving, listening to problems, and pointing out alternatives to make the backpacking and camping a little easier.

Group discussions around the nightly campfire focused on daily interactions among peers and interactions among Ss and staff. Behavior rehearsal was often used to allow Ss to try out new behaviors and get feedback from staff and peers.

An equipment checklist was kept for each S, listing all of his belongings. This list was checked daily to count the loss of equipment or clothes (see Table 4).

Ss' responses to time limits were kept daily. S was counted late if he had not completed an assignment within the time allotted or if he did not respond to a signal whistle call for a group gathering. Since the camp area could be as large as ⅛th of a mile in diameter, a whistle system was used to contact Ss. One whistle blow meant to look at and become visible to signaling staff (S desired could then be hand-signaled to come to the staff member). Two whistle blows meant that all Ss should get to the signaling staff at a walking pace. Three whistle blows meant get to signaling staff as fast as possible.

Staff knew that the expectations, physical discomfort, and responsibility of STEP could overwhelm any child. However, no part of the mountain activities was beyond the capabilities of an 8- to 11-year-old

TABLE 4

Equipment Checklist

Dates

Backpack							
Sleeping Bag							
Poncho							
2 Cups							
Spoon							
Pocketknife							
Flashlight							
Boots							
Tennis shoes							
Short pants							
Long pants							
2 T-shirts							
3 Prs. socks							
2 Sets underwear							
1 Sweater or Sweatshirt							
1 Jacket or another Sweatshirt							
1 Ski hat							
1 Glove							
1 Dish towel							
1 Hand towel							
Toothbrush							
Fishing gear							
Optional gear, list below:							

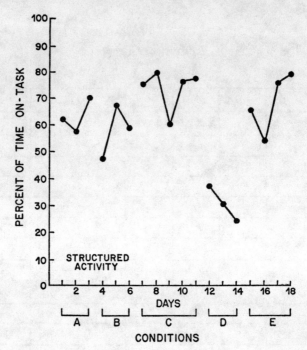

FIGURE 1. Percent of time on-task during structured hour.

child. If *S*s behaved in an appropriate manner and complied with the rules (staff imposed or natural), *S*s could survive somewhat comfortably.

RESULTS

Wilcoxon's Matched-Pairs Signed-Ranks Test was used to determine significance of change on all measurements.

The change in appropriate classroom behavior for the structured math period is shown in Figure 1. The formula used to calculate percentage of on-task behavior was:

$$\% \text{ on-task} = \frac{\text{Total intervals of on-task behavior}}{\text{Total intervals observed}}$$

Where: total intervals of on-task behavior includes intervals of approval, compliance, appropriate interaction with teacher, appropriate interaction with peers, volunteering, attending, and initiation to teacher.

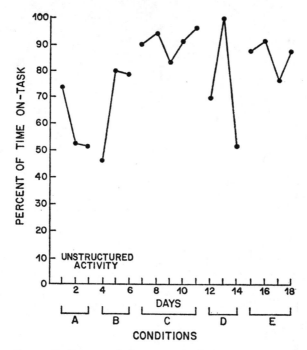

FIGURE 2. Percent of time on-task during unstructured hour.

During Condition A (baseline), on-task behavior was observed at an average of 64% of the time (Figure 1). During Condition B (introduction of cards), on-task behavior lowered to 58%. For Condition C (six out of seven behaviors), on-task behavior increased to 76% (this increase over baseline is significant at .005). During Condition D (return to baseline), the on-task behavior dropped to 31% (this drop is significant at the .005 level). In Condition E (all behaviors appropriate), on-task behavior increased to 67% (this increase was significant at the .005 level).

The changes in the on-task behavior for the unstructured, free choice period are shown in Figure 2. During Condition A, on-task behavior was observed at 59%; during Condition B, on-task behavior increased to 67%; during Condition C, on-task behavior escalated to 89% (this increase over baseline is significant at the .005 level); Condition D saw a decrease to 73% on-task behavior (this decrease is significant at the .01 level); during Condition E, on-task behavior increased to 84% (this increase is a significant increase over baseline at the .005 level).

TABLE 5

Wide Range Achievement Test as Measured by
Pre-Test, Post-Test, and Change

	Mean Pre-Test Grade Level	Mean Post-Test Grade Level	Mean Change
Reading	5.5	5.9	+.4
Spelling	4.1	4.3	+.2
Arithmetic	3.55	3.8	+.25

A one-day follow-up observation three months after termination of STEP saw Ss in their normal classroom at an average on-task level of 83%, while Ss' peers were performing at 84% (indicating no significant difference between Ss and peers).

Results from The Wide Range Achievement Test (Table 5) given as a measure of academic improvement indicated an average gain in reading of .40 grade level, in spelling, of .20 grade level, and in arithmetic, of .25 grade level. Although these were higher than the normal gain of .10 grade level expected over the summer, they were not statistically significant.

Frequency counts of items lost on the backpacks as recorded by the equipment checklist are shown in Figure 3. On the first backpack (4 days), 20% of all items were lost by the last day. On the second backpack (7 days in duration), the loss decreased to 17% of all items. By the end of the third backpack (7 days in duration), only 7% of all items were missing. The decrease in equipment losses is significant at the .005 level.

Observation on response to time limits (completing tasks in a set amount of time) was kept on the backpacks, and results are shown in Figure 4. On the first backpack, Ss were not ready within the time limits an average of 21% of the time; on the second backpack, this was reduced to 7%; and on the third backpack, this decreased further to 2%. This change is significant at the .005 level.

The results from the Louisville Behavior Checklist are shown in Table 6. Ss demonstrated a movement toward a score of 50.00 (the norm established for the test) on all 15 of the sub-scales, with the mean variance from the norm reduced on 14 of the 15 sub-scales. Both of these changes are significant at the .005 level. Miller et al. (1972) conducted a test-retest study on the Louisville Behavior Checklist over the same time interval on a normal population and found no significant difference using a rank order correlation test of significance.

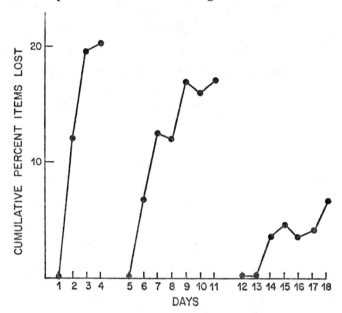

FIGURE 3. Cumulative percent of equipment lost.

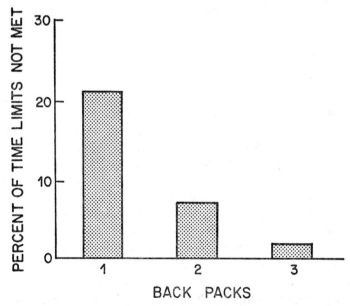

FIGURE 4. Percent of time limits not met.

TABLE 6

THE LOUISVILLE BEHAVIOR CHECKLIST

Mean Standard Scores, Mean Variance from Norm,*
and Movement Toward Norms on
Pre-test and Post-test

| Sub-scales | Mean Standard Scores | | | Mean Variance from Norm* | | |
	Pre-test	Post-test	Movement Toward Norm	Pre-test	Post-test	Movement Toward Norm
Infantile Aggression	67.62	63.38	+4.24	18.00	13.69	+4.31
Hyperactivity	68.08	63.77	+4.31	17.31	14.08	+3.23
Antisocial	70.54	64.54	+6.00	21.46	17.31	+4.15
Aggression	69.85	65.00	+4.85	19.85	15.23	+4.62
Social Withdrawal	65.77	60.08	+5.69	16.00	12.54	+3.46
Sensitivity	66.54	58.92	+7.62	17.15	9.85	+7.30
Fear	62.54	55.62	+6.92	13.15	7.00	+6.15
Inhibition	66.62	59.69	+6.93	17.08	11.08	+6.00
Learning Disability	71.62	62.23	+8.89	20.85	16.64	+4.21
Total Disability	71.85	64.23	+7.62	21.00	15.00	+6.00
Academic Disability	69.38	62.15	+7.23	19.38	16.77	+2.61
Immaturity	70.92	59.23	+11.69	21.23	12.77	+8.46
Normal Irritability	62.69	58.00	+4.69	13.62	9.23	+4.39
Pro-Social	42.85	47.92	+5.07	13.15	17.31	—4.16
Rare Deviancy	80.63	66.46	+14.17	32.46	19.62	+12.84

* Norm for all scales is 50.00.

DISCUSSION

STEP findings regarding home-based reinforcement and therapeutic camping support the results of previous investigators; however, the effect of both techniques in one program has not previously been demonstrated. In addition, STEP had many unique facets: (1) long-term delayed reinforcement; (2) a maximum intensity program which left Ss in their home environment; (3) short-term treatment; (4) no interference with S's normal school year; (5) no emphasis on performance by teacher as instruments of change; (6) less expense than institutionalization; and (7) generalization to new behaviors.

During STEP, the explicit reinforcement for improved home and school behavior was delayed as much as 14 days. Most programs emphasize the immediacy of reinforcement as a major factor in modifying behaviors. It was hypothesized that delayed reinforcement would aid in generalization. Although this cannot be proven by this study, the be haviors of Ss did significantly change with a delayed reinforcement format.

Institutionalization had been considered for 50% of the Ss. The Louisville Behavior Checklist (Miller, 1967), given prior to the program, demonstrated that Ss' scores deviated from the normal population at the .005 level of significance. By maintaining S in his home environment, the problem of generalization from an inpatient setting to the home environment was eliminated.

STEP was designed as a time-limited program (39 days/8 consecutive weeks) which involved multiple behavioral changes in multiple settings. Because of the limited amount of time in which to effect changes, expectations of Ss were extremely high and very demanding from the moment they entered STEP. In order to survive, Ss had to respond immediately and positively, which they did. Rather than receive reinforcers for small approximations to final expected behaviors, Ss were required to make large gains in very short time periods. STEP findings support the hypothesis that, when Ss are faced with an unalterable situation which demands positive behavioral changes, those changes will be made.

STEP was held during the summer months. This meant no interruption of the regular classroom routine and alleviated the possibility of identifying Ss as exceptional or problem children to educators and peers.

Teacher attention in the simulated classroom was kept below 8% during all conditions. Many classroom studies emphasize the importance of social reinforcement in modifying classroom behavior. Because of past resistance by teachers to apply social reinforcement to problem students, it was felt that this should not be used as an instrument of change as it would make generalization more difficult. Token economies have been shown to be effective but, again, educators are often hesitant to apply these techniques. If parents are used as the instrument of change, teacher's expectations are decreased. The limited effort required by teachers to maintain S's appropriate behavior enhanced the continuation of the school reporting cards in all S's normal classrooms.

Including staff time devoted to program design, implementation, follow-up, and research, the program cost $80.00 per week per child to the Mental Health Center. (Parents' fees were on an ability to pay basis and covered approximately 25% of the stated cost.) Institutionalization can cost upwards of $200.00 a week.

The intent of STEP was to change Ss' inappropriate behaviors and generalize these behaviors to many settings. Parent and teacher reports indicate that Ss' behaviors have improved in all settings. Preliminary six-month follow-up data support these reports.

The results of STEP would probably not have occurred without motivated parents. Parents were willing to follow a prescriptive approach and carry out the treatment demands. It is unlikely that the magnitude of behavioral change could have been accomplished without parent involvement and support.

The risks of a mountain backpacking activity, which places many demands and expectations on Ss, must be emphasized. Losing one's way, accidents, poor judgment, and bad weather can cause severe consequences that seldom occur in a therapist's office. Expectations placed on the Ss must be carefully determined to assure success.

From program results, it cannot be determined which component (parent, school, mountain activities) had the greatest impetus in promoting behavioral change in Ss. The authors suspect that therapy components delivered simultaneously had more impact than if elements were delivered at separate times.

The Ss in the study were drawn from a very select population. The Ss had failed in prior treatment, in school, and in family functioning. They could verbalize their position in life and were very much in contact with the hopelessness of being a loser. Ss were shocked into change, were reinforced for the change, and then expected to change again. The challenges they faced were both emotional and physical; throughout the summer, they conquered increasingly difficult tasks. Ss learned to reinforce each other and take pride in what they could do correctly. "I will make it, you will make it, we will make it" was the clear verbal and nonverbal message staff related to the Ss. By the end of the second backpack, the Ss echoed this message to each other, to the staff, and to Mother Nature.

REFERENCES

BAILEY, J. S., WOLF, M. M., and PHILLIPS, E. L.: Home based reinforcement and the modification of pre-delinquent classroom behavior. *J. Appl. Behav. Anal.,* 3, 223-233, 1970.

COBB, J. A., and RAY, R. S.: Manual for Coding Discrete Behaviors in the School Setting. Social Learning Project, Oregon Research Institute, 1971.

JASTAK, J. F., and JASTAK, S. R.: The Wide Range Achievement Test. Wilmington, Del.: Guidance Associates of Delaware, 1965.

LOUGHMILLER, C.: *Wilderness Road.* Houston: U. of Texas, Hogg Foundation for Mental Health, 1965.

McNEIL, E. B. (Ed.): Therapeutic camping for disturbed youth. *J. Soc. Issues,* 13, 1-62, 1957.

McNEIL, E. B.: Forty years of childhood. *Mich. Quart. Rev.*, 1, 112-118, 1962.
MEYERS, T.: *Camping for Emotionally Disturbed Boys.* Bloomington, Ind.: Indiana U. Press, 1961.
MILLER, L. C.: The Louisville Behavior Checklist for Males 6-12 Years of Age. *Psychol. Reports*, 21, 885-896, 1967.
MILLER, L. C., HAMPE, E., BARRETT, C. L., and NOBLE, H.: Test-retest reliability of parent ratings of children's deviant behavior. *Psychol. Reports*, 31, 249-250, 1972.
NELSON, C. M., WARRELL, J., and POLSGROVE, L.: Behaviorally disordered peers as contingency managers. *Behav. Ther.*, 4, 270-276, 1973.
RICKARD, H. C., and DINOFF, M.: Shaping adaptive behavior in a therapeutic summer camp. In: L. P. Ullman and L. Krasner (Eds.), *Case Studies in Behavior Modification.* New York: Holt, Rinehart, and Winston, 1965.

Section II

TRAINING PARENTS IN GROUPS

6

A Group Treatment Program for Parents

VIRGINIA TAMS
and
SHEILA EYBERG

The program described in this paper evolved from a group treatment program for mothers of 7- to 12-year-old children referred to the Department of Medical Psychology at the University of Oregon Medical School. All of the children exhibited high rates of acting-out behaviors at home, and often at school as well. Acting-out behaviors include aggressiveness, destructiveness, disobedience, hyperactivity, temper tantrums, and any high-rate activity which is annoying to the parents or teacher. Group, rather than individual, treatment for the mothers was initiated in an effort to decrease cost in terms of professional time and to decrease the waiting period for the clients referred. It soon became evident, however, that the group approach offered additional advantages, including a sense of mutual understanding and sharing among the group members. Through the sharing process, learning and application of behavior principles were effected by a combination of peer and professional input. There was an emphasis on developing problem-solving skills in the parents, in addition to modifying undesirable child behavior patterns. The present program incorporates feedback from mothers in the earlier groups.

The program is designed to include both parents, if available, as well as parents of children who have behavior problems other than acting-out. The program is amenable to use with parents of both problem and non-problem children, and could be adapted for use with teachers. Including

101

nonproblem children and teachers in the program could result in primary intervention or even prevention of moderate to severe problem behaviors. Because of the large number of referrals of children with moderate to severe behavior problems, priority must be given to parents of these children at the Medical School.

The group program now includes parents of children ranging in age from 2 to 12 years. For potential group members who have children from 2 to 6 years of age, the initial evaluation includes observation of structured mother-child and father-child interactions, in addition to a parent interview which focuses on specific interaction sequences of the child with important adults and children in his or her life at home, school, and other settings. From the interview and observations, detailed information is obtained concerning the strengths and weaknesses of the parents, child, and parent-child relationship. The specific observations and interviews are derived from Hanf's (Hanf, 1968; Hanf and Kling, 1973) individual treatment program for parent-child pairs. The initial evaluation of parents with older children, those between 7 and 12 years old, includes the structured parent interview as well as unstructured interviews and observations of the child and parents, individually and conjointly. In order to assess the effectiveness and generalization of the intervention process, similar observations and interviews are conducted upon completion of the nine-week program, as well as at three- and six-month follow-up sessions.

Also used in the assessment of program effectiveness are an attitudinal and a behavioral measure, both of which each parent completes at the first and last group meetings and again at the three- and six-month follow-up sessions. The Bipolar Adjective Checklist (Becker, 1960), which has been used in assessing pre- to post-treatment changes in global parent perceptions of children (Patterson, Cobb, and Ray, 1973; Eyberg and Johnson, 1974), serves as the attitudinal measure. The checklist contains 47 bipolar adjectives to be rated on a 7-point scale and is scored on the basis of five factors labeled Relaxed Disposition, Withdrawn-Hostile, Lack of Aggression, Intellectual Efficiency, and Conduct Problem (Patterson and Fagot, 1967).

The Behavior Inventory (Eyberg and Tams, 1973), which is designed to assess changes in specific problem behaviors, serves as the behavioral measure. The inventory contains 45 relatively frequently occurring and observable behavior problems assembled from a number of case records. In assessing program effectiveness, both of the scales on the inventory are used. The first, a 3-point scale, obtains frequency estimates of each behavior. The second scale requires that the parent decide whether or not each behavior at the judged frequency level constitutes a problem. Of special interest and a possible discussion topic is the comparison of two parents who agree on the problem frequency rating for their child, but who disagree on the attitudinal rating. More specifically, both of a child's parents may circle the "often or always" position in the frequency scale, yet one parent circles the "yes" position in the attitude or "Is this a problem?" scale while the other circles the "no" position.

Over the course of the nine-week program, the parents attend a weekly two-hour discussion group, read the book *Parents Are Teachers* (Becker, 1971), and complete exercises in the Becker book as well as handouts designed to increase generalization of behavior principles introduced. During the first eight weeks, the parents read the Becker book and are requested to complete the first written exercise at the end of each chapter assigned. This exercise, which involves completing important sentences from the chapter, provides an excellent opportunity for review and for strengthening the learning of key concepts. Each week the parents review and discuss the major points and relevant examples contained in the assigned reading. They also discuss possible applications of behavior modification principles introduced in the reading and by the group leaders. They are encouraged to critically evaluate all material presented and attempt to answer their own questions concerning the material.

To aid the parents in applying the principles to which they have been introduced, they are provided with one or more handouts to be completed each week. Although only one child in a family is assessed and discussed at the group meetings, parents are urged to apply the principles learned to all of the children at home and are provided with additional handouts as needed. In addition to the assigned readings, the weekly discussion includes a review of the behavior principles being applied, ways to modify parent application of the principles based on the data or results recorded on the handouts, and methods of presenting specific programs and other procedures to obtain child cooperation. An example of a discussion topic is the solicitation of child input into either the basic format of a token program or the application of the program; this input could include the selection of reinforcers to be earned.

Throughout the program, the emphasis is on training the parents in the effective use of positive, nonaversive procedures in shaping their own and their child's behavior in order to facilitate a positive parent-child relationship. The group leaders model the use of these procedures by reinforcing comments that reflect parent motivation to improve their relationship with the child primarily by positive means. Also, to the extent possible, the leaders ignore parent comments which do not reflect this motivation. When necessary, the leaders redirect the discussion to maintain the focus on relevant issues and to give each parent an opportunity to enter into the discussion. Also, during the weekly discussions, the group leaders supplement parent comments when appropriate. Over the course of the program, the necessity for supplementation decreases. This decrease is accompanied by encouraging and reinforcing active parent participation. This process is congruent with the primary goal of the program—that parents develop positive problem-solving skills that are applicable to difficulties besides those existing at the time of referral or at the first group meeting. In accordance with this goal of increased parent independence and skill in coping with problems is the policy of encouraging parents to call one another during and after the program to share successes and seek help in handling particularly difficult problems.

Program Format

At this point, a more detailed description of the program will be presented. The description is designed to serve as a guide for conducting the program. Throughout the nine weeks there is considerable repetition of key concepts presented in the reading and handout assignments, as well as by the group leaders. This repetition enhances parent learning, incorporation, and generalization of the important principles.

First Session

During this session, the parents introduce themselves and briefly describe the child in their family on whom they will focus during the program. An overview of the program is presented, and the importance of regular attendance is stressed. The parents are informed that if they miss two consecutive meetings, they will be placed on a waiting list for the next group if they wish to complete the program.

The desirability of focusing on changing one behavior at a time is related by the group leaders. Noncompliance is designated as the first undesirable behavior to be decreased since (a) it occurs in virtually all families, (b) it can be modified with relative ease because it occurs frequently, is observable, and need involve only the parent and child, and

Handout 1

Between sessions 1 and 2 Child's name ______________

Desirable behavior to be counted: Compliance

Frequency of occurrence on:

Day 1 llXXllllXXX
Day 2 lXllXXXXllXl
Day 3 ______
Day 4 ______
Day 5 ______
Day 6 ______
Day 7 ______

Other desirable behaviors observed:

Day 1 Friday	1.	finished his breakfast	Day 5	1.	
	2.	dressed himself		2.	
	3.	hung up his clothes		3.	
	4.	watched TV quietly		4.	
	5.	went to bed on time		5.	
Day 2 Saturday	1.	made his bed	Day 6	1.	
	2.	set the table		2.	
	3.	played well with his brother		3.	
	4.	helped his dad in the yard		4.	
	5.	helped wash the dishes		5.	
Day 3	1.		Day 7	1.	
	2.			2.	
	3.			3.	
	4.			4.	
	5.			5.	
Day 4	1.				
	2.				
	3.				
	4.				
	5.				

FIGURE 1

(c) it is amenable to relatively rapid modification by positive methods which can later be applied to other problem behaviors. After the positive modification methods of attending to and reinforcing desirable behavior are introduced and discussed, the first handout (see Figure 1) is distributed. Compliance is selected as the first behavior to be increased by the application of positive methods. The leaders explain that compliance was selected because it is a desirable behavior and is clearly incompatible with noncompliance, the behavior chosen to be decreased. The parents are requested to give a minimum of ten positive commands each day. Positive commands include statements such as "Please pick up your coat," and exclude "negative" statements like "Please *don't* throw your coat on the floor." Each time either parent gives a command, he or she places a tally mark on the handout. If the child complies, the parent slashes the tally to make an "X" which serves to remind the parent to reward the child for complying. If the child does not comply, the parent leaves the original tally and says nothing to the child. Noncompliance, then, is ignored. To emphasize further the importance of reinforcing desirable behavior on a daily basis, in addition to rewarding compliance, the parents are to list five desirable child behaviors outside the area of compliance. At this point the parents give examples of behaviors they could list on the handout. Chapter 1 in Becker, which presents an overview of principles relevant to parenting as well as the effects of positive reinforcement and punishment in everyday life, is assigned.

Second Session

At the beginning of this session, parents receive a "Compliance Graph" (see Figure 2) which is designed to reflect changes in the percentage of child compliance on a weekly basis and is distributed to the parents at each of the remaining sessions. Throughout the program, parents compute and graph the compliance percentage from the command-comply data discussed previously. The percentage data are closely examined at each session, and possible reasons for fluctuations are entertained by the parents with a focus on coping with and preventing possible future decreases in compliance.

The command-comply data used in computing the percentage of child compliance also serve as the basis for a point system designed to systematically increase compliance. The parents receive a handout (see Figure 3) which provides space for recording the command-comply data as well as specific parent-child interaction sequences following child noncompliance. In subsequent meetings, the sequences of interactions are examined, and the parents discuss means of increasing their use of nonaversive techniques to decrease undesirable child behavior. In the lower portion of the handout, the parents are to record each reward they give the child. They are told that the reward total is expected to be greater than five, which was the minimum goal of the previous week's reinforcement assignment.

Handout 2

Child's name _____

COMPLIANCE GRAPH

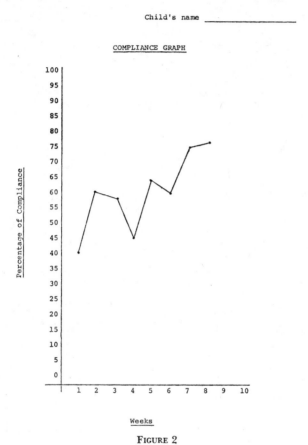

Weeks

FIGURE 2

The compliance point system, mentioned previously, provides that children from 7 to 12 years old receive one point each time they comply with a parent command. When 25 points are earned, the parents are to praise the child for complying and to give him or her a previously selected activity reinforcer, such as a trip to the park. At this point, parents are encouraged to name and discuss other possible reinforcers. Over the course of the remaining sessions, reinforcer and procedural adjustments in the compliance point system are made as appropriate. When the percentage of compliance remains close to 75% for two consecutive weeks, the parents are aided in devising a series of procedures in order to re-

Handout 3

Between sessions 2   and 3   Child's name _____

Desirable behavior: Compliance _____

Contract: When you earn 25 points, you can go to the park with Bob.

Day	Daily Point Total	Frequency of Occurrence	Exactly what I said and/or did each time it failed to occur (unless exactly same done) and how my child responded to each thing I did
1 Mon.	9	XXIXIXI IXXIXIX X	1) I threatened him with stick—he then obeyed 2) I went after him—he hit me—I yelled at him to go to his room—he stomped off to his room yelling names at me. 3) I ignored him and then I (over)
2 Tues.	7	IXIIXXXI IXXXI	1) I ignored him for awhile—then I yelled at him to do it and he did 2) I said if he didn't do it I'd tell his dad and he'd fix him—he did it 3) I just let it go—he went out and played 4) I did same as(1)
3			
4			
5			
6			
7			

Make a tally each time you praise your child.

Day:	1	2	3	4	5	6	7
Tally:	⊬⊬ II	III					

FIGURE 3

move or "fade out" the activity reinforcer. The procedures are arranged in a manner which allows for the maintenance of compliance by occasional verbal reinforcement. The process often involves gradually increasing the number of points required for obtaining a reinforcer within a specified time length.

Parents with children between 2 and 6 years of age receive an additional handout relevant to the point system. Each time the child complies, he or she places or helps the parent place one large token such as a happy face in one of the squares which are arranged in rows of five squares each. When the child has filled one row or has earned five tokens, a specified reward is received, often gum or a small toy, as well as an explanation for the nonverbal reward. Congruent with the continued group focus on the desirability of using positive methods to modify undesirable behavior, Chapters 2 and 3 in Becker are assigned.

Third Session

At the third meeting, two handouts designed to aid the group members in increasing both the quantity and quality of their rewards are presented. On the first of these handouts (see Figure 4), the parents describe a number of desirable child behaviors as well as specify their recognition of these behaviors to the child. The second handout (see Figure 5) lists labeled or specific verbal rewards such as "I like it when you clean your room," and specific physical rewards like a gentle squeeze of the arm. Distribution of this handout provides a transition into a presentation by the group leaders on the advantages of labeled as opposed to unlabeled rewards such as "Good boy," as well as the positive effects of accompanying labeled with physical rewards. The parents are to read Chapter 4 in Becker, which discusses token reinforcement systems, for the next session. In preparation for designing a token program, they are urged to consider which problem behaviors and rewards might be included in a program for their child.

Fourth Session

"Progress Chart" is the label of the handout (see Figure 6) on which each parent records the token program developed during this session for the child. Although parents who have completed the assignments relevant to designing token programs provide substantial input into the program design, the group leaders give considerable guidance in order to maximize the likelihood of establishing a successful program. On the Progress Chart, three to six behaviors parents wish to see increased or further developed in their child are listed as "Tasks." All of the listed behaviors are clearly observable and specifically enough defined for easy monitoring by the parents and child. The child receives one point for completing each specified task. A point total and reward, decided upon

Handout 5

Between sessions _3_ and _4_   Child's name _____

Desirable behavior: _Compliance,_ _____

Contract: When you earn _25_ points, you can _get an ice-cream cone._

Frequency of occurrence on:

Day: 1. _\IIXXX\IXXX_ 2. _XXIIXIXXXX_ 3. _____ 4. _____
5. _____ 6. _____ 7. _____ Total Points: _____

Day	First five behaviors incompatible with noncompliance	What you said or did to reinforce each behavior
1 Wed.	cleaned up spill helped grandpa sweep put away toys sang to us asked me to color with him	A thorough job! Thank you for helping. It looks good. (hug) You sang very well. I like to color with you.
2 Thurs.	emptied the garbage cleaned up room helped brother mend torn spelling paper played quietly while I was on phone scraped off dishes	That helps me when you do your chores! you really straightened that up fast! That sure looks better. I'm glad you didn't bother me on the phone. (squeezed arm) You did a good job. Thanks!
3		
4		
5		
6		
7		

FIGURE 4

by the parents and child, are recorded on the Progress Chart. When the child's point total equals the number recorded on the chart, the specified reward is given.

Congruent with the stated program goal of developing parent independence in solving existing as well as "new" problems, the group leaders

Handout 6

EXAMPLES OF SOCIAL REINFORCEMENT

VERBAL

I like it when you _____. (clean your room, eat quickly, help me without being asked, play so quietly)

That's a great _____. (tower, fort, game, picture)

You're really doing a good job of _____. (helping me, baking that cake, sawing that wood, building the model)

Those _____ are really _____. (cookies, colors; good, pretty)

You're doing just what I asked and so _____. (quickly, fast, neatly, happily)

I like the way you _____. (helped Dad today, took care of your sister, played without fighting with your friends)

The way you're _____ is really fantastic. (dressed, working hard at your homework)

That's (pointing) _____. (great, really pretty, good, carefully done)

I really like (enjoy) _____ with you. (playing, shopping, working)

You can really pick interesting (fun) _____. (ways to keep busy, games to play, things to do)

Now you're _____; that's so _____. (cleaning, coloring, making your bed; nice, pretty, helpful)

You're doing such a _____ job; that's _____ than I could do! (careful, neat; better, nicer)

PHYSICAL

Ruffle hair
Squeeze arm
Pat on head, back, hand
Hug
Kiss

FIGURE 5

Handout 7

Between sessions 4 and 5

Child's name _____

PROGRESS CHART

Command-comply contract: When you earn 30 points, you can have Mary over for lunch

Command-comply data

Day: 1. \\\XXXXXII\X   2. X\XX\I\X\\XX   3. _____

4. _____   5. _____   6. _____   7. _____

Task	Day 1 Friday	Day 2 Saturday	Day 3 Sunday	Day 4	Day 5	Day 6	Day 7
Make bed without being asked	☆	☆					
Finish breakfast within 1/2 hour	☆		☆				
Play with brother 1/2 hour without hitting	☆	☆	☆				
Feed the dog at 5:00	☆	☆	☆				
Be in bed by 8:30	☆	☆	☆				
DAILY TOTAL	4	3	4				

Write contract for new token program in space at right.

When you earn 20 points, you can Stay up until 9:00 this week.

rapidly decrease their active involvement in the discussions of modifications of the token programs. Within a three-week period, the parents themselves are able to evaluate effectively almost all of the proposed modifications. Many of the changes effected are similar to those described in relation to the compliance point system. Behaviors may be deleted when they occur at least 72% of the time (5 out of 7 days) for a two-week period, and substitutions or additions are made as appropriate. Like the point system, the token program is faded out on a gradual basis. The likelihood of reintroducing a token program at some future time and the possible means of reintroduction are discussed. Chapter 6 in Becker, which presents the futility of most criticism in effectively decreasing undesirable behavior, is assigned at the end of the fourth session.

Fifth Session

To emphasize further the application of positive methods in modifying behavior, the parents make brightly colored reminder cards with slogans from the Becker chapter assigned for this session. "Catch your child being good," "Reward improvement," and "Don't wait for misbehavior" are illustrative slogans. Many parents also design their own reminder phrases. Reactions of the parents and children to the cards, which the parents post in easily observable places in their home, are discussed at the following session.

In order to facilitate the involvement and cooperation of every family member in developing a positive family atmosphere, the parents receive a handout (see Figure 7) for recording every comment of praise and criticism spoken during a ten-minute period when the family is together and not engrossed in an activity like watching television. Most families elect to record during dinner. This assignment is derived from a chapter exercise in Becker. For the next session, parents are to read Chapter 7, which contains examples of positive reinforcements that supplement and expand upon those listed on the handout distributed to the parents during the third session.

Sixth Session

Since the praise-criticism data are collected for two one-week periods, in line with Becker's suggestion, the parents again receive the relevant handout. The group members frequently verbalize the expectation of the group leaders that a comparison of the data from the first and second week will indicate improvement, as defined by a decrease in criticism and

Handout 8

Between sessions __5__ and __6__   Child's name _____

PRAISE AND CRITICISM

Put a tally in the appropriate column whenever you give a praise or critical comment toward any family member during the time you are counting.

Time during which you are counting: ___6:00 — 6:10___   a.m.   (p.m.)

Day	Praise Comments	Total Praise	Critical Comments	Total Criticism
1 Tues.	ll	2	lll	3
2 Wed.	lll	3	llll	4
3				
4				
5				
6				
7				

FIGURE 7

an increase in praise comments. A handout (see Figure 8) is provided for recording the first week's data. This handout is distributed again at the next meeting to allow for easy comparison of the data for the two-week period and to serve as a referent for the discussion.

Handout 9

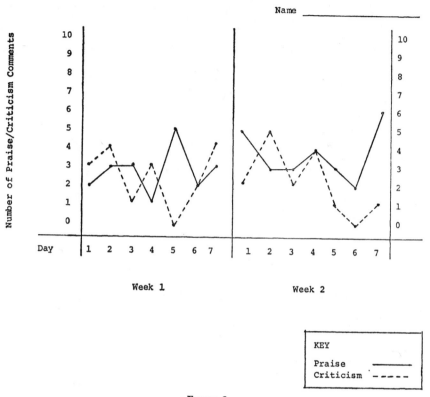

FIGURE 8

Although it is expected that the parents have become comfortable with
and proficient in their use of praise, another handout (see Figure 9) on
positive reinforcement is distributed to aid them in further increasing
the variety and general quality of their rewards. On this handout, the
parents are to record the first five verbal praises they give the child each
day and make a notation if a token is given along with any of the listed
praises. During the subsequent meeting, parents review one another's
data and tend to support and reinforce primarily those parents who listed
an equal or greater number of praises not related to their child's point
system or token program.

The first chapter in the Becker book (Chapter 8) dealing with punish-

Handout 10 (page 1 of 2)

Between sessions _____ and _____   Child's name _____

Write down the first 5 praises given each day (exact words you used).
Put a T by the number if a token was also given.

Day		Praise Given
1	1.	That's great! You put a period after every sentence.
Wed.	2.	Thank you for putting away the jar (smile and hug).
T	3.	You did a good job of making your bed today.
	4.	I'm glad you changed your shirt — you look very neat.
T	5.	Your teeth look very shiny — and I didn't even have to remind you!
2	1.	Wow! Did you ever do the dishes fast and well!
Thurs. T	2.	I'm happy that you made your bed already.
T	3.	You and Jim sure play well together now (ruffle hair).
	4.	Thanks for helping Dad fix the back door.
	5.	That's a good idea. I never would have thought of putting those colors together, but they look nice!
3	1.	_____
	2.	_____
	3.	_____
	4.	_____
	5.	_____
4	1.	_____
	2.	_____
	3.	_____
	4.	_____
	5.	_____

FIGURE 9

ment or cueing the child by nonpositive means is then assigned. Also assigned is a handout (see Figure 10) which requires the parents to list any remaining undesirable child behaviors, the ways they presently attempt to handle these behaviors, and the ways they could cope with them more effectively.

Handout 11

Between sessions _____ and _____   Child's name _____

Current undesirable behavior(s)	Usual way you handle the behavior(s)	Possible better way to handle the behavior(s)
Goes to a friend's house on way home from school without telling me	Sometimes I ignore him and sometimes I tell him I must know where he is.	Have a snack ready for him only if he comes right home
Almost constantly wants me to come see how he's doing on his fort when I sit down to write a letter	Usually I tell him to go work on it some more and I'll be out to look at it soon	Set the timer for 5 minutes — if he doesn't come in before it rings go and praise him — otherwise send him to his corner for 3 minutes
Doesn't come in when I call him for dinner	I have him eat alone when he finally comes in	Tell him he won't get any dessert unless he comes in by 6:00

FIGURE 10

Seventh Session

During this session, parents encourage one another to discover and effect nonaversive means to decrease the behaviors they listed on the last handout. For coping with those behaviors which are threatening to the child or other persons, as well as those especially resistant to modification by positive methods, the response-cost and time-out procedures are presented by the group leaders. An example of response-cost would be deducting a given amount of money from the child's weekly allowance each time the specified undesirable behavior is exhibited. An example of time-out would be sending the child to a specified corner or room free from possibly-rewarding stimuli for a short time period, like ten minutes, each time the designated undesirable behavior is displayed.

At this point, the group leaders caution the parents to specify commands and house rules in the form of direct statements such as "Please go to bed now," rather than in the form of questions or indirect state-

Handout 12

Between sessions _____ and _____   Child's name_____

PUNISHMENT CHART

(Use <u>only</u> if problem has not been reduced by positive methods.)

Undesirable behavior selected: Hits little brother_____

Punishment to be used: Every time he hits his brother he will be sent

to his room for 5 minutes_____

Day	Frequency of occurrence	Frequency of follow through with punishment
1 Friday	||	||
2 Saturday	|||	||
3		
4		
5		
6		
7		

FIGURE 11

ments like "Will you please go to bed now?" The latter form is permissible only if the parents are willing to accept "No" for an answer. Furthermore, when the parents actually wish to give the child a choice, it is suggested that they specify the viable alternatives to the child. For instance, a parent could say, "Would you like to go to bed right after the TV program or right now so there will be time for me to read you a story?" Giving the child a choice between alternatives acceptable to the parents, as illustrated in the previous example, is more likely to increase the child's independence and decision-making ability than is telling the child exactly what to do.

When child compliance does not occur within a reasonable time following the issuance of a direct command, it is suggested that the parent either remind the child of a planned reward for compliance such as, "As soon as you make your bed you can go out and play;" or, if appropriate, warn the child of a planned aversive consequence for noncompliance like, "Please pick up your coat now or you'll have to stand in the corner." The warning gives the child two options: to comply and thus avoid the negative consequence as well as receive at least a verbal reward; or to fail to comply and thus receive the specified consequence and no reward. With house rules, it is advised that the parents and child specify the consequence for breaking them at the time the rules are made. The importance of following each infraction with the consequence is stressed. After the negative consequence has been applied for noncompliance or a rule infraction, however, no further punishment for that instance of undesirable behavior is meted out.

Parents whose children continue to exhibit threatening or especially change-resistant undesirable behavior receive a handout (see Figure 11) which provides for describing the behavior, a punishment technique, and the rate of parent follow-through with the technique. The desirability and possible ways of changing to positive methods in order to decrease the incidence of undesirable behavior are discussed by the group members. The results of implementation of the various methods are discussed at the subsequent sessions. The parents are assigned Chapter 9 in Becker, which reviews ways to teach a child to generalize specific rules and ways for parents to foster desirable child behavior.

Eighth Session

To again emphasize the desirability of generalizing the principles learned throughout the program, parents complete the final handout

Handout 13 (page 1 of 2)

Between sessions _____ and _____ Child's name _____

Rewrite the following rules so that they are stated positively:

1. You <u>can't</u> play outside <u>unless</u> you finish your homework.

   When you finish your homework, you can play outside.

   _____

2. You <u>can't</u> come to dinner <u>until</u> you hang up your school clothes.

   You can come to dinner as soon as you hang up your school clothes.

3. If you <u>don't</u> eat your peas, you <u>won't</u> get any dessert.

   If you eat your peas, you can have some dessert.

   _____

4. If you come home <u>late</u> from Susan's house, you <u>can't</u> watch TV after dinner.

   _____

   _____

Write what you should do after these behaviors occur:

1. Goes to bed on time.

   Reward him by reading him a story at bedtime.

   _____

2. Does not leave the yard when told to stay there.

   Give him a hug and tell him he can stay out and play longer because he stayed in the yard like he's supposed to.

3. Has temper tantrum.

   Take him firmly to his room and have him stay there until he has been quiet for 3 minutes.

4. Cleans his room without being asked.

   Tell him how much it helps make the whole house look better.

FIGURE 12

Handout 13 (page 2 of 2)

5. Plays cooperatively with **sister.**

   Allow him to play outdoors with his friends for 15 extra minutes after dinner.

6. Dawdles at dinner.

   _____

   _____

7. Makes bed 7 days in a **row.**

   _____

   _____

8. Interrupts mother while **she is** on phone.

   _____

   _____

9. "Talks back" to mother.

   _____

   _____

10. Says something **nice to mother.**

   _____

   _____

FIGURE 12 *(cont'd)*

(see Figure 12), which is based on an exercise from Chapter 9 in the Becker book. This handout provides the parents with an opportunity to demonstrate their own knowledge of effective and appropriate methods for consequating a variety of behaviors, most of which have not been discussed or encountered previously by the parents. The first part of the handout requires the parents to rewrite the negatively stated rules in a positive manner; the second part requires the parents to state what they should do following the occurrence of the desirable and undesirable child behaviors listed in order to increase or decrease the likelihood of repetition by the child. The last chapter in the book, which exemplifies how the principles of behavior modification can be applied successfully to many problem behaviors, including dependency, lack of confidence, withdrawal, and acting-out, is assigned. This assignment, like the final handout, is congruent with the major program goal of enhancing the parents' ability to cope effectively with problems with their children that might arise in the future.

Ninth Session

During the final session, the parents summarize the general behavior modification principles presented throughout the nine-week program, in addition to discussing practical applications of the principles. The parents then comment on one another's participation in and progressive changes evidenced during the nine-week program. At this point, the group leaders relate their observations and impressions of each parent's participation. Parents are then encouraged to comment on and offer suggested changes in the program, including the involvement of the group leaders. Arrangements for the postgroup assessments are made at the end of the session.

PROGRAM EVALUATION

Although the final data from the parents who have completed the program have not been analyzed, the program, subjectively speaking, has met with success. This subjective impression is supported by the very low parent dropout rate, the consistent decrease in the reported frequency, number, and severity of problem behaviors over the course of the program, the maintenance of change or continued decrease in problems through the six-month follow-up period, and the number of positive comments regarding the program by the parent participants. The reasons for success which have been suggested by parents who have completed the program include the following:

1. The program is explicit and clear, and provides numerous opportunities for comparison of the incidence of specific problems initially existing with those present at later times.

2. The parents quickly become aware that many families have similar difficulties and that there are ways, often not notably discrepant from methods they have tried at some time in the past, to alleviate existing problems and even prevent future moderate to severe difficulties.

3. The parents see that they not only receive but can give support and helpful suggestions in the group.

4. The stress on and encouragement of generalization of the application of the principles learned to other children in the family, as well as to the parents themselves, serve to remove the initial family focus on and differential treatment of the child referred. These changes, in turn, tend to improve the general family atmosphere.

5. The parents in each family discover that, when they rather consistently employ similar, primarily positive, methods of handling difficulties, the general family atmosphere and their own marital relationship, which frequently are marked initially by tension and disharmony, improve both during and after the program.

SUMMARY

A behavior modification program designed to teach parenting skills to parents of children between 2 and 12 years old has been described in this paper. Although the program was discussed primarily in terms of its use with parents of children with moderate to severe behavior problems, it is amenable to use with parents of nonproblem children.

During the nine-week program, parents attend a weekly two-hour discussion group, read Becker's book *Parents Are Teachers*, and complete chapter exercises and handouts designed to increase generalization of principles presented in the book and by the group leaders. Pregroup, postgroup, and follow-up measures to assess program effectiveness and generalization include parent-child observations and interviews, and parent completion of the Bipolar Adjective Checklist and the Behavior Inventory. Independence and skill of parents in effectively handling problems with their children are maximized through active parent participation as an integral part of the entire intervention process.

REFERENCES

BECKER, W. C.: The relationship of factors on parental ratings of self and each other to the behavior of kindergarten children as rated by mothers, fathers, and teachers. *J. Consult. Psychol.*, 24, 507-527, 1960.

BECKER, W. C.: *Parents Are Teachers*. Champaign, Ill.: Research Press, 1971.

EYBERG, S. M., and JOHNSON, S. M.: Multiple assessment of behavior modification with families: Effects of contingency contracting and order of treated problems. *J. Consult. and Clin. Psychol.*, 42, 594-606, 1974.

EYBERG, S., and TAMS, V.: A behavior modification mothers' group treatment program. Paper presented at the Annual Meeting of the Oregon Psychological Association, Sun River, Ore., May 1973.

HANF, C.: Modifying problem behaviors in mother-child interaction: The standardized laboratory situations. Paper presented at the meeting of the Association of Behavior Therapies, Olympia, Wash., 1968.

HANF, C., and KLING, J.: Facilitating parent-child interaction: A two-stage training model. Unpublished manuscript, U. of Oregon Medical School, 1973.

PATTERSON, G. R., COBB, J. A., and RAY, R. S.: A social engineering technology for retraining the families of aggressive boys. In: H. E. Adams and J. P. Unikel (Eds.), *Issues and Trends in Behavior Therapy*. Springfield, Ill.: Charles C Thomas, 1973. Pp. 139-224.

PATTERSON, G. R., and FAGOT, B. I.: Selective responsiveness to social reinforcers and deviant behavior in children. *Psychol. Record.*, 17, 369-378, 1967.

7

Comparing Group and Individual Methods for Training Parents in Child Management Techniques

●

KAREN E. KOVITZ

A systematic trend advocating the use of a triadic model of therapeutic intervention has emerged in recent years in the research and applied literature of contemporary child psychology. Within this framework, paraprofessionals and indigenous nonprofessionals have been trained to function as direct therapeutic agents. The feasibility and effectiveness of this approach have been well documented in studies of parent-mediated treatment of children with behavior problems (Berkowitz and Graziano, 1972; Johnson and Katz, 1973). Most of the studies cited in these reviews have employed either individual or group methods for training parents to use operant techniques in child management.

Studies describing the training of individual couples or single parents have shown parent-mediated intervention to be effective for a range of behavior problems and a wide variety of treatment procedures. However, several variables related to evaluating the overall efficacy of the parent-mediated approach seem to have been neglected in the majority of individual parent training reports. For example, monetary and time expenditures have seldom been included. In addition, procedures aimed at

This study is based in part upon a thesis submitted to the Department of Educational Psychology, University of Calgary, in partial fulfillment of the M.Sc. degree. The author wishes to thank Drs. Lorna Cammaert (Chairperson), Roy Brown, and Eugene Edgington for their helpful suggestions as members of the thesis committee. Special thanks to Drs. Lee Handy and Eric Mash for their assistance throughout the project, and grateful appreciation to Dr. Roy Ferguson, Director of Psychology, Alberta Children's Hospital, whose cooperation made the study possible.

124

facilitating the maintenance and generalization of parent behaviors have rarely been reported.

Studies employing group methods for training have also demonstrated the feasibility and success of parent-mediated treatment of behavior problems. Of greater importance, perhaps, have been their contribution toward developing procedures for identifying crucial variables in training and their effects upon process and outcome measures. Several other developments have emerged from studies of group training. More frequent accounting of cost in relation to benefit has occurred. The importance of assessing effects of training on parent behaviors in addition to the traditional assessment of children's behavior has been realized. Finally, the need for controlled, group, experimental designs in examining various training strategies has been recognized.

Some investigations have used both group and individual methods for training each mediator. These studies have shown that a combination of individual and group methods can result in significant and reliable change in parent and child behaviors, but the relative contribution and important parameters associated with each method of training are difficult to determine.

Two studies (Peine, 1971; Mira, 1970) have attempted to assess various aspects of parent training in relation to group or individual methods. In so doing, they have provided some basis for comparing outcome following group or individual training. Peine (1971) investigated the effects of different training variables (lecture only versus lecture plus contingency contracting) on parent attendance, punctuality, and participation. One of the experimental groups received individual training. The data showed that contingency-managed groups were more responsive than lecture-only groups to all aspects of the training program and that there were no differences in parent behavior for group and individual participants after training. Relative costs for each method of training were not reported. Peine cautions against interpreting the latter finding as conclusive since a number of uncontrolled variables prevented the use of a formal group design. Mira (1970), on the other hand, reported differences for group and individual conditions. Group was not as effective, according to the criteria of total professional time expended and successful outcome, as individual training. However, limitations in the design of the study and in data reporting make assessment of the comparability of individual and group training methods difficult.

In summary, effective parent-mediated treatment of behavior problems appears to have been demonstrated where individual, group, or a combination of both methods for training parents have been employed. Additional research is needed to identify important general parameters in parent training and to evaluate the relative efficacy of various training and treatment strategies. Procedures for investigating these issues should include multiple sources of data, cost-benefit analysis, and controlled experimental designs.

The present investigation, as one part of a broader study, examined procedures for delivering and evaluating parent training services. The general objectives of the study were: to demonstrate accountability in a clinical as well as a research context within the parent-mediated treatment model; to systematize a method for both investigating variables related to training and organizing the findings; and to provide information on an initial and crucial treatment dispensation decision when child management problems may be involved, i.e., whether to work with individual parents or groups of parents in training them as treatment mediators. The following research areas were of major interest: first, to determine the feasibility of training parents using a low cost, intensive, and systematic training program; second, to evaluate the effectiveness of the systematic training program and compare it with the informal training offered within the scope of traditional treatment services at the children's hospital; and third, to examine the relative efficacy of group and individual methods for training parents in child management techniques.

METHOD

Subjects

Ss in the study included 20 two-parent families (mediators) and their respective, identified target children. Fourteen of these families were selected to participate in the experimental training program upon meeting the following criteria: two parents were living at home, both had signed the behavior contingency contract (Figure 1), and they had submitted the $50 deposit; the target child was between the ages of 6 and 12 years, was reported by parents to be exhibiting several high-rate deviant behaviors, and had not been medically diagnosed as psychotic, brain-damaged, or seriously physically handicapped. Six families participated in the control training program and were selected from hospital treatment records according to the above demographic and behavioral criteria.

Procedure

Assignment. Ss were randomly assigned to one of two experimental conditions—group or individual training. The Group Training Condi-

FIGURE 1

INDIVIDUAL CONTRACT

In order for us to work cooperatively and effectively together, mutual expectations should be clearly stated. The following contract specifies the responsibilities which you should be willing to undertake. It also sets out the consequences for doing so.

RESPONSIBILITY	CONSEQUENCE
1. I will attend weekly meetings.	$3.00 if both parents attend ($1.00 if only *one* parent attends)
2. I will collect and bring in complete data on the behavior of my child for *each* meeting.	$2.00 each week
3. My spouse and I will observe and record some specified behaviors of our child, simultaneously but independently, at home, twice per week.	$2.00 each week for collection *and* submission
4. My spouse and/or I will be responsible for completing various weekly readings and written home assignments and bringing these to weekly meetings.	$2.00 per week

Thus, an opportunity to earn back $48.00 of the $50.00 fee, required for admission to this program, is given according to the conditions specified above. The $2.00 charge will cover the cost of materials and equipment required to implement the course. The monies forfeited by failure to meet the above responsibilities will be pooled and donated to ....

In addition to the monetary system outline, fulfilling responsibilities 1 through 4 will earn the right to participate in *clinic time*. This is a 10-minute period available to *each* family at the end of each session to discuss questions and problems pertaining to that family's needs. An opportunity for feedback on the points raised is thus available.

We, ..., agree to try

....

to fulfill the responsibilities as outlined above, and agree to the terms of this contract.

I, ...,

in return for your cooperation in the above, will agree to serve as a teacher and resource person, provide encouragement and support, and will undertake to carry out the program as well as the distribution of the above consequences.

tion consisted of nine couples, five of whom met together with a consultant one night a week, and four of whom met together with the same consultant on a different night of the week. The Individual Training Condition comprised five couples, each of whom met with the consultant once per week. Ss were included in the Control Training Condition if they had recently completed a treatment program which had included some parent-mediated behavioral intervention in child management problems.

Training

All group and individual systematic training was conducted in a meeting room at a children's hospital in Calgary. The format for training included lectures, videotaped demonstrations, discussion, reading materials (e.g., Becker's *Parents Are Teachers,* Patterson and Gullion's *Living with Children*), and written home assignments. Session content was similar to that described by Walder et al. (1967); however, greater emphasis was placed upon developing competence in each of three skill areas, and these were taught in succession rather than concurrently: (1) defining, monitoring, and graphing behavior; (2) principles of reward and punishment; and (3) techniques of child management. Training was aimed at developing knowledge of general behavioral principles and skills.

Several other modifications in commonly reported procedures were made. First, the program was designed to elicit maximum parental responsibility for the design, administration, and evaluation of treatment strategies; therefore parent behaviors (attendance, punctuality, and assignment completion) that have been shown to influence the outcome of training were placed under formal contract (Peine, 1971; Peine and Munro, 1973; Patterson and Reid, 1970). An attempt was also made to "match" these responsibilities with proportionally weighted consequences. Second, training procedures were designed to be practical and inexpensive to administer within an established clinical setting. Thus, intensive training was restricted to six weeks, and parent report data were deemed acceptable. Several studies (Johnson and Bolstad, 1973; Peine, 1972) have reported reliable data where parents have been subject to periodic monitoring as provided for in the present study. Further details of the training program are available in *A Training Guide for Leaders in Techniques of Child Management* (Kovitz, 1973).

(a) *Group Training Condition.* Mediators in the Group Training Condition (GTC) met together with the consultant once a week for 3½ hours, for six weeks. Session 1 included training in defining, recording, and graphing the frequencies of selected behaviors presented on video-tape. Following lecture and demonstrations, parents were instructed to rate the behavior of an analogue target child in terms of its frequency within a 20-second interval and its quality defined by (D) Deviant/Disruptive, (A) Acceptable, or (P) Passive. Clinic time was made available for each family to discuss ideas and problems associated with monitoring behavior, and group as well as consultant feedback was encouraged. Session 2 followed a similar format. The content included basic principles of reward and punishment. All contingencies described in the contract were in effect. Session 3 focused on applying techniques of reinforcement. Sessions 4, 5, and 6 involved instruction in program design and application of techniques for changing behavior. Cautions to bear in mind in program planning, modifications in design, and circumventing program failure were discussed.

(b) *Individual Training Condition.* Mediators in the Individual Training Condition (ITC) each met with the consultant once a week for 1½ hours, for six weeks. The content and format for ITC participants were identical to those outlined for GTC.

(c) *Control Training Condition.* Mediators participating in the Control Training Condition (CTC) had received some exposure to at least one of the following: instruction in behavioral principles, monitoring behavior, and contingency management. The duration of treatment ranged from 4 months to 1½ years. It was assumed that couples who had undergone individual "informal training" would provide a useful and meaningful comparison group for the systematic training program.

Evaluation

Three procedures for data collection were employed to assess the effectiveness of the systematic training program and to compare group and individual methods for training; they were: (1) evaluation of progress; (2) evaluation of outcome; and (3) cost-benefit analysis. Comparisons between systematic and traditional programs were limited to those data provided by outcome measures.

Progress measures. Progress measures were selected to yield an estimate of mediators' participation and commitment to the training program. Data were collected during training on attendance, punctuality, and completion of assignments.

Outcome measures. Several instruments were used to assess the effects of systematic training on mediator and target child behavior. A 21-item multiple choice concept test (Kovitz, 1973) tapped knowledge of general behavioral principles, observation skills, and intervention strategies. Mediator behavior was also assessed by means of the Children's Report of Parent Behavior Inventory (CRPBI) designed by Schaeffer (1965) to measure children's perceptions of their parents' child-rearing behaviors. In the shortened version (Cross and Aron, 1971) used in this study, eight factors are identified which sample specific parent behaviors— acceptance, control by guilt, nonenforcement, child-centeredness, hostile control, lax discipline, positive involvement, and instilling persistent anxiety. Separate reports for mother and father were obtained from each child.

Outcome of training on children's behavior was evaluated by parental report on two rating instruments—the Devereux Child Behavior Rating Scale (DCBRS) and the Behavioral Evaluation Index (BEI). The DCBRS (Spivack and Spotts, 1965) yields scores on 17 factors. Seven of these, collectively labeled "behavioral control factors," were used in the present study: proneness to emotional upset; need for adult contact; anxious-fearful ideation; impulse ideation; inability to delay; social aggression; and unethical behavior. The BEI is an adaptation of the Behavioral Research Project's Home Follow-up Evaluation (Tharp and Wetzel, 1969). Each referral behavior for the target child is rated according to a 5-point index of improvement. The BEI provided a global measure of perceived change in presenting problems, reported by parents.

A behavioral measure was also used to evaluate outcome of training on target behavior. Frequency data were collected at home by mediators in the systematic training program. Interrater reliability was determined for each mediator pair and ranged from .84 to .96. Since parents were encouraged to identify target behaviors for intervention, not all children had the same behaviors specified. All children did, however, have at least one example of noncompliant behavior listed among their referral problems. Thus a class of "noncompliance," represented by a single behavior on an idiosyncratic basis for each child, was selected to represent a direct behavioral measure for assessing the effect of training on child behavior.

Cost-benefit analysis. Monetary and time costs were calculated in relation to measures of progress, outcome, and consumer satisfaction, in order to assess cost-benefit for the systematic training program. Costs to program sponsors and recipients were determined separately.

Assessment of *Ss* in the Group and Individual Training Conditions was carried out on three occasions: pretraining, posttraining, and at follow-up approximately one month later. Mediators completed the concept test and the DCBRS on each occasion and the BEI at posttraining and follow-up. Target children whose parents participated in the systematic training programs were seen by the consultant for assessment at intake, posttreatment, and follow-up intervals at which time the CRPBI was administered.

Ss in the Control Training Condition were assessed at the end of treatment. Mediators completed the concept test, the DCBRS, and the BEI. The CRPBI was administered to the target children.

RESULTS

Findings related to the evaluation of the systematic training program, the comparison of systematic and control treatments, and the comparison of group and individual methods are described according to the data collection procedures.

Progress Measures

The data on progress variables for GTC and ITC clearly indicated that, for both treatments, attendance was extremely regular for all sessions, and assignments were completed 99 percent of the time. Mediators tended to arrive on time but, where tardiness occurred, it was twice as likely for ITC participants.

Outcome Measures

Analyses of posttreatment data, related to the effect on mediators' and target children's behavior of participating in systematic versus informal training, yielded the following results.

Group differences were found on the concept test $(F_{1,18}=42.61$ and $p<.0001)$ with mediators in the systematic program achieving significantly higher scores. There was no difference between the two groups for scores ascribed to mediators on the CRPBI (for mothers or fathers), or for ratings assigned to children on the DCBRS. A difference between groups was found on the BEI $(F_{1,18}=4.49$ and $p<.05)$; parents in the systematic training program reported significantly greater improvement in target children's referral problems than did parents in the control program.

Analysis of the effect of systematic training over time (pretraining, posttraining, and follow-up), and method of training (GTC and ITC), yielded the following results.

For the concept test, the Time was significant $(F_{2,22}=30.32$ and $p<.0001)$; however, there was no difference between group and individual training methods.

A multivariate analysis of variance on mothers' CRPBI scores showed the Time effect to be significant ($F_{16,30}$=2.26). A step-down test revealed that children reported mothers' use of nonenforcement and hostile control to decline significantly over the course of training ($F_{2,22}$ and $p<.002$; and $p<.02$ respectively). There was no difference between GTC and ITC for mothers on the CRPBI.

A multivariate analysis of variance on fathers' CRPBI scores yielded a significant effect for time of testing with $F_{16,30}$=2.39. The step-down test showed that children reported a significant reduction in fathers' control by guilt during the training program ($F_{2,22}$=10.75 and $p<.0007$). There was no difference between GTC and ITC.

No differences between Group and Individual methods of training were found on the DCBRS. Tests of the Time effect and the Time X Method interaction were significant with $F_{14,22}$=3.85 and $p<.0008$, and $F_{28,59}$=1.95 and $p<.02$ respectively. The step-down test for the Time effect indicated that "proneness to upset," anxious-fearful ideation," and "impulse ideation" occurred less frequently as training progressed. The step-down test for the interaction showed that impulse ideation changed significantly over time with method of training; however, GTC 2 differed from both GTC 1 and ITC from pretest to posttest on this variable.

The Newman-Keuls *a posteriori* procedure was used to determine where the differences across time occurred for each of the significant effects. Results indicated that, for all variables investigated, significant changes occurred from pre- to posttraining, and pretraining to follow-up tests.

Results of the ANOVA for data obtained from the BEI yielded no significant differences for either method of training or between posttesting and follow-up testing.

In order to determine the effect of systematic training across time on noncompliant behavior, product moment correlations were calculated for individual Ss between the frequency of noncompliance and progressive days in the training program. The level of significance was determined by randomization* (Edgington, 1969). The correlations for individual Ss appear in Table 1. To investigate whether a significant decrease in the

---

* Randomization was carried out by randomly sampling 1000 random permutations of the frequency data over 35 days and, for each of these 1000 samples, a product moment correlation was calculated. Following this, the proportion of the 1000 correlations having as large an absolute value as that of the obtained coefficient was determined, and that proportion was the probability value associated with the obtained coefficient.

TABLE 1

Test of Trends in Noncompliant Behavior Across Time

Subject	Correlation (Day x Frequency)	Probabilities*
1	—.56	.001
2	—.48	.003
3	—.59	.001
4	—.57	.001
5	—.62	.001
6	—.42	.006
7	—.72	.001
8	—.65	.001
9	—.82	.001
10	—.62	.001
11	—.41	.013
12	—.16	.188
13	—.56	.001
14	—.77	.001

* Determined by randomization.

frequency of noncompliance occurred over time in treatment, a combined probability over all Ss was computed. A logarithmic transformation of this value (Guilford and Fruchter, 1973) was treated as a chi square statistic. This analysis yielded highly significant results at $p<.001$, where chi square obtained was equal to 172.03 with 28 degrees of freedom ($\chi^2_{.001}=56.89$). An ANOVA for unequal sample size, carried out on the correlation between frequency of noncompliance and consecutive days in treatment, with level of significance determined by randomization,** was used to assess the effect of method of training on the frequency of noncompliant behavior. No significant differences were found between children whose parents participated in the Group or Individual Training Conditions ($F_{2,11}=1.223$, $p=.34$).

Cost-benefit

Mean cost-benefit per family for each training method is reported in Table 2. No significant difference in reported satisfaction, on a program evaluation questionnaire, for Group and Individual training participants was found.

** The 14 values (one per S) were randomly divided 1000 times into three groups, with 5, 5, and 4 in each group, to determine what proportion of those random divisions provided as large a value of F as the obtained value of F.

TABLE 2

Mean Cost-Benefit per Family for Each Training Method

Variable	Cost ITC*	GTC**	Variable	Benefit ITC	GTC
Cost to Recipient			*Progress Measures*		
Monetary	$3.20	$4.22	Attendance	100%	99.1%
Time	11 hrs.	23 hrs.	Punctuality	11.3 min.	6.2 min.
			Assignments completed	99.1%	99.0%
Cost to Sponsor			*Outcome Measures*		
Contact Time	11 hrs.	6.9 hrs.	Concept Test	SI†	SI
Extra Time	10 min.	40 min.	Devereux Child Behavior Scale	SI	SI
			Children's Report of Parent Behavior	SI	SI
			Noncompliance	SI	SI
			Mean Satisfaction Rating	4.21	4.03

* Individual training condition.
** Group training condition.
† Significant improvement.

DISCUSSION

The present study was designed to investigate the practical feasibility and effectiveness of a low-cost, systematic training program for parents; to compare the outcome of an intensive training program with the outcome of informal training offered within a more traditional treatment program; and to compare the relative efficacy of Group and Individual methods for training. Results of the study showed that conceptual and behavioral skills can be taught to parents in an efficient and systematic fashion within a six-week training period, and that these skills can then be transferred by parents to ameliorate behavior management problems in the home. Pretraining to posttraining changes were demonstrated in parent and child behaviors, and these were maintained at follow-up. In addition, the present investigation suggested that low-cost, intensive, and systematic training procedures appear to be at least as effective as informal, longer training offered within the context of traditional treatment methods. Furthermore, group training was shown to be just as effective as individual training in progress and outcome of parent-mediated intervention.

Informal and Systematic Training

Two of the outcome measures, the concept test and BEI, significantly differentiated Ss in informal and systematic training conditions. These results suggest that parents do acquire more knowledge regarding behavioral principles and techniques when these are deliberately and systematically taught. Acquisition of these skills may, as Patterson (1969) suggests, facilitate maintenance and generalization of treatment effects. The results of informal and systematic comparisons also showed that greater improvement is reported in children's referral problems for participants in the systematic training program. It may be, however, that the higher ratings reflect relative dramatic and rapid gains that occurred in that program—compared to possibly more gradual improvement during informal training—rather than absolute changes in behavior. Long-term follow-up research is needed to investigate the implications of this finding.

Neither the specific rating of target children's behavior (DCBRS) nor the measure of perceived mediator behavior (CRPBI) significantly differentiated systematic and informal training groups. Based on pre- to post-training changes observed for experimental group Ss, similarity in these outcome measures may reflect improvement following treatment for participants in both groups. The conclusions that may be drawn with respect to the systematic and informal training comparisons are somewhat limited in light of the fact that a posttest-only control group design was employed.

Systematic Training: Group and Individual Methods

Results of the present study confirmed previous findings with respect to the facilitating effect of contracting for various progress measures on mediator participation and commitment to the training program. It would appear that even better participation, with respect to attendance, punctuality, and assignment completion, was found in this study than in other published reports (e.g., Peine and Munro, 1973). It is unlikely, however, that this is due simply to the use of contingency contracting; rather, it is possible that Stuart's (1971) idea of proportionally weighting privilege and responsibility terms of the contract, as used in the present study, may have augmented the efficiency of contracting for participation.

Comparative analyses of individual and group training methods revealed that there were no significant differences between groups on any of the outcome measures. Significant changes for both groups from pretraining to posttraining, and pretraining to follow-up were found for all measures.

The systematic training program was oriented toward bringing about some specific changes in mediators' behavior, such as (1) less reliance upon covert control and aversive methods, and more frequent and consistent use of positive consequation in child management, and (2) acquisition of a set of transferable problem-solving skills. Significant changes across time for individual and group participants on both the concept test and the CRPBI provided some validation for these goals. Not only did parents show great gains in theoretical and applied knowledge of behavioral management but, in addition, variables on the CRPBI that were expected to sample behaviors related to (1) did reflect change. Children reported a significant decrease in mothers' nonenforcement and in their use of hostile control, as well as a strong tendency for mothers to use firmer discipline and less control by guilt. Children also reported a significant decrease in control by guilt for fathers as well as a tendency for them to use firmer discipline, more enforcement, and less hostile control.

Analysis of the effect of systematic training on target children's behavior using frequency of noncompliance as the criterion was consistent with parent ratings of child behavior on the DCBRS. The fact that significant changes were not observed from posttraining to follow-up for target children on the BEI was also consistent with data on the effects of training over time, i.e., significant differences between posttraining and follow-up were not evident for any of the measures.

The need for careful accounting of cost in relation to benefit in the delivery of mental health services has been pointed out by several investigators (O'Dell, 1974; Johnson and Katz, 1973). In part, the present study was designed to investigate the practical feasibility and efficiency of low-cost parent training.

Cost-to-recipient figures indicated that GTC participants tended to pay more for the training program, i.e., they forfeited slightly more of their deposit. In addition, the contact time commitment per family was greater for GTC (23 hours) than ITC (11 hours). Benefit to recipients who participated in group or individual training was similar in that progress variables reflected high commitment and participation, outcome measures showed significant improvement during training which was maintained through the follow-up period, and reported satisfaction was very high.

The sponsor's cost to administer the program via group or individual methods showed that it was just as effective, but much less expensive, to provide group training.

Implications

The results of this study suggest several implications for the administration and delivery of treatment services. First, the possibility is raised of applying contingency management to participation behaviors, in a variety of treatment services, to increase efficiency and commitment. Second, a short-term, systematic, and educational program for training parents may provide a desirable alternative or adjunct to traditional therapy methods where problems in child management are involved. Third, in arriving at an initial treatment decision, i.e., whether to work with an individual family or a group of parents, salient features of the sponsors' and recipients' needs and available resources should be given careful consideration. Perhaps with the accumulation of more complete data on consumer satisfaction and cost-benefit, clients and sponsoring agencies will be willing and able to make joint recommendations regarding such treatment decisions.

Future studies should continue to document details of training and evaluation, outline variables and parameters of parent training, and describe cost-effectiveness.

REFERENCES

BECKER, W. C.: *Parents Are Teachers*. Champaign, Ill.: Research Press, 1971.

BERKOWITZ, B., and GRAZIANO, A.: Training parents as behavioral therapists: A review. *Behav. Res. and Ther.*, 10, 297-317, 1972 .

CROSS, H. J., and ARON, R. D.: The relationship of unobtrusive measures of marital conflict to remembered differences between parents. Proceedings, 79th Annual Convention of the Americal Psychological Association, 6, 365-366, 1971.

EDGINGTON, E. S.: Approximate randomization tests. *J. Psychol.*, 72, 143-149, 1969.

GUILFORD, J. P., and FRUCHTER, B.: *Fundamental Statistics in Psychology and Education*. New York: McGraw-Hill, 1973.

JOHNSON, C., and KATZ, R. C.: Using parents as change agents for their children: A review. *J. Child Psychol. and Psychiat. and Allied Disciplines*, 14, 181-200, 1973.

JOHNSON, S. M., and BOLSTAD, O. D.: Methodological issues in naturalistic observation: Some problems and solutions for field research. In: L. A. Hamerlynck, L. C. Handy, and E. J. Mash (Eds.), *Behavior Change: Methodology, Concepts and Practice*. Champaign, Ill.: Research Press, 1973.

KOVITZ, K. E.: *A Training Guide for Leaders in Techniques of Child Management*. Unpublished manuscript, University of Calgary, 1973.

MIRA, M.: Results of a behavior modification training program for parents and teachers. *Behav. Res. and Ther.*, 8, 309-311, 1970.

O'DELL, S.: Training parents in behavior modification: A review. *Psychol. Bull.*, 81, 418-433, 1974.

PATTERSON, G. R.: A community mental health program for children. In: L. A. Hamerlynck, P. O. Davidson, and L. E. Acker (Eds.), *Behavior Modification and Ideal Mental Health Services.* Calgary: U. of Calgary, 1969.

PATTERSON, G. R., and GULLION, M. E.: *Living with Children.* Champaign, Ill.: Research Press, 1968.

PATTERSON, G. R., and REID, J. B.: Reciprocity and coercion: Two facets of social systems. In: C. Neuringer and J. Michael (Eds.), *Behavior Modification in Clinical Psychology.* New York: Appleton-Century-Crofts, 1970.

PEINE, H.: Training parents using lecture-demonstration procedures and a contingency-managed program. Unpublished doctoral dissertation, U. of Utah, 1971.

PEINE, H. A.: The elimination of a child's self-injurious behavior at home and school. *School Application of Learning Theory,* 4, 1972.

PEINE, H. A., and MUNRO, B. C.: Behavioral management of parent training programs. *Psychol. Record,* 23, 459-466, 1973.

SCHAEFFER, E. S.: Children's reports of parental behavior: An inventory. *Child Devel.,* 36, 413-424, 1965.

SPIVACK, G., and SPOTTS, J.: The Devereux Child Behavior Scale: Symptom behaviors in latency age children. *Amer. J. Ment. Deficiency,* 69, 839-853, 1965.

STUART, R. B.: Behavioral control of delinquency: Critique of existing programs and recommendations for innovative programming. In: L. A. Hamerlynck and F. W. Clark (Eds.), *Behavior Modification for Exceptional Children and Youth.* Calgary: U. of Calgary, 1971.

THARP, R. G., and WETZEL, R. J.: *Behavior Modification in the Natural Environment.* New York: Academic Press, 1969.

WALDER, L. O., COHEN, S. I., and DASTON, P. G.: Teaching parents and others principles of behavior control for modifying the behavior of children. Progress Report, U.S. Office of Education, 32-31-7515-5024, 1967.

Section III

SOME NEW APPROACHES TO PARENT TRAINING

8

Teaching Conflict Resolution Skills to Parents and Children

BARCLAY MARTIN
and
CRAIG TWENTYMAN

The domain of troubled parent-child interactions can be divided some-what arbitrarily into two broad aspects: (1) those features involving how the parent and child *talk* about the problem, that is, how they attempt to reach some agreement about what is to be done about the problem, and (2) what, in fact, they *do* about it when the occasion arises. In the past, quite different theoretical and therapeutic strategies have been associated with these two aspects of parent-child behavior—expressive, "feeling" oriented therapies with the former, and behavior modification with the latter. A primary goal in our current research is to explore the apparent contradictions between the two approaches and see to what extent they can both be usefully incorporated within modification procedures.

The expressive therapy approach in its purest form is best exemplified by Thomas Gordon's *Parent Effectiveness Training* (1970), and behavior modification approaches to parent-child problems have by now been described by many authors (e.g., Becker, 1971; Krumboltz and Krumboltz,

The second named author is not involved in the current research program at North Carolina. He conducted a pilot experiment at the University of Wisconsin which served as an essential first step in the development of both the assessment and intervention procedures described in this paper. Judith Lippmann, David McNeill, and Sandra Mills are serving as therapists in the current research, and their contributions are much appreciated. This research is supported by a grant, MH 22750, from the National Institute of Mental Health.

141

1972; Patterson and Gullion, 1968). Several points of contrast can be made between these orientations. Within the behavioral tradition, relatively little attention has been given to the expression of emotion and verbal communication, it being assumed for the most part that positive emotional or attitudinal changes will follow desirable changes in behavior produced by contingency management procedures. Gordon, on the other hand, disavows any explicit use of rewards or punishments in child-rearing. He sees this as a one-sided use of parental power and points out that sooner or later parents run out of power; the day of reckoning comes when the parents bemoan the fact that they have lost their influence over their son or daughter. Gordon also points out that the application of the principles of behavior modification is not such a simple matter; what starts out sounding easy—rewarding good behavior and ignoring or mildly punishing bad behavior—can become a complicated business. The effective reinforcers have to be identified and occasionally changed, behavior may have to be shaped gradually from easy to more difficult forms, the relative effects of immediate versus delayed reinforcements have to be considered, certain material rewards must be faded out in time, the programs have to be applied with consistency, and so on.

The gap between the two approaches should not be exaggerated, however. Ginott (1965), basically an exponent of the expressive therapy viewpoint, nevertheless emphasized the importance of firm rule enforcement and limit setting; meanwhile behavior modifiers have recently entered the field of conflict resolution, especially in dealing with conflicts between parents and teen-age children or between husband and wife. In part, the difference may simply be a matter of deciding which behaviors we want to change—noncompliance, hitting, talking back, withdrawal, or crying versus emotional-verbal communication and how to negotiate agreements about conflicts. Do we want to teach children to "behave" or to participate in decision making, or both? If one teaches communication and conflict resolution skills by reinforcement and modeling procedures, then the basic methodological difference between the two approaches would seem to vanish, assuming that operational measures of such variables as emotional communication can be reasonably attained. Gordon, in fact, does advocate modeling as an effective teaching device both as a way for parents to influence their children and as a way for trainers to influence parents. It is also a little hard to believe that subtle and not-so-subtle social reinforcement does not occur in the context of Gordon's parent groups even though he decries the planned use of such contingencies by parents.

In the discussion to follow, we shall use the term "contingency management" to refer to traditional operant behavior modification and "conflict resolution" to refer to both communicational and negotiating aspects of problem-solving behavior. The overall aim of our research is to determine for what kind of families with what kind of problems either of these two approaches or some combination of the approaches is effective. For purposes of the present paper, however, we shall concentrate on procedures for teaching conflict resolution skills, since work in this area is still relatively new.

Assessment of Conflict Resolution Skills

From time to time, parents and children engage in an interactive sequence that we call a problem interaction. These sequences are initiated in various ways, e.g., the parent makes a demand and the child does not comply, or the child asks the parent to do something and the parent refuses; the parent has had a frustrating day at work or a fight with the spouse and jumps on the child over some minor matter, or the child has had an upsetting experience at school and is unusually grumpy and out-of-sorts upon arrival at home. Whatever the initiating act, the sequence will tend to follow its own typical course and outcome for that parent and child. The parent may press the child with questions, more directly blame and criticize, or become angry and yell or slap. The child in turn may withdraw from the interaction, cry, become sullen, or counterattack verbally or physically. Both participants are likely to wind up in a state of distress.

As part of the preintervention assessment procedure, we obtain direct measures of how parents and children talk to each other in solving troublesome problems. After a recurring problem has been identified, a given parent and child are asked to reach agreement about how to handle this problem, and their subsequent interaction is videotaped. The following excerpt illustrates certain features of ineffective conflict resolution. Unfortunately, the ineffective qualities of the interaction are considerably muted without the visual and auditory aspects of the original videotape.

George's mother corrects him during violin practice, and both of them eventually become upset. They are trying to reach agreement about how to handle this problem.

> Mother: Well, what do you think? What do you suggest that we
> could. . . .
> George: Don't correct me.

Mother: How can I not correct you ever? How would you learn? If I don't ever correct you?
George: Uh, I don't have to learn.
Mother: Well, then, there's no point in taking violin, and we decided that that was a good thing for you to do, right?
George: Well, I didn't like it. Ever. You know that.

✔   ✔   ✔

Mother: Well, you know, one way that I wouldn't get angry would be if when I correct, I really see that you were trying to change what you were doing, rather than just ignore . . . for instance when I say, "O.K. stop."
George: Yeah, but I have to finish the measure.
Mother: Well, but often you try to finish the piece.
George: No, I don't.
Mother: You see? And that just doesn't work. It gets me upset.
George: Not, not.
Mother: So what can we do?
George: Nothing.

✔   ✔   ✔

Mother: Oh, I'm not sure that this is going to help too much.
George: I know, I'm sure it won't. (hopeless tone of voice)
                    (21 second pause)
Mother: Well, we certainly tried.
                    (13 second pause)
Mother: And I don't see that there is anything really new that we haven't tried.
George: I know. There's nothing to do but drop it. Drop it, drop it. Drop it.
Mother: But then you wouldn't . . . first of all we need the . . .
George: Piano, piano, instead, instead.
Mother: You'd still have to be corrected on the piano.
George: I know, I know, I know. (whining, petulant)

A coding scheme which should permit some quantification of those features related to effective and ineffective problem solving is being developed to apply to this kind of interaction. Generally speaking, "effective" refers to discussion that results in a more complete expression of points of view and in agreements that are complied with. The nine parent and four child categories in current use are shown in Table 1. Excesses of parent Direct Power, Direct Blame, and Indirect Blame are expected to be detrimental to successful problem solving, as are excesses of Child Opposition, Giving In, and Withdrawal.

TABLE 1

Coding Categories for Parent - Child Interaction

Parent	*Child*
1* Direct Power	1* Stubbornly Opposes Parent
2 Indirect Power	2* Gives in Passively
3* Direct Blame	3* Withdraws from Problem Solving
4* Indirect blame	4* Asserts Own Point of View
5 Reasons and Explanations	
6 Requests for Opinion	
7 Expression of Opinion or Proposal	
8* Expresses Own Feelings	
9* Reflects Child's Feelings, or General Point of View	
0 (For both parent and child) Any Expression Not Scored in Other Categories	

* These categories have been found to have adequate reliability (interrater correlations range from .78 to .94) and also are the categories that the intervention more specifically attempts to decrease or increase.

Intervention for Conflict Resolution

In teaching conflict resolution skills, the basic strategy is to break up the old ways in which parents and children talk (or don't talk) about their problems and provide training in new responses. The old habit patterns are frequently strong, and it is necessary to use highly structured and firmly applied procedures to facilitate the learning of the new responses. The therapist who does not remain firmly in control in the early stages of the intervention will find the parents and children quickly lapsing into their former patterns.

The general aims of the intervention procedures can be summarized as follows: parents are taught to minimize the use of arbitrary power, direct and indirect blaming, and long lectures; more positively, they are taught (1) to express their feelings or desires directly, briefly, and with as much intensity as they actually feel, (2) to listen to their children and reflect back what they are expressing about their feelings, wants, and general point of view, and (3) after this interchange of affect and desires, to reach specific agreements with the children that are mutually acceptable. We make it clear to the parents that we are not necessarily advocating equal power for parents and young children, but we are advocating some *reasonable input* from the child. In some cases, the problem is primarily a communicational one, and there is nothing to reach agreement about. In this case, the third part of the procedure would be omitted.

Children are taught to assert their point of view (likes, dislikes, wants, and feelings) with a minimum of antagonistic opposition, passive giving in, or withdrawal. Thus far, however, we have tended to emphasize the positive with children and have not focused as much on reducing the ineffective features of their interactions, as we have with parents.

The intervention process utilizes the following training sequence. In the case of a mother and her son, for example, the mother is first given some brief practice alone in Feeling Expression and Listening-Reflection, as we label these two response styles. This is done by asking her to respond to several hypothetical situations and giving feedback in terms of her performance. An audiotape model of a mother expressing her feelings or listening-reflecting in the prescribed manner is used as part of this procedure. The mother being instructed is told not to *ask* questions, blame, or give a lecture when practicing either Feeling Expression or Listening-Reflection.

The child, who has been sitting at a table with coloring books and other materials in another part of the room, is now asked to join the parent. An identified problem is selected, and the child is first asked to express his point of view to the parent—"I want you to tell mother what you like or don't like about (refer to situation), what you want to happen, or how it makes you feel. . . ." Some young children find it hard to comply with or even to understand verbal instructions of this kind and, accordingly, we supplement the instructions with two aids. First, a digital counter is placed in front of the child, and he is told that when he is talking and saying something about what he feels (as above), then the "penny box" will click, the numbers will increase, and afterwards he will get one penny for every five points obtained. During the actual training, the face of the counter is hidden by a small cardboard screen so that the child's visual gaze and attention are not totally directed toward the counter. Second, an audio modeling tape is played on which another child is asked to do the same thing—in this case, tell his mother his feelings about her constantly nagging at him to pick up his clothes. This modeling tape also includes a mother who reflects back to the child what she hears about his feelings and desires. The mother in treatment is told that she is going to be asked to reflect her child's feelings and wants, and to listen to how the model mother does this. After listening to the model tape, the child and mother proceed to express and listen-reflect, respectively. They are interrupted and reminded of the instructions if they deviate too far from the required responses.

In the second phase, the procedure is reversed and the parent is given the Express Feelings instructions including specific requests not to ask questions, blame, or give a long lecture. The child is told to listen to the parent and be ready to tell the parent later what he hears. We have learned that the parent's expression must be kept brief if the child is to remember it. It comes as a shock to some parents to discover how little the child does absorb of what they have to say. The child can again earn points and pennies by telling the parent, more or less accurately, the main messages that the parent has given. A model tape is played of a mother expressing and a child listening-reflecting.

The third phase of the Conflict Resolution procedure involves asking the parent and child to first offer as many possible solutions as they can to the problem, and then try to reach agreement on a solution acceptable to both. They are permitted to interact freely, except that a mother, for example, is interrupted if she begins to ask too many questions, blame, or lecture.

Research Findings

Lanelle Taylor (1974) has recently completed a small study in which a version of this procedure was used to help mothers and children resolve conflicts arising from the fact that a retarded sibling lives in the home. A retarded child can create various kinds of psychological stress for the normal sibling. For example, normal siblings may feel resentful because parents devote more time and energy to the retarded child, or resentful because they are asked to assume various responsibilities for the retarded child; they may worry that there is something wrong with them, too, perhaps some hidden defect; out of a sense of guilt they may assume too much responsibility for the retarded child and behave in a self-sacrificing way; discussions of institutionalization may arouse their own fears of rejection. Needless to say, this can be an emotionally charged area for the parents, and they may have learned to avoid much open communication about it because of the painful emotions that are aroused.

Taylor essentially used the procedures described above except that she used videotaped models enacting *both* effective and ineffective problem-solving strategies applied to the emotional problems associated with having a retarded sibling. The "penny box" was also omitted with these 5- to 11-year-old children. Five experimental mother-child dyads were given two sessions of intervention (for a total of approximately 100 minutes) spaced a week apart and a postintervention assessment session one week after the second intervention session. Four control dyads received the same pre- and postintervention assessments but were told simply to continue talking to each other at home about these problems during the two-week waiting period. Pre- and postintervention assessment included both the direct measure of parent-child interaction previously described and a true-false questionnaire completed by the child that included a number of subscales referring to different kinds of problems or concerns associated with having a retarded sibling.

Some evidence for the validity or generality of the interaction assessment procedure is shown by correlations between certain interaction measures and questionnaire measures obtained at preintervention. Child Withdrawal correlated .78 ($p < .01$, one tailed test) with a subscale reflecting hyper-responsibility for the retarded sibling. Child Antagonistic Opposition correlated —.88 ($p < .01$, one tailed test) with the hyper-responsibility subscale. In other words, children who withdrew and were unable to communicate their concerns about the retarded sibling to the mother seemed to have an overconcern about the welfare of the retarded sibling. We would need more information to fully understand this relationship, but it suggests that the child may be attempting to allay some anxiety or other troubling emotions by being excessively good and responsible. Also, child Antagonistic Opposition as measured from the Interaction Test correlated .61 (p < .10, one tailed test) with a subscale in which the child said that the parent shows favoritism toward the retarded child.

Mothers were also asked to fill out the questionnaire as they thought their child would. It was thus possible to compute discrepancy scores between mother and child. An overall index of ineffective problem-solving behaviors based on a combination of several of the categories obtained from the Interaction Test correlated .67 ($p < .05$, one tailed test) with a false-negative measure of questionnaire discrepancy; that is, mothers who failed to answer true to many problems and concerns to which the child had answered true showed ineffective problem-solving behaviors in the Interaction Test. Thus, mothers who were low in problem-solving skills were relatively insensitive to what was troubling their children. The false-negative questionnaire discrepancy also correlated .68 ($p < .05$, one tailed test) with Child Gives In Passively and .17 ($p < .02$, one tailed test) with Child Appropriate Assertion. Mothers who do not know what is bothering their children tend to have children who give in passively and do not appropriately assert themselves. This makes sense—whatever the historical causes of the current interaction may be, it will be hard for a mother to know what is troubling her child if the child simply acquiesces and never asserts a point of view.

Taylor's intervention was only moderately successful. We remind you that it was 100 minutes long! The treatment mothers relative to the control mothers showed significantly greater decrease in Direct Blame ($p < .002$) on the Interaction Test, and treatment children showed significantly greater decrease in Withdrawal ($p < .01$) and significantly greater increase in Appropriate Assertion ($p < .05$). Other trends in the expected direction were present but, with these small N's, they did not reach statistical significance. Decreases in false-negative discrepancy on the questionnaire were not significantly greater for the treatment than the control group. A closer look at some of the individual dyads in this study clearly showed that two sessions were not enough to modify the ineffective response styles of a couple of mothers, but the results were generally encouraging.

Last September a larger study was begun that is still under way. In this research we are not working with one kind of focused problem, as did Taylor, but instead have included families in which there are various kinds of recurring problems between parents and children. Families have been recruited via a form letter and brief questionnaire sent to *all* parents of first, second, and third grade children in the Chapel Hill, N. C., public schools.

Our intervention procedures include both conflict resolution and contingency management training. The latter primarily involves the use of reward programs and mild punishment programs (time-out or withdrawal of a privilege). In the main study we are assessing the effectiveness of the whole treatment package against a minimal treatment condition. In the latter, the parents are given a brochure that describes in some detail and with examples what we are trying to teach, and are told to read this and try to put it into practice. The treatment group is further divided into two groups, one in which fathers are included in the treatment process and one in which fathers are not included. For all families in this study, fathers have indicated a willingness to participate. Assessment involves not only the pre- and postintervention videotaping of mother-child problem-solving behavior, but also a rather exacting procedure for collecting data from mothers over the telephone. The mother is asked to keep track of all problem interactions and is telephoned daily (excluding weekends) for seven consecutive days. The

TABLE 2

Mean Frequencies of Problem Interactions per 10 Hours, Pre- and
Postintervention, as a Function of the
Three Treatment Conditions

CONDITION	MEASURES			
	Problem Interactions		Prolonged* Problem Interactions	
	Pre	Post	Pre	Post
Father (N = 6)	3.75	0.89	2.43	0.37
No Father (N = 5)	2.38	0.62	2.05	0.33
Minimal (N = 5) treatment	1.87	1.62	1.15	0.82

* See text for definition of Prolonged Problem Interaction.

telephone interviewers are trained to get a sequential, behavioral description of each problem interaction and, borrowing from Watergate technology, we tape the mother's telephone descriptions (with her permission, of course). These descriptions are then typed on 3" x 5" cards, shuffled into a random sequence, and rated by judges into one of several categories.

Pre- and postintervention assessment measures have now been obtained on about half of the total anticipated sample. The mother-reported telephone data for this partial sample look promising, as can be seen in Table 2. The data under the second columnar heading, Prolonged Problems, are probably the most important. Prolonged problems are problem interactions which endured for more than two interchanges and which tended to show some escalation of distress on the part of either parent or child—in other words, more serious and debilitating sequences as compared to briefer and less emotionally upsetting ones. Sharp drops in the frequency of these prolonged problems are shown in both treatment groups, compared to a much smaller drop in the minimum treatment group. No particular trends have emerged thus far between the father and no-father conditions. The mismatch or initial problem rates for the three conditions will be reduced when some of the remaining families can be included. The trends, however, remain the same in the present data if one achieves a better match by looking only at families which have initial prolonged-problem frequencies of less than 3.0 per 10 hours. Statistical inference, however, will have to wait completion of the study.

To show that one can effect immediate changes is necessary, but it is not in itself a particularly exciting finding. Assuming that this prerequisite is accomplished, what are some of the more specific, and in our opinion, more interesting questions? First, we plan to see if a low-cost (in terms of professional input) telephone monitoring and booster-session procedure is more effective than no monitoring at all during a six-month follow-up period. Second, as the number of families in the study increases, we hope not only to see if including father makes a difference in the changes (and persistence of change at the six-month follow-up) in mother-child problems, but to assay the role of father-mother conflict on these changes. The most obvious hypothesis is that it will be necessary to include father when marital conflict is high but less necessary when it is low. Third, in a concurrent study now under way, we are beginning to compare the effectiveness of the conflict resolution procedures with the contingency management procedures and at the same time are attempting to see what kinds of disturbed parent-child interactions respond better to one or the other. It may be, for example, that with somewhat older, more verbal children, whose disturbed behavior is more neurotic-conflicted in nature, conflict resolution alone may solve many problems and make explicit contingency management programs unnecessary. With other parent-child dyads, especially those in which the parent is relatively helpless in the face of an aggressive, out-of-control child, some form of contingency management may be necessary before meaningful verbal communication can be achieved.

In sum, then, the long-term goal of all our researches is to identify the kinds of families and the kinds of problems that are best helped by specific aspects of these various procedures. The evolving nature of the intervention should be emphasized. What we have is not a finished product ready to be marketed, but procedures that still need revision and continuing evaluation.

REFERENCES

BECKER, W. C.: *Parents Are Teachers*. Champaign, Ill.: Research Press, 1971.

GINOTT, H.: *Between Parent and Child*. New York: Macmillan, 1965.

GORDON, T.: *Parent Effectiveness Training*. New York: Peter H. Wyden, 1970.

KRUMBOLTZ, J. D., and KRUMBOLTZ, H. B.: *Changing Children's Behavior*. Englewood Cliffs, N. J.: Prentice-Hall, 1972.

PATTERSON, G. R., and GULLION, M.: *Living with Children: New Methods for Parents and Teachers*. Champaign, Ill.: Research Press, 1968.

TAYLOR, L. S.: *Communication Between Mothers and Normal Siblings of Retarded Children: Nature and Modification*. Unpublished Ph.D. thesis, U. of North Carolina, Chapel Hill, 1974.

9

Conjoint-Behavior Therapy: The Modification of Family Constellations

WALLACE L. MEALIEA, JR.

During the past decade, an increasing number of studies have reported the use of parents as change agents to modify their children's behaviors (Johnson and Katz, 1973; Patterson and Reid, 1973; Wahler, 1969a). Although the data are not unequivocal, these studies indicate that cooperative and fairly articulate parents are able to understand the basic principles of behavioral analysis and apply these principles to modify their children's behavior. Typically, the programs have been concerned with the modification of a specific behavior, such as tantrums, talk-outs, aggression, and bed wetting. Although the data show that these behaviors can be changed, there has not been a great deal of support to indicate that these changes hold up over time or that they generalize.

Many researchers have recognized the need to develop treatment programs that not only modify specific behaviors, but also enable generalization to occur (Stuart, 1969; Patterson, 1971). As Patterson et al. (1967) state, "Effective social engineering would require not only that the effects generalize but that they persist. . . . The members of the child's social environment are the final arbiters in determining the practical outcomes of intervention programs. This being the case, it seems reasonable to consider the reinforcement schedules of the parents or the members of the peer group as representing the primary focus of an intervention program . . ." (p. 182).

This position is consistent with the results of Wahler's (1969b) study which suggest that changes in behavior do not necessarily generalize across situations unless environmental support is provided to maintain them. Indeed, the behavioral model strongly indicates that a thorough

152

understanding of the interface between individuals and their environments is one of the necessary factors if change is to take place (Kanfer and Saslow, 1969). However, too frequently behavior modifiers develop programs based on the belief that all that is required to change the behavior of individuals and their interaction with their environments is the acceleration or deceleration of single dimensions of performance (Willems, 1973; Burger, 1972). As Davison (1969) indicates, such a narrow perspective denies the topographical and functional complexity of behavior.

To avoid such a narrow perspective, a therapist, when viewing the parent as a potential change agent, must not lose sight of the complexity of the interactions that exist between parent and child. Although the behavior of some children can be changed without reference to underlying family pathology (Patterson, 1971), behavior modifiers should not ignore the possibility that some children do exhibit deviant behavior because of the pathogenic interactions that exist between their parents. The contribution of family therapists (Ackerman, 1958, 1966; Bell, 1961) who have alerted us to the child's sensitivity to disruption in the family unit should not be denied. In fact, the important issue is not whether this disruption is considered to be neurotic or psychotic in nature, or whether behavioral or exchange theory is used to describe the interactions between the parents. Recognition of the interactions between the parents and the quality of the relationship that exists in their marriage is the important fact. If the relationship between the parents is ignored and not considered as part of treatment, there is not only the possibility of a child's behavior not changing, but also the serious possibility of further deterioration in the family unit (Bergin, 1971). Willems (1973) gives an example of the impact of a narrow spectrum operant approach to modifying the interaction between a mother and child. The mother engaged in a high frequency of nagging behavior, which was modified after training in contingency management. The nagging decreased; however, the mother experienced an increase in tension and somatic complaints and ultimately abandoned the family unit. The insensitivity of the behavior modifier to the mother as a person who had her own personal concerns and needs is inexcusable; however, this type of insensitivity is too frequently exhibited by behavior modifiers (Burger, 1972).

The present paper focuses on an approach to family intervention in a situation in which a child's deviant behavior reflects pathogenic exchanges between husband and wife. This approach can be described as conjoint-behavior therapy because it is an attempt to amalgamate the major advantages of both orientations. The basic assumption of this approach is that changing the child's behavior is only the first step in producing changes in the family constellation which, hopefully, will then support future change in the child.

Marital therapy in which husband and wife are treated jointly is a relatively recent advance in psychotherapy and even more recent in the area of behavior therapy (Liberman, 1970; Ely et al., 1973; Gurman, in press). Although many marital therapists use a psychodynamic model as the basis of their treatment (Ackerman, 1958, 1966), an analysis of the various approaches indicates that the work by Haley (1963) and Satir (1964), which emphasizes interpersonal relations and the breakdown in communication as the major component in marital dysfunction, is very compatible with the behavioral model. To the communication theorists, such as Haley and Satir, the family is defined as a system with its own rules, roles, expectations, and other mechanisms (including specific reinforcement contingencies) which help to produce and to maintain the deviant behaviors of its members. Within families, patterns of behavior develop that are cyclical and repetitive, and that contribute to the disruption and distress experienced by some or all of the family members. The deviant behavior of the child or of any other family member is considered to be symptomatic of family disturbances; however, the deviant behavior is functional and tends to support and perpetuate the family structure.

The communication theorists describe human interaction in game-like terms. That is, there are rules, both covert and overt, that govern the interactions among the players. How the rules evolved is not of critical importance; the present interaction of the players and the influence the rules have on future behavior are the important factors. The system is considered pathological when the rules are set in such a way (typically covertly) that the family is locked into a self-defeating pattern that is not open to change. The goal of treatment is to bring about a change in the family system. The family therapist promotes change by not subscribing to the current rules and by pinpointing conflicts that are a result of the faulty communication networks that exist within the family unit. This is accomplished by making the members aware of the communication patterns and other patterns of interaction that exist within the family. The primary focus of treatment is changing those patterns which cause family disturbances—for example, inducing changes in the homeostatic system of the family, producing shifts in incapacitating power struggles among the family members, pointing out destructive coalitions, triangles, and scapegoating, and articulating the rules and how they are established (Ferreira, 1967; Haley, 1963; Jackson, 1968; Satir, 1964).

The behavioral approach to family therapy is also concerned with the interactions that exist among the family members. These interactions are based on the notion of reciprocity; that is, the response-reinforcement relationships among the family members are contingent upon each other (Azrin et al., 1973; Stuart, 1969). The optimal interaction would be one in which the members of a family frequently reinforce each other for behaviors that are supportive of a happy, healthy family constellation. However, the pattern of reciprocity that a given family develops may be pathogenic in that the exchanges among family members support deviant behavior. If a pathogenic exchange exists, the behavior modifier must pinpoint what behavior is maladaptive and what contingencies are continuing the behavior. At this point in the treatment process, the communication and behavioral approaches have a common focus; however, the mode of intervention, particularly the role played by the therapist, is significantly different for each approach.

The major limitation of the communication approach is the lack of a technology for facilitating change. The communication therapist is relatively nonactive; this therapist relies primarily upon fulfilling a role as a model for clear and accurate communication within the treatment session to provoke the impetus of change. On the other hand, the behavior therapist actively intervenes by requiring the patients to take responsibility for change not only within the treatment sessions, but more importantly in their everyday living. Not only must the individuals within a family become aware of the relationships and interactions that take place, but they must actively attempt to modify the reinforcement contingencies that perpetuate their present family constellation.

An Attempt at Integration

The choice of treatment depends on the goals of both the family and the behavior modifier. Some parents are quite ready to have the therapist take responsibility for treatment; they may even agree to take part in a training program to develop the skills necessary to modify their child's behavior. Not infrequently, however, parents will reject any attempts to involve them in the change process. Typical responses are, "We brought our daughter to the clinic because she was a problem in school.

. . . Our marriage relationship is fine. . . . Sorry, but our daughter is the one with the problem." In such situations, the behavior modifier has to decide whether to work only on the child's behavior, with the concomitant risk that, if change does take place, it may not continue over time, or to terminate the contact. If, however, the parents are open to intervention in their lives and the goals of therapy are the more general ones of growth to greater responsibility and choice, greater individualization, and remediation of unrealistic expectations on the part of all family members, as well as attacking the family patterns that are antagonistic to reciprocity within the family unit, then an attempt to integrate the behavioral with communicative approaches seems reasonable.

Conjoint-behavior therapy has the goal of providing parents with the skills and resources necessary to be able to:

a. Pinpoint which behaviors or lack of behaviors are maladaptive in their children;
b. Effectively observe and record these behaviors;
c. Become aware of the arrangements and contingencies in the home that support these behaviors;
d. Develop and evolve treatment strategies that will change these behaviors;
e. Become aware of their own personal interactions as husband and wife, father and mother that influence the climate of the home and have significant impact on the lives of their children;
f. Become aware of the many positive reinforcers that are present even though there may be difficulties in the marriage;
g. Develop new areas of reinforcement and reestablish former reinforcers to increase the chance of reciprocity in their relationship;
h. Become aware of the nonreciprocal aspects of their relationship, i.e., pinpoint the occurrence of noncontingent reinforcement, when one spouse reinforces the other without this reinforcement being reciprocated;
i. Establish an awareness of each other as persons, and acknowledge the mutuality of the relationship and the need to form a broad base of reinforcement that will allow for change and growth.

Method of Treatment

Conjoint-behavior therapy initially focuses on the child's behavior problem and the training of the parents to modify the specific behavior.

When this initial goal is accomplished, the focus shifts to the parents and their interactions with each other.

I. Phase One: Initial Interview. An extensive interview based on Kanfer and Saslow's model for behavioral analysis is conducted with the entire family. A home visit is made to get a total picture of the family. If the child is in school and the problem is also school related, there is a visit to the school to interview teachers and to observe the child in the classroom setting.

The parents are given a detailed explanation of the model that will be used in treatment and are given copies of *Living with Children* (Patterson and Gullion, 1968), which they are required to read before the next session. These sessions with the parents serve the following purposes: (a) they provide support for the parents in order to develop their confidence in themselves as potential change agents; (b) they provide them with information concerning behavioral techniques; and (c) they demonstrate procedures and techniques.

During this time, baseline data are collected on the child's behavior. This may entail observing in the home and/or having the parents come to the clinic to interact with their child. At the clinic this is videotaped and played back to the parents to make them aware of the type and variety of exchanges that take place among the members of the family. Video feedback is one of the more effective techniques used to modify behavior. Often it is impossible to convince an individual parent of the role he or she is playing in the family without the feedback provided by video (Bernal, 1969; Alger and Hogan, 1967; Berger, 1970).

Following the training of the parents in the basic language of behavior modification, the initial program for their problem is developed. At this time, decisions on treatment are made, such as type of program (such as home token system), type of records to keep, pinpointing of reinforcers, and establishment of consequences.

II. Phase Two: Implementation of program. The parents come to weekly sessions to report what is happening at home. Home visits are made to observe the parents interacting with the child. Audio- and video-tapes are made in the clinic and home of the parents' interactions. Changes are made in the program as required to meet the parents' level of responding.

III. Phase Three: Parent interactions. Once the program has been established and is working, the focus shifts to the parents and the kind of interactions that occur between them. At this point some parents become uncomfortable because the shift is away from the specific problems of the child to the exchanges that take place between themselves. The parents are seen without the child during this period. The structure of the marriage and the covert and overt rules that govern the interactions in the marriage are isolated and explored in depth. Following Stuart (1969) and Knox (1971), an attempt is made to view the marriage in a behavioral framework and establish specific goals and behaviors for which the couple can work.

The parents should have developed an understanding of a social-learning or reinforcement interpretation of behavior from their involvement with the modification of their child's behavior. Their task during Phase Three is to clearly define the reinforcement contingencies that exist within their marital relationship and isolate the sources of marital discord.

Evaluation

The evaluation is twofold. The first question asked is: Did the behavior of the child change, and is it continuing to change? This is decided by such means as records, teachers' reports, and evidence of new behaviors. The second question is: How are the parents getting along, what are their subjective feelings about their relationship and its impact on the child? Are the parents generating new programs or modifying the old program to fit the changes that have taken place in the child? This is decided from the partners' subjective evaluation of their marriage.

The above approach is time-consuming in terms of client and professional time. For those families that are basically healthy and in which the child's negative behavior is a reflection of inappropriate learning or lack of information on the part of the parents, it is more economical to treat the specific behavior. However, for the family that has evolved pathogenic patterns of interaction that elicit and foster deviant behavior in the child, the long-term development and change in the child may be dependent upon a change in orientation and style of interaction in the parents. For this to take place the parents must be recognized as individuals with concerns and problems that have to be resolved, new learning must take place, and a greater awareness of interactions and the implications these have for the family as a unit must emerge.

Cases

The following cases describe five families that were seen for treatment.

Case #1. Dan was a 12-year-old boy who was referred for treatment for encopresis. He was the oldest son in a family that consisted of his mother, father, a younger brother and sister, and a maternal grandmother. Dan had been seen by a clinical psychologist, a social worker, a psychiatrist, and his family physician for treatment. His encopretic behavior occurred in the home and at school (range from zero to three episodes a day). His parents were also concerned about his inability to be on time, i.e., late getting up, getting to breakfast, school, and other scheduled appointments, and his irresponsible behavior around home, i.e., not doing assigned chores such as making bed, keeping room tidy, helping around house.

An analysis indicated that Dan was highly reinforced at home and in school for his encopretic and tardy, irresponsible behavior. At school he was allowed to leave the classroom and return home whenever he had an "accident," which occurred very conveniently at the time of exams or when assignments were due. At home his mother engaged in a game of hiding his soiled pants whenever she found a set that Dan had previously hidden. Mother also kept a well-stocked drawer of clean underpants for Dan's use. If Dan was late for breakfast and school, his mother would drive him to school (although he lived within a few blocks of the building). If he did not carry out his household chores, his mother or grandmother did them for him. Except for the father, who dissociated himself from the situation with the statement, "Who wants a kid that shits his pants," everyone in the family was very solicitous and understanding of Dan's problems.

Dan and his parents agreed to establish a contingency management program. A token system was established, and Dan contracted to earn certain rewards, such as time with his Dad, and to avoid certain negative outcomes, such as losing his privileges of watching TV, having snacks, reading comics, and going to movies. Within five weeks of the ten-day baseline period, Dan's encopretic behavior and tardiness were brought under control both at home and in school. The most effective reinforcer was time with his father, and this increase in interaction between Dan and his father was a significant step towards later changes in the father's role in the family.

The success of the program in changing Dan's behavior helped convince the parents that a similar analysis and program would help their own marital relationship. Dan's mother was very upset by the feedback she received via video of the overwhelming possessive role she played in the family. She became aware of the reinforcement she had been giving Dan for his maladaptive behavior and realized it was serving a need, i.e., having someone depend on her, that compensated for limitations in the relationship with her husband. Mother and father had grown distant from each other; father did not like a son who "shit his pants" and consequently buried himself in the family business. The parents contracted for behavior each wanted the other to exhibit; they rearranged their living schedule to have more private time together. They also clarified and resolved the roles to be played by all family members, particularly that of the grandmother, who tended to ally herself with her daughter and against her son-in-law. After five months of treatment the family had resolved most of the conflicts that had caused friction in the family unit. An eight-month follow-up indicated that Dan's problem behavior had not recurred, and the members of the family felt very good about the family situation.

Case #2. George was a 14-year-old boy who was referred for encopresis. A detailed work-up by the Pediatric and Psychiatric Departments of the State University indicated that his difficulty was psychogenic in nature. George was the oldest son in a family that consisted of his divorced mother, a younger sister, and his mother's common-law husband. Although George's mother expressed concern about his behavior, it became clear that she was reinforcing this behavior by her inconsistent attitude toward it, i.e., vacillating from punishing, to ignoring, to pleading for him to stop the behavior. Her common-law husband removed himself from the problem with the statement, "He ain't my kid." George's mother had no difficulty in adopting a contingency-management program to modify his behavior. Limits were placed on George's behavior with negative and positive consequences contingent on whether or not he soiled his pants. George earned the right to play basketball, watch TV, buy records, have access to his comic book collection, and go to shows with his friends by going to the toilet in time. Since he indicated a desire to spend time with his "stepfather," this also was made a positive consequence.

In the marital phase of treatment, a good deal of time was spent on redefining the "stepfather's" place in the family and increasing his level of involvement. Initially mother was hesitant to make demands on him because of the common-law nature of the marriage. The "stepfather" was interested in the family, but in the past his wife had placed few demands on him, asking only that he provide material support and security for the family. The mother became aware of her limited expectations and communicated openly to her husband her fear that, if she asked him to get involved, he would desert her as her first husband had. The lack of communication had resulted in a somewhat neutral and unsatisfying family situation. The family was seen for eight months, during which time a restructuring of roles and the establishment of new ways of interacting were accomplished. A 12-month follow-up indicated no recurrence of George's encopretic behavior, and both Mother and Father expressed satisfaction with their new mode of relating.

Case #3. Billy was a seven-year-old boy who was referred because he had frequent crying spells at home and in school. In fact, they ranged from zero to ten or more episodes a day. Billy was the oldest son in a family that consisted of his mother, father, and four younger sibs. Billy was above average in intelligence and doing well in school, except for his crying. Any attention by his mother or his teacher to his behavior that was even remotely critical brought on crying. He also cried himself to sleep at night. In Billy's case a formal behavioral program was not established because of his vulnerability and excessive concern with censure. He had overwhelming feelings of being bad and evil, and was certain that God observed and kept account of all his "bad behavior," such as asserting himself, sucking his thumb, and arguing with his siblings.

Billy's mother was a bright, articulate, college-educated woman who was left alone for long periods of time with her five children because her husband's job required much out-of-town travel. Treatment initially focused on Mother's response to Billy, particularly the long sessions she would have with him each time he cried, trying to probe and find out what was making him so unhappy. She realized that her attention to her son's unhappiness completely outweighed all other responses she made to him, especially since she had four younger children. She also became aware of subtle pressure she was putting on him to be "good," which was completely misinterpreted by Billy. He viewed much of his own behavior as evil and was deeply frightened of the chance of losing his mother's love. In fact, the exchange that developed between Billy and his mother is a classic example of the repetitive pattern of one behavior being highly reinforcing of a second behavior which is interpreted by both parties as inappropriate. Billy's mother began, very carefully at first in order to minimize the chance of being interpreted as rejecting him, to shift her attention from crying behavior to Billy's more appropriate behaviors.

The marital phase of treatment consisted of a great deal of individual counseling with Billy's mother (because of the father's work schedule, he was not available often) and intermittent joint sessions with both parents. The mother became aware of her deep dissatisfaction with having to be both father and mother to her children and her resentment toward her husband for placing her in this position. The major decision made by the father was to take a new job that would allow him to be at home and play a more appropriate and reinforcing role as husband and father. Treatment took place over a period of seven months, and a two-year follow-up indicated that Billy was no longer crying and was exhibiting normal behavior for a nine-year-old boy. Both mother and father indicated satisfaction with the structure of their married life.

Case #4. Sammy was a 17-year-old retarded male who was initially referred for enuretic behavior. An analysis of the situation indicated that the parents were interested not only in the enuresis, but also in his lack of social and self-help skills. Sammy was a tragic example of an individual who was labeled "retarded" (psychological testing showed that he could read, write, and had a WAIS Full Scale IQ of 75) and consequently learned how to behave in such a manner. His parents were oversolicitous and placed no limits on his behavior. He was given free access to the family's store and its supply of such things as pop, candy, comics, and TV. The parents engaged in inconsistent behaviors; for example, for a period of time they set alarm clocks to go off every hour during the night and got Sammy up to go to the toilet. (He still wet the bed every night, however.)

After a baseline period of one week, a token system was established that allowed Sammy to earn points to acquire the good things in life, such as pop, candy, TV, comics, and time for fishing with Dad. The points were earned by staying dry at night, washing himself, brushing his teeth, dressing himself within a time limit, and helping clean up his room. The enuretic behavior was brought under control within a two-week period, and the self-help behavior also increased within the first month of the program.

Although the program was successful in producing significant changes in Sammy's behavior, his parents failed to uphold the contracts and began to reinforce him noncontingently. This resulted in rapid extinction of Sammy's gains, and he returned to his baseline level of maladaptive behavior. His parents would reestablish the program but in a short time became inconsistent in following it. During the third month of treatment, Sammy's mother was hospitalized for a week; during this period, his father completely ignored the program and allowed Sammy to behave in any way he wanted. The father's rationalization was that it was too upsetting for Sammy to have his mother in the hospital.

Following the mother's return to the home, an attempt was made to reestablish the program; however, the father was concerned with his wife's health and would not be bothered keeping track of Sammy's behavior. Neither parent expressed a willingness to continue the treatment or to involve themselves in exploring their own relationship. The father was convinced that his wife was going to die. If she did, Sammy would probably have to be institutionalized. After four months, treatment was terminated, and a one-year follow-up indicated that Sammy's behavior was still maladaptive (his mother was still living). The temporary success of the program had no impact on Sammy's parents' view of him. As his father fatalistically stated at the follow-up interview, "After all, Sammy was retarded."

Case #5. Tony was a 15-year-old boy who was referred for frequent temper outbursts at home and in school. Tony was the younger child in a family that consisted of his mother, father, and his 16-year-old sister Terrie. Tony's outbursts had resulted in his being suspended from school; they had become so intense that he had threatened to kill his sister with a kitchen knife. His parents were also concerned with his uncooperative behavior around the home, e.g., his refusal to clean his room, help with household chores, listen to his parents' requests to come home on time, or do homework.

An analysis of the family indicated that there was little mutual reinforcement exhibited between any of the family members. Mother worked days, while father worked two jobs during the day and night and on weekends. The children were pampered, spoiled adolescents who received any material object demanded without having to reciprocate. Tony and Terrie each had a horse, a dog, and a snowmobile. They made insatiable demands on their parents' rather limited financial resources. If a demand was denied, both Tony and Terrie would have temper outbursts. Although they only cursed at their mother or father, Tony and Terrie did get into physical fights with each other. Since Terrie was larger than her brother, he had begun to protect himself by threatening to stab her if she continued to hit him.

The parents were overworked, tired, basically inept individuals who felt completely helpless in their dealings with their children. The father's traditional pattern of behavior was to lose his temper (which had been the model for Tony) and hit the family member who had angered him.

He was approaching sixty, however, and no longer had the ability to physically handle his children, both of whom were bigger and stronger than he. Initially, all members of the family agreed to try a contracting system that would attempt to specify the expected behaviors for each family member. Surprisingly Tony and Terrie quickly worked out mutual contracts that stated each other's boundaries and areas of cooperation, such as caring for the horses and dogs. They also established goals for working around the house and assisting their mother with many of her household chores.

After a baseline of two weeks, the contracts went into effect. For a period of three weeks there was a marked improvement in both Tony's and Terrie's behavior. A crisis occurred, however, when father unilaterally changed the terms of the contract with his children. He demanded that they stay home from an earned activity and help him. When the children refused, he deprived them of their snowmobiles. The result was a return to temper outbursts and general uncooperative behavior. This pattern continued intermittently for a period of three months. The family would reestablish the contracts, all would go well for a period of time, then father would unilaterally change the contingencies.

An attempt was made to work with the father and mother and get them to cooperate with the program. The parents had a very unhappy, nonreinforcing relationship. The mother felt overwhelmed by the disruption and unhappiness in the family. She spent most of her time working in a restaurant and then coming home to cook and clean and get caught up in the fights between the children and her husband. The father was continually tired from long hours of work; he felt victimized by his family and the demands made on him. The paradox of his behavior was the lack of control he had over the situation and the futility of his attempts to reestablish control through temper outbursts. Treatment dragged on intermittently for a period of seven months. The parents expressed many of their concerns but were unable to effectively come to grips with problems in their marriage. The question of control was the central issue that could not be resolved. Although the children did respond and live up to their contracts, the father would not tolerate this system. He interpreted the contracts as usurping his role as the father in the family. The father constantly stated that he should have respect from his family; his own father demanded respect and was quick to use the whip if it wasn't given. Tony's father could not acknowledge the incongruity between his demands and what actually happened in the family. Tony and Terrie had become somewhat aware of the maladaptive aspects of their own behavior and began to think in terms of leaving the family. In the school setting, Tony's temper outbursts became less frequent and did not cause any more difficulty. In the family situation, however, the exchanges among the members, although less violent and physical, were still basically negative. Father and mother remained intensely unhappy with their plight, and the children talked openly about leaving the family when they came of age.

In all five cases, the parents did initiate behavioral programs that modified their children's deviant behavior; however, in two of the cases the changes extinguished, basically because the parents did not continue the program. These results suggest that, as with any treatment program, the final disposition depends upon the expectations of the participants and their willingness to engage in the change process (Lazarus, 1971).

Although the outcome of the presented cases suggests that conjoint-behavior therapy is a fruitful approach to be considered by the family therapist, the data do not clearly indicate whether or not the change in the children's behavior was necessarily dependent upon a change in the marital relationship of the parents. In order to empirically investigate this relationship, a study should be conducted that would place families with problem children into three groups: child-focused, parent-focused, and family-focused. The child-focused group would have parents trained in behavioral management techniques and would attempt to have the parents modify the child's behavior independent of any direct change in their own relationship. The parent-focused group would train the parents to modify their own behavior, similar to the Azrin et al. (1973) program, without any direct reference to the child's behavior. The family-focused group would attempt to use the conjoint-behavior therapy approach to make the parents aware of the interactions in the family unit. The comparative efficacy of these three groups in having an impact on the child's behavior should provide an answer to whether or not a change in parents' interactions with each other facilitates and prolongs changes in their children's behavior.

REFERENCES

ACKERMAN, N. W.: *The Psychodynamics of Family Life*. New York: Basic Books, 1958.

ACKERMAN, N. W.: *Treating the Troubled Family*. New York: Basic Books, 1966.

AZRIN, N. H., NASTER, B. J., and JONES, R.: Reciprocity counseling: A rapid learning-based procedure for marital counseling. *Behav. Res. and Ther.*, 11, 365-382, 1973.

ALGER, I., and HOGAN, P.: The use of videotape recordings in conjoint marital therapy. *Amer. J. Psychiat.*, 123, 1425-1430, 1967.

166 *Behavior Modification Approaches to Parenting*

BELL, J. E.: *Family Group Therapy*. (Public Health Monograph No. 64, U.S. Department of Health, Education and Welfare). Washington, D. C.: U.S. Government Printing Office, 1961.

BERGER, M. M. (Ed.): *Videotape Techniques in Psychiatric Training and Treatment*. New York: Brunner/Mazel, 1970.

BERGIN, A. E.: The evaluation of therapeutic outcomes. In: A. E. Bergin and S. L. Garfield (Eds.), *Handbook of Psychotherapy and Behavior Change: An Empirical Analysis*. New York: John Wiley, 1971. Pp. 217-270.

BERNAL, M. E.: Behavior feedback in the modification of brat behaviors. *J. Nerv. and Ment. Disorders*, 148, 375-385, 1969.

BURGER, H.: Behavior modification and operant psychology: An anthropological critique. *Amer. Educ. Res. J.*, 9, 343-360, 1972.

DAVISON, G. C.: Appraisal of behavior modification techniques with adults in institutional settings. In: C. M. Franks (Ed.), *Behavior Therapy: Appraisal and Status*. New York: McGraw-Hill, 1969. Pp. 220-278.

ELY, A. L., GUERNEY, B. G., and STOVER, L.: Efficacy of the training phase of conjugal therapy. *Psychotherapy: Theory, Research and Practice*, 10, 201-207, 1973.

FERREIRA, A. J.: Psychosis and the family myth. *Amer. J. Psychotherapy*, 21, 186-197, 1967.

GURMAN, A. S.: The effects and effectiveness of marital therapy: A review of outcome research. *Family Process*, in press.

HALEY, J.: Marriage therapy. *Arch. Gen. Psychiat.*, 8, 25-46, 1963.

JACKSON, D. D. (Ed.): *Communication, Family and Marriage*. Palo Alto: Science and Behavior Books, 1968.

JOHNSON, C. A., and KATZ, F. C.: Using parents as change agents for their children: A review. *J. Child Psychol. and Psychiat.*, 14, 181-200, 1973.

KANFER, F. H., and SASLOW, G.: Behavioral diagnosis. In: C. M. Franks (Ed.), *Behavior Therapy: Appraisal and Status*. New York: McGraw-Hill, 1969. Pp. 417-444.

KNOX, D.: *Marriage Happiness*. Champaign, Ill.: Research Press, 1971.

LAZARUS, A. A.: *Behavior Therapy and Beyond*. New York: McGraw-Hill, 1971.

LIBERMAN, R.: Behavioral approaches to family and couple therapy. *Amer. J. Orthopsychiat.*, 40, 106-118, 1970.

PATTERSON, G. R.: *Families: Applications of Social Learning to Family Life*. Champaign, Ill.: Research Press, 1971.

PATTERSON, G. R., McNEAL, S., HAWKINS, N., and PHELPS, R.: Reprogramming the social environment. *J. Child Psychol. and Psychiat.*, 8, 181-195, 1967.

PATTERSON, G. R., and GULLION, M. E.: *Living with Children*. Champaign, Ill.: Research Press, 1968.

PATTERSON, G. R., and REID, J. B.: Intervention for families of aggressive boys: A replication study. *Behav. Res. and Ther.*, 11, 383-394, 1973 .

SATIR, V.: *Conjoint Family Therapy*. Palo Alto: Science and Behavior Books, 1964.

STUART, R. B.: Operant-interpersonal treatment for marital discord. *J. Consult. and Clin. Psychol.*, 33, 675-682, 1969.

WAHLER, R.: Oppositional children: A quest for parental reinforcement control. *J. Appl. Behav. Anal.*, 2, 159-170, 1969. (a)

WAHLER, R.: Setting generality: Some specific and general effects of child behavior therapy. *J. Appl. Behav. Anal.*, 2, 239-246, 1969. (b)

WILLEMS, E. P.: Go ye into all the world and modify behavior: An ecologist's view. *Representative Res. in Soc. Psychol.*, 4, 93-105, 1973.

10

Group Assertion Training for Mothers: A Family Intervention Strategy

MARTIN E. SHOEMAKER

and

TERRY L. PAULSON

Assertion training, singly and in combination with other behavioral therapies, has become the treatment of choice in dealing with a wide variety of clinical problems. Morrow (1971), in a bibliographic survey of behavior therapy literature between 1950 and 1969, includes over 50 examples of its clinical application since the pioneer works of Salter (1949) and Wolpe (1954, 1958).

Since the inception of assertion training as an application of Pavlov's learning theory to neurotic disorders, its rationale and techniques have greatly broadened. One technique has been a group procedure in which the therapist (assertion trainer) gathers a homogeneous sample of clients with similar target problems and instructs them on how to change their nonassertive and timid behaviors. The efficacy of this treatment has been verified by empirical research with socially anxious college students (Hedquist and Weinhold, 1970; Rathus, 1972), neuropsychiatric inpatients (Booraem and Flowers, 1972; Eisler et al., 1973), and in clinical reports by Fensterheim (1972) and Lazarus (1968).

Reviews on the allocation of child-rearing functions in the American family are almost unanimous in favor of maternal preeminence in disci-

The authors are grateful for the assistance of Sally Friedlob, who served as audio-tape rater, and to Dr. Paul W. Clement for his timely supervision and critical reading of the manuscript.

pline and nurturance activities (Clausen, 1966). However, the fact that mothers often display frustration and various discipline and marital difficulties indicates a definite need for improved parent and family management skills. Behavioral analysis of mothers who seek clinical help for the above discloses frequent response excesses, such as anxiety, withdrawing from conversations, angry outbursts, accusatory statements, self-neglect, and response deficits—"I" statements, initiating conversations, positive statements of praise, opinions, or requests.

In an attempt to deal clinically with these behaviors, the present investigators developed a group procedure which uses the basic assumptions and strategies of assertion training. The focus was on the content and consequences of unassertive maternal behavior and on the effects of positive changes and increased self-expression on family interaction patterns. The study attempted to assess the frequency change in specific target verbalizations of both mother and father, and the general behavior control of the problem child for whom help was originally sought.

METHOD

Subjects

Sixteen mothers were selected out of a child guidance parent population after initial experiences with operant parental management techniques demonstrated a basic unassertive communication style. The children's presenting problems ranged from general noncompliance with parental requests at home to severe "acting out" behavior. Eight mothers signed contracts to participate in one of the two groups. They were told that the groups were designed to teach them "how to be a more effective mother and wife." The Ss were white middle-class mothers with a mean age of 36.8 years and a mean education of 12.8 years.

Design

The Ss were randomly assigned to one of two groups—a no-wait group (Group 1), or a wait group (Group 2). Separate groups were created by manipulating the waiting period before treatment of the second group, an adaptation of the postponed-therapy control design (Campbell and Stanley, 1966; Rogers and Dymond, 1954). Each group met ten times—twice a week for five weeks—1½ hours per session. Group 1 also participated in a five-week follow-up procedure while Group 2 was being treated.

Procedure

In-group variables were divided into (a) didactic material, (b) behavioral focusing, and (c) modification strategies. The first included a general introduction of the group to the goals and strategies of assertion training as a specific treatment approach for increasing communication skills. The primary purpose of this introduction was to structure expectancies toward change in specific verbal target behaviors, in contrast with more traditional forms of group therapy and analysis. *S*s were informed of the disadvantages of their present unassertive response patterns. For example, one of the *S*s was overly apologetic to her husband whenever she wanted him to do something. This stance had made it extremely difficult for this woman to secure assistance openly from him, particularly in the area of the children's discipline. The results of this pattern were definitely reflected in the noncompliance of the target child and in marital tension.

After appropriate cognitive and perceptual sets were initiated, behavioral focusing was explained in terms of Alberti and Emmons's (1970) tripartite comparison of assertive, aggressive, and withdrawing (nonassertive) verbal response styles. The content and consequences of these styles were discussed and criteria for each response category established.* (See Table 1.)

The primary modification strategy was the shaping of appropriate assertive responses through the use of discriminative tokens (white poker chips) given by the trainer and group members to other group members as immediate positive feedback (Hastorf, 1965; Krasner, 1962; MacPherson, 1972). Red and blue tokens were used as negative feedback for aggressive and withdrawing responses respectively. *S*s reported each week on specific verbal interactions at home and, as the responses were reported, tokens were given according to the tripartite criteria. The content of the verbalization was the major focus. The following is a taped excerpt illustrating the token use early in the discrimination training.

> FIRST MOTHER: Yesterday I told my boy that I was very disappointed in his English grade and felt like getting him a tutor if he didn't improve. (She receives several white tokens.) I also told him that I was glad his other classes were okay. (She again receives white tokens.)

---

* Many sources beyond Alberti and Emmons (1970) were used in developing these criteria. A few of the most helpful would include Fensterheim (1972), Rathus (1972), Salter (1949), and Wolpe (1969).

TABLE 1

Response Criteria for Discrimination of Response Styles

A. *Assertive Response Coding:* The action of declaring oneself, speaking up for one's rights or needs, trusting oneself; of stating, this is who I am, what I think and feel; (it) characterizes an active rather than a passive approach to life, an open, direct, honest, and appropriate expression of what a person feels and thinks. The assertive statement is usually expressed in the form of an explicit first person pronoun statement, e.g., "I think that we should start now," "I feel upset when. . . ." It can imply an assertion without the pronoun "I" or "we" being used, e.g., "Can you help me with this problem?" "Thank you for your help," or "That seems very unfair to me." The content of such assertions would express one of the following three areas:

1. *Feeling Talk* (*expression of emotional quality*), e.g., "I get uptight when you . . ." "That's fantastic; I feel happy you . . ."

2. *Thinking Talk:*
   a. The expression of likes or dislikes (opinions);
   b. A statement of active disagreement or agreement;
   c. The giving or receiving of a compliment;
   d. Initiation of problem-solving talk (owning a problem);
   e. Stating a suggestion or solution.

3. *Asking Talk:*
   a. Asking for clarification or help;
   b. Expression of non-negotiable requests.

B. *Nonassertive Response Coding* (may be of two types):

1. *Aggressive Responses:* Those which carry the desire for self-assertion to extremes. They tend to be overexpressed and self-enhancing at the expense of another. Aggressive statements commonly result in a "put-down" feeling on the part of the recipient and generate a mood of hostility, defensiveness, and humiliation; they may provoke a fight or other negative reactions. They are usually expressed in the second or third person, e.g., "You are a bigot!" "You make me sick!" "That's about enough out of you!" They usually require an exclamation point. The following are categories of aggressive verbal statements:

   a. Threatening or provoking;
   b. Sarcasm, malicious joking;
   c. Insult;
   d. Blaming;
   e. Name-calling;
   f. Interruption of another speaker (unless a right, e.g., if he or she had been interrupted or the other speaker was attempting to change topics);
   g. Other.

TABLE 1 *(continued)*

2. *Withdrawing Responses:* These are characterized by an inhibited or avoidance communication and deny the feelings or opinions of the subject. These types of verbalizations weaken or squash the true feelings of the individual in an attempt to reduce anxiety or avoid negative situations. Examples of this passive type of response would be: "Oh, that's all right, I didn't want it anyway"; "Oh, it's nothing"; "Well, my suggestions aren't any good, you do it by yourself." They usually occur in one of the following categories:

    a. Inappropriate or over-apologetic stance;
    b. Extreme or continuous self-criticism;
    c. "Keeping the peace" or "Don't rock the boat" stance;
    d. Inappropriately changing the subject;
    e. Interjecting laughter or joking to release tension (if avoiding question);
    f. Refusal to speak when spoken to (after a question);
    g. Curt answers to avoid the issue, e.g., "I don't know." ("I do not feel like talking" is appropriate and is rated as an assertion.)

TRAINER: I like the way you told him how you felt even if part of what you felt was negative.

FIRST MOTHER: It was really hard to keep from exploding at him, but I hardly ever do. I usually don't say anything when I'm mad. (She receives a blue token from the trainer.)

SECOND MOTHER: Why did you give her a blue token? I don't understand why she shouldn't avoid a fight. (She receives a white token from the trainer.)

TRAINER: Thanks for asking for clarification. I gave her a blue token for withdrawing and not correctly expressing her anger. She will probably take it out on him sooner or later and, if she persists in hushing up these negative feelings, her boy will never learn to use negative feedback.

FIRST MOTHER: If I had told him what I really wanted to, everybody would have given me red chips for being aggressive (group laughs).

TRAINER: Not necessarily. Red tokens are not for feeling angry, but for attacking someone rather than asserting how you feel in first-person "I" statements.

A co-trainer recorded all token interactions and, at two intervals (fifth and tenth sessions), general token "receiving" and "giving" patterns were discussed. Trainer token giving was purposely faded as the group proceeded and familiarity with response criteria improved. For example, after the token interaction tables were summarized for the fifth session, it was discovered that one *S* was clearly not giving any negative feedback (red or blue chips). This was discussed in the group, and the *S* was able to relate how hard it has always been for her to stand up to anyone publicly or say anything critical. After this discussion, a more specific behavioral focus in terms of appropriate negative feedback was assigned to her, and the final-session token report revealed increased frequency of giving both red and blue tokens.

Modification procedures also included two other learning approaches —modeling and rehearsal. The individual components and the effects of these procedures, isolated and in combination, have begun to be studied in detail (see Eisler et al., 1973; Friedman, 1971; McFall and Lillesand, 1971; McFall and Marston, 1970). The present investigation used the term "modeling" to describe a process of role playing performed for a specific verbal response to be observed by a specific group member. Rehearsal was the practicing of a specific verbal response or sequence of verbal responses by a group member. Modeling was used to illustrate a particular response and was followed by overt rehearsal and coaching until the *S* reported a comfortable state (Subjective Units of Disturbance Scale< 25) (Wolpe, 1969) and good response acquisition. Token feedback was given throughout all these procedures. Other *S*s not directly involved were encouraged to covertly rehearse the appropriate responses.

Extra-group variables included selected readings in *Your Perfect Right* (Alberti and Emmons, 1970) and behavior assignments to be completed at home. The assignments were used to facilitate both in-group material and generalization in the natural environment of desired target behaviors. For example, one *S* was married to a chronic alcoholic husband, and she had difficulty not engaging him in a fight when he came home late after drinking. One of her assignments was to "ask for distance" from her husband when he had been drinking as a means of not arguing and stopping an aggressive interaction. Her assignment was to say instead, "I'll discuss it with you in the morning." Concurrently this same *S* was encouraged to compliment her husband when he did things she liked or when they did recreational events together as a family. Other *S* assignments might include asking for time alone or away from family, making clearer and more consistent requests of children, and saying "no" to inappropriate family demands.

After the fifth session, scheduled inter-subject telephoning was assigned for completion between group meetings Each *S* received one support-feedback phone call per week. The telephoning was implemented to continue support and feedback between group meetings and provide social reinforcement beyond the context of the group environment.

Follow-up (Group 1 only) consisted of a continuation of the support-feedback phone conversation for a five-week period. Ss were instructed to give positive social reinforcement for reports of assertive behavior and assistance in correcting unassertive responses. A post-follow-up survey revealed that Ss had completed their respective calling assignments.

TECHNIQUES OF MEASUREMENT

The families (Mother-Father-Child) of both groups were evaluated three times at five-week intervals. Group 1 (no-wait) received pretherapy (pre), posttherapy (post), and follow-up (FU) evaluations. Group 2 (five-week wait) received a pretherapy (pre$_1$) evaluation at the same time as Group 1. After five weeks, Group 2 received another pretherapy (pre$_2$) evaluation followed by five weeks of intervention and posttherapy (post) evaluation.

The primary measure was an adapted version of the Inventory of Marital Conflicts (IMC) developed by Olson and Ryder (1970). The IMC uses a forced conflict interaction technique developed to provide behavioral data on decision-making processes and conflict resolution in couples. It consists of 18 vignettes of typical marital conflicts which each couple tries to resolve.

In the present study, four vignettes were randomly selected for each evaluation period. After a preliminary reading of conflict items purposely slanted to produce husband-wife discrepancies, each couple was placed together in a room for a 20-minute discussion session. These sessions were audio-recorded, and the tapes were independently scored by a blind rater using the same tripartite response criteria used in the group discrimination learning. The regular IMC scoring system was not used. Individual frequencies were collected for assertive, aggressive, and withdrawing verbalizations by both spouses. Data reliability checks taken between rater and trainers before each scoring session produced satisfactory correlation coefficients of $r = .83, .81,$ and $.88$.

Mothers completed a 30-item self-report measure, the Rathus Assertiveness Schedule (RAS) (Rathus, 1972). Both parents also rated the behavior of the original target child using the Devereux Child Behavior Rating Scale (DCBRS) (Spivack and Spotts, 1966). The DCBRS focuses only on current behavior (last two weeks). Face validity was used to establish a cluster of scales measuring general behavioral control, e.g., distractibility, impulse ideation, social aggression, and unethical behavior. Raw scores of 6 out of 17 scales (1, 11, 14-17) were converted into standard scores with a mean of 50 and a standard deviation of 10.

One-way repeated-measures analyses of variance (Winer, 1962) were separately computed on husband and wife for each of the three behavioral categories. When an F ratio reached a significance level of .05, Duncan's Multiple Range Test (Edwards, 1968) was performed on all pairs of means within groups for each repeated measure. For Group 1, mean comparisons were performed between the following pairs: pre-post, post-FU, and pre-FU. For Group 2, mean comparisons were performed between the following pairs: pre_1 -pre_2 (Control period), pre_1 -post, and pre_2 -post.

RESULTS

Conflict Resolution (IMC)

The results of the mother-father interaction on the IMC procedure are summarized for Groups 1 and 2 in Table 2. In Group 1, wives significantly increased their assertive statements ($p < .05$) following treatment and again between the post and follow-up evaluations. They also decreased aggressive statements significantly between pretherapy and follow-up evaluations. Although not participants in the training, husbands also exhibited significant changes in assertive statements between pretherapy and follow-up evaluations. Neither wives nor husbands had significant changes in withdrawing statements.

Table 2 also shows that, during the control period for Group 2, (pre_1 -pre_2), comparison scores on all IMC measures were not significant. In the same group following treatment, however, husbands and wives significantly increased assertive statements ($p < .05$) between pre_2 and post-therapy evaluation; likewise, they significantly decreased aggressive statements during the same period. Again on all comparison scores of withdrawing statements, no significant differences were found between observation periods.

Rathus Assertiveness Schedule (RAS)

Table 3 shows that F ratios on the RAS did not reach the confidence level of .05; therefore, the wives did not demonstrate significant change in their self-report of assertiveness. However, all Ss moved in the projected direction.

TABLE 2

Summary of the One-Way Repeated-Measures Analyses of Variance for
Wives and Husbands of Groups 1 and 2 on the IMC.

Dependent Variable	F*	P	Duncan's Range**			Criterion
GROUP 1—IMC						
Wives						
			FU	Post	Pre	
Assertive	14.504	.002	88.5	59.7	39.9)	increase
Aggressive	6.696	.016	1.4	(12.5	13.5)	decrease
Withdrawing	3.069	.096				decrease
Husbands						
Assertive	7.914	.010	82.2	(57.0	42.8)	increase
Aggressive	1.602	.254				decrease
Withdrawing	1.341	.363				decrease
GROUP 2—IMC						
Wives						
			Post	Pre_1	Pre_2	
Assertive	29.957	.001	87.1	(32.3	29.9)	increase
			Post	Pre_2	Pre_1	
Aggressive	8.730	.008	0.01	(19.0	22.4)	decrease
Withdrawing	1.584	.446				decrease
Husbands						
			Post	Pre_2	Pre_1	
Assertive	9.783	.006	77.0	(38.0	33.6)	increase
			Post	Pre_1	Pre_2	
Aggressive	5.161	.038	0.01	(23.1	24.0)	decrease
Withdrawing	1.432	.468				decrease

* All *F*s have 2 and 9 degrees of freedom.
** For group 1, "Pre," "Post," and "FU" indicate pretherapy, posttherapy, and follow-up, respectively. For group 2, "Pre_1," "Pre_2," and' 'Post" indicate $pretherapy_1$, $pretherapy_2$ and posttherapy, respectively. The entries below these labels are the group mean scores. Any two means not joined within parentheses are reliably different at the .05 level or better. Any two means joined within parentheses are not reliably different.

Child Behavior Rating Scales (DCBRS)

On the final measure, a subjective rating of the original problem child's behavior (DCBRS), parents in both groups perceived positive behavior control changes; however, only mothers' ratings were significant ($p < .05$). Differences in parental ratings following the control period of Group 2 were not significant (Table 3).

In-group Data

Although formal statistical analyses were not performed on in-group behavioral data, frequency counts demonstrated that all *S*s increased in

TABLE 3

Summary of One-Way Repeated-Measures Analyses of Variance for
Wives and Husbands of Group 1 and 2 on the DCBRS and
Wives only on the RAS.

Dependent Variable	F*	P	Duncan's Range**			Criterion
RAS— (wives only)						
Group 1	.7011	.521				increase
Group 2	.4223	.668				increase
GROUP 1—DCBRS						
			FU	Post	Pre	
Wives	7.849	.011	(44.92	46.12)	52.7	decrease
Husbands	3.188	.090				decrease
GROUP 2—DCBRS						
			Post	Pre$_1$	Pre$_2$	
Wives	5.779	.024	49.33	(54.16	54.49)	decrease
Husbands	1.621	.250				decrease

* All *F*s have 2 and 9 degrees of freedom.
** For group 1, "Pre," "Post," and "FU" indicate pretherapy, posttherapy, and follow-up, respectively. For group 2, "Pre$_1$," "Pre$_2$," and "Post" indicate pretherapy$_1$, pretherapy$_2$, and posttherapy, respectively. The entries below these labels are the group mean scores. Any two means not joined within parentheses are reliably different at the .05 level or better. Any two means joined within parentheses are not reliably different.

the accumulation of white tokens for assertive behavior and decreased in
the negative token feedback as the sessions progressed. Also, the number
of tokens given per session by each member increased.

DISCUSSION

The effectiveness of assertion training has been largely verified through
case reports and group experimental studies with normal populations,
e.g., college students. In the present study, the *S*s were drawn from a
population of parents who reported child-rearing difficulties and general
family problems. The results support the following conclusions:

(1) Mothers who seek help for family communication problems can be
trained fairly rapidly in a group to be more assertive and less aggressive
in problem-solving situations with their husbands.

(2) A change in attitude about one's own assertiveness, at least those
cognitive behaviors assessed by self-report measures, does not necessarily
coincide with observable changes in target response frequencies. In the
present study, mothers who became more assertive with their husbands

did not report significant changes in general assertiveness, which was measured by the RAS.

(3) Husbands not involved in the group training respond in similar situations with the same significant verbal changes as their wives. Assertive verbalization seems to stimulate more of the same. Parenting techniques adapted from client-centered models of psychotherapy (Gordon, 1970) have suggested similar results between family members using nondefensive verbalization skills.

(4) Follow-up strategies among group members, particularly assignments in the natural environment, have the definite value of increasing and strengthening the appropriate responses practiced originally in the group. Most of the *S*s reported significant changes at home as a result of their assertive behavior, and these positive consequences, e.g., getting more help from husband, actually increased the target behaviors. As mentioned earlier, however, stimulus generalization outside of the home was not objectively demonstrated.

(5) Assertion training is a valuable tool for the behavior therapist working with parents as the major modifiers of their children's problem behaviors. Mothers who gain skills in self-expression and verbal discipline rate their children as significantly improved without the child having direct therapeutic contact with the professional therapist.

This study has attempted to explore the effects of assertion training beyond the trained *S*s behavior—in this case, on other family members' behavior. However, future research is needed to verify these procedures in other population groups, e.g., minority group families, and with *S*s not previously involved in any form of therapy. Also, this investigation cannot say whether the improved ratings given to the children by the *S*s were a function of attitude change on behalf of the *S*s, e.g., sense of improved abilities, or actual change in the behavior frequency. Independent behavioral ratings of mother-child interaction and the general behavioral control of the child are recommended.

A recent survey of family therapists' practices by the Group for the Advancement of Psychiatry (1970) revealed that, in 85% of all families seen for treatment, these practitioners perceive the primary goal of treatment to be improved communication. Assertion training for mothers offers a parsimonious and viable treatment strategy with specifiable objectives for attaining this goal.

REFERENCES

ALBERTI, R. E., and EMMONS, M. L.: *Your Perfect Right: A Guide to Assertive Behavior*. San Luis Obispo: Impact, 1970.

BOORAEM, C. D., and FLOWERS, J. V.: Reduction of anxiety and personal space as a function of assertion training with severely disturbed neuropsychiatric inpatients. *Psychol. Reports*, 30, 923-929, 1972.

CAMPBELL, D. T., and STANLEY, J. C.: *Experimental and Quasi-Experimental Designs for Research*. Chicago: Rand McNally, 1966.

CLAUSEN, J. A.: Family structure, socialization, and personality. In: L. W. and M. D. Hoffman (Eds.), *Review of Child Development Research*, Vol. 2. New York: Russell Sage Foundation, 1966.

EDWARDS, A. L.: *Experimental Design in Psychological Research*. New York: Holt, Rinehart, and Winston, 1968.

EISLER, R. M., HERSEN, M., and MILLER, P. M.: Effects of modeling on components of assertive behavior. *J. Behav. Ther. and Exper. Psychiat.*, 4, 1-6, 1973.

FENSTERHEIM, H.: Behavior therapy: Assertive training in groups. In: C. J. Sager and H. S. Kaplan (Eds.), *Progress in Group and Family Therapy*. New York: Brunner/Mazel, 1972.

FRIEDMAN, P. H.: The effects of modeling and role-playing on assertive behavior. In: R. D. Rubin, H. Fensterheim, A. A. Lazarus, and C. M. Franks (Eds.), *Advances in Behavior Therapy*. New York: Academic Press, 1971.

GORDON, T.: *Parent Effectiveness Training*. New York: Peter H. Wyden, 1970.

Group for the Advancement of Psychiatry. Report No. 78, *The Field of Family Therapy*. New York: 1970.

HASTORF, A. H.: The reinforcement of individual actions in a group situation. In: L. Krasner and L. P. Ullman (Eds.), *Research in Behavior Modification*. New York: Holt, Rinehart, and Winston, 1965.

HEDQUIST, F. J. and WEINHOLD, B. K.: Behavioral group counseling with socially anxious and unassertive college students. *J. Counseling Psychol.*, 17, 237-242, 1970.

KRASNER, L.: The psychotherapist as a social reinforcement machine. In: H. H. Strupp and L. Luborsky (Eds.), *Research in Psychotherapy*. Washington, D. C.: American Psychological Association, 1962.

LAZARUS, A. A.: Behavior therapy in groups. In: G. M. Gazda (Ed.), *Basic Approaches to Group Psychotherapy and Group Counseling*. Springfield, Ill.: Charles C Thomas, 1968.

MacPHERSON, E. L. R.: Selective operant conditioning and deconditioning of assertive modes of behavior. *J. Behav. Ther. and Exper. Psychiat.*, 3, 99-102, 1972.

McFALL, R. M., and LILLESAND, D. B.: Behavior rehearsal with modeling and coaching in assertive training. *J. Abnorm. Psychol.*, 77, 313-323, 1971.

MORROW, W. R.: *Behavior Therapy Bibliography 1950-1969*. Columbia: U. of Missouri Press, 1971.

OLSON, D. H., and RYDER, R. G.: Inventory of marital conflicts (IMC): An experimental interaction procedure. *J. Marriage and Family*, 32, 443-448, 1970.

RATHUS, S. A.: An experimental investigation of assertive training in a group setting. *J. Behav. Ther. and Exper. Psychiat.*, 3, 81-86, 1972.

ROGERS, C. R., and DYMOND, R. F.: *Psychotherapy and Personality Change*. Chicago: U. of Chicago Press. 1954.

SALTER, A.: *Conditioned Reflex Therapy*. New York: Farrar, Strauss and Giroux, 1949. (Republished: New York: Capricorn, 1961).

SPIVACK, G., and SPOTTS, J.: *Devereux Behavior Rating Scale Manual*. Devon, Pa.: Devereux Foundation, 1966.

WINER, E. J.: *Statistical Principles in Experimental Design.* New York: McGraw-Hill, 1962.

WOLPE, J.: Reciprocal inhibition as the main basis of psychotherapeutic effects. *Arch. Neurol. and Psychiat.,* 72, 205-226, 1954.

WOLPE, J.: *Psychotherapy by Reciprocal Inhibition.* Stanford: Stanford U. Press, 1958.

WOLPE, J.: *The Practice of Behavior Therapy.* New York: Pergamon Press, 1969.

11

Some Possible Effects of Parent Self-Control Training on Parent-Child Interactions

JOE H. BROWN, A. M. GAMBOA, JR., JOHN BIRKIMER, and ROBERT BROWN

Recent investigations (Patterson et al., 1972) have demonstrated that parents can be trained to alter the maladaptive behavior of their own child. Presumably the effects of these changes are brought about by altering the reinforcing contingencies in the child's environment. When the child displays an inappropriate response, the parent is trained to introduce an extinction or punishment contingency; conversely, when the child responds in an appropriate manner, positive reinforcements are given.

While the effects of behavioral programming have proven efficacious in training parents, little attention has been given to the maintenance of these effects. Too often the results have been short-lived, for positive behavior change has faded as contact with the trainer has diminished (e.g., Patterson, 1973). One method of helping maintain the effects of these programs is to transfer the control from the trainer to the client. The cardinal feature of self-control is that it is the individuals themselves who are the agents of their own behavior change (Thoresen and Mahoney, 1974). The role of the person in this change has been a long-standing issue. Skinner (1953), among others, has maintained that all instances of self-control are ultimately maintained by external variables, while Bandura (1969) has pointed out that most instances of human

180

behavior result not only in environmental consequences, but also in self-evaluative reactions.

In an attempt to synthesize some of the common features found in various forms of self-control, Thoresen and Mahoney (1974) propose the following tentative definition: "A person displays self-control when in the relative absence of immediate external constraints, he engages in behavior whose previous probability has been less than that of alternatively available behaviors." In short, the self-controlling person engages in responses that have been relatively unlikely in previous situations.

To exercise self-control individuals must understand what factors influence their actions and how they can alter those factors to bring about the changes they desire. According to Stuart (1972), the alteration of those factors in order to facilitate behavior change is itself a demonstration of self-control. Given any behavior of a child, the parents have the choice of either suppressing undesirable behavior or accelerating desirable behavior. While the suppression of undesirable behavior is an immediate way to handle a specific problem, parents who truly utilize self-control techniques will be more likely to use praise or positive reinforcement to increase the probability of continued positive behavior in the future.

One could conceptualize this as a choice situation in which the individual can choose either the immediate punishing contingencies, to attempt to suppress the problem behavior, or the distant contingencies, which will probably have greater long-range benefits for the parent and the child. Thus, the tentative definition points up three important features of classical self-control phenomena: (1) they always involve two or more alternative behaviors; (2) the consequences of those behaviors are usually conflicting; and (3) the self-regulatory pattern is usually prompted and/or maintained by external factors such as its long-term effects. It should be noted that behavior cannot be considered as self- or externally controlled; rather, it must be viewed on a continuum from external to self-control. To date, however, self-control has not been examined on a continuum. Self-control efforts have involved a mixture of self-observation, environmental planning, and behavioral programming (Mahoney, 1972; Stuart and Davis, 1972). Yet, there is some question as to the optimal combination of these procedures over time for groups of individuals across a variety of performance areas.

The present study sought to examine the effects of the use of behavioral programming and self-control procedures by parents on parent-child interactions. Furthermore, the self-control procedures utilized here

placed few external controls upon the parents (i.e., parents were permitted to select their own treatment programs).

METHOD

Experimental Situation

The present investigation was conducted in a school for children with
special problems. This particular school—a re-education school (RE-ED),
Title II of Elementary-Secondary Education Act—is designed to supplement services and to demonstrate new approaches to educational problems. Referrals come from various schools in a six-county area of North
Central Kentucky. They may be initiated by the classroom teachers,
counselors, school social workers, or principals. Applicants must be
"between six and twelve years of age, with average or above average
potential, and unable to function in a regular classroom." Each child
spends Monday through Friday noon at the center and returns home
for the weekend. Parents receive consultant services while the child is
enrolled at the center. Thus, rather than permanently institutionalizing
the child, RE-ED serves as a "halfway house" in which both the parent
and child can acquire new patterns of behavior.

Subjects

The RE-ED staff identified 12 mothers who they thought could benefit
from special consultation. While the level of disruptive behavior had
been reduced at the center, parents continued to report high levels of
disruptive behavior at home. In short, while some of the behaviors were
being controlled through reinforcement contingencies in the residential
setting, satisfactory generalization to the home environment was reported
as not occurring.

PROCEDURE

Training

Each parent initially received three hours of instruction on pinpointing and recording behaviors. At the end of the three-hour session, each
parent had demonstrated the ability (1) to differentiate between observable behavior and nonobservable labels for behavioral categories
and (2) to accurately record each occurrence of the observable behavior.
Observable behavior had been defined as "behaviors one can see or
hear." Parents had been required to observe three role-playing incidents

and record the frequency of observable behavior with 100% accuracy. In addition, each parent had also been asked to demonstrate her ability to identify and record the antecedent and consequent events of each behavior.

Next, each parent was asked to specify two problematic target behaviors for her child. The mothers then observed their children for the ensuing weekend to validate the two previously identified target behaviors. The weekend observation took the form of entering on a log-form in a packet of such forms supplied by the authors each problem behavior, the apparent antecedent event, and the result or consequence of the behavior. These packets are described in more detail below. Following the weekend observation, some parents identified a new target behavior which presented a "greater problem" than the previously specified behavior (s).

Phase I: Baseline

Once each parent had operationally defined her target behaviors for the child, she was asked to keep a baseline record of the behavior and its antecedent and consequent events. Each occurrence of a problem behavior was to be recorded by the parents, but for data analysis purposes the experimenters reduced the record to separate "episodes" of the problem behavior; that is, when obvious chains of behavioral interactions between the parent and child developed, such that the parent response to the child misbehaviors led the child to immediately repeat the misbehavior, the resulting chain of misbehaviors was scored as a single episode. This often occurred when the child refused an initial parental request. By scoring such chains as more than one episode, the experimenters would have confounded the rate of misbehavior with both the child's and the parent's persistence.

General Procedures

Parent training sessions were scheduled on Fridays, when parents arrived to take their children home, and on Sunday evenings, when parents were scheduled to return their children to the center. The scheduling of these sessions helped to increase the rate of attendance since parents were necessarily at the center at these times. Each parent received a data packet for Friday, Saturday, and Sunday. The data packet contained places to enter (1) the time when the child "got up" and "went to bed," (2) each antecedent-behavior-consequence combination, and (3) the time of onset and termination of each behavior. Each parent picked up her data packet on Fridays and discussed procedures with the trainers for obtaining accurate observations over the coming weekend. On Sunday evenings, parents and trainers analyzed their observations and discussed changes for the next weekend.

Phase II: Behavioral Programming

The mothers received treatment packets containing procedures for accelerating adaptive behaviors and decelerating maladaptive behaviors. Parents were asked to ignore unacceptable behaviors which they could tolerate and implement time-out procedures for those behaviors that exceeded their tolerance level. Parents were asked to praise desirable behaviors each time they occurred. In some instances a point system was utilized in which a child was required to "obey a list of rules." Points were accordingly exchanged for back-up reinforcers such as "food" or "special activities." This treatment phase usually lasted two weekends (six days).

Phase III: Self-Reinforcement

Self-reinforcement procedures were implemented for the mothers once the reinforcement procedures (Phase II) had demonstrated their effects in increasing the level of desirable behavior or reducing the rate of maladaptive behavior in the children. The primary purpose of this phase was to help parents become more systematic in their use of reinforcement procedures. If parents could learn to control their own behavior, it is likely that they would be more effective in controlling the behavior of their children. Parents were instructed to present themselves with a reward after having exhibited a desirable behavior. For example, a parent might say to herself, "I am a good mother," each time she praised a child's desirable behavior or ignored an undesirable behavior. In other instances parents chose to treat themselves with a cigarette or a cup of coffee, contingent upon a desired performance. In individual cases where reinforcement procedures (Phase II) reduced the level of disturbed child behavior to near zero, self-reinforcement procedures were not implemented.

RESULTS

Reliability

It was virtually impossible in the present study to enter the home for observations and obtain what would appear to be a representative sample of normal interaction within the family. While an independent observer was not employed in the study, there was corroborative evidence to support the accuracy of the observations. For example, observations were handwritten. Furthermore, the nature of the "data forms" required each mother to record separate patterns of behavior rather than simply to code prespecified behaviors or tally the frequency of a behavior. Thus the accuracy of the reported observations seems to be more dependent on the parents' descriptions of their observations in behavioral terms. Unobtrusive measures helped validate the reported data, too. Where parents indicated that they had left the data forms at home, they often changed pens or indicated they were unable in the new setting to collect data of a prespecified behavior or tally the frequency of a behavior.

In addition, parents' "emotional reactions" corresponded to their recorded observations. During baseline, a parent returning data often appeared distraught and upset and reported, "I had a bad weekend with my child." On such occasions, her data were consistent with her appearance and verbalizations. During treatment, many volunteered comments like, "I can't believe how easy it is when you know how," and appeared more relaxed and happy. On these occasions their data would show substantially lower misbehavior rates. Also during treatment, parents often reported in their logs general unexpected improvements in the quality of their children's behavior: "She asked me if she could help with the dishes. She only did that one other time in her life." Finally, the parents' continuation of treatment procedures and the application of those procedures by some parents to other children are most consistent with the reported success of the procedures.

While independent observations were not made in the home setting, teachers recorded the same target behaviors in the center. Although teachers were unable to record observations for all the children, the frequency of observed behavior corresponded to parents' records.

Case Reports

In case reports one through four, each parent identified "noncompliance" behaviors as problematic. These parents complained that their children refused to comply when asked to do something; consequently, each parent was instructed to make a request of the child each hour. For example, the parent might ask, "Please clean up your room," or, "Will you stop running through the house?" Each of these demands served as an antecedent to the "compliance" or "noncompliance" behavior. By following the instructions to make a request each hour, parents were able to obtain stable representation of the frequency of compliance or noncompliance behaviors. The frequency level of compliance or noncompliance behaviors might otherwise drop as a result of not making a request of the child.

A compliance behavior was defined as an appropriate response by the child to the *initial request* of the parent; anything else was recorded as a noncompliance behavior. Noncompliance was recorded if the child ignored the initial request and/or the mother made a second request of the child. (Again, parents generally recorded their specific request, the behavior—verbal and motor—of the child, and their or the child's consequent behavior. For data analysis, "compliances" and "noncompliances" were scored.)

Mark: Subject 1. Mark initially ignored all requests his mother made. Mother reported that Father made few demands of Mark, but the child usually complied. Mother was asked to sit down with the father and agree on a set of responsibilities for Mark. For each compliance behavior, Mark was permitted ten minutes with Dad in the garage or ten minutes at Grandpa's. Figure 1 shows the frequency of compliance and noncompliance behaviors for baseline and treatment phases. The frequency of noncompliance decreased from a mean of 10.2 at baseline to 6.5 the second weekend, to 3.6 the third weekend. The average number of noncompliances during self-reinforcement (Phase III) decreased slightly from 3.6 to 3. Behaviors were recorded across a four-day period the second weekend (Phase II) because Mark remained home. A marked reduction in noncompliances occurred the first day treatment was initiated, but they increased sharply the second day. Further inspection of the data indicated that the mother was neglecting to praise the child for compliance behaviors on the second through the fourth days of the second weekend (Phase II). The mean number of compliance behaviors increased from two at baseline to six during self-control.

Ginny: Subject 2. The mother initially reported that Ginny refused to comply with or complained about doing anything that she requested. Following the first weekend of baseline, however, it became apparent that Mother and Father were often making similar but individual requests of Ginny at the same time, and making surprisingly many "spur-of-the-moment-requests" for chores. Further, the child was rarely given time to play.

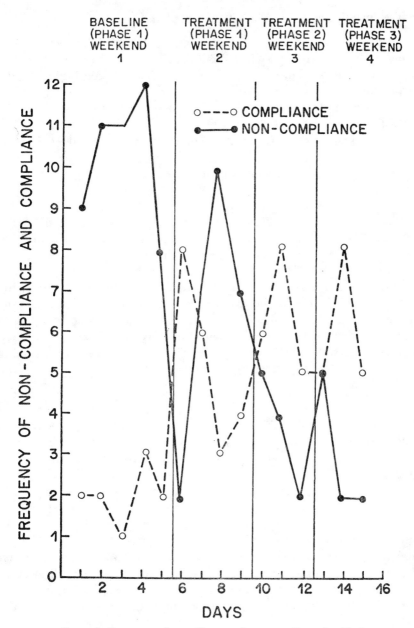

FIGURE 1. Frequency of compliance and noncompliance for Mark.

Treatment procedures (Phase II) required that:

(1) Mother and Father together make a list of jobs the children could be "reasonably expected to do";

(2) A certain amount of free time be designated, contingent on the completion of each job;

(3) Each child be contracted with to complete "his fair share of the tasks";

(4) Making children do anything other than the "contracted tasks" be "studiously avoided";

(5) Minor disturbances be ignored and compliance behaviors be praised.

When examining the effects of treatment one notes that the frequency of nonresponses dropped from a mean of 16 at baseline to 2 in treatment (Phase II). Likewise a concomitant increase from 3 to 35 compliances was recorded.

In addition to observing Ginny's marked improvement in complying with parental requests, the parents were successful in implementing treatment with Ginny's two brothers at home. Twenty-nine compliances were recorded for Chris in the same three-day period, and 14 compliances were recorded for Mike until he injured his hand severely, making some of his tasks difficult or impossible.

James: Subject 3. In addition to a high level of noncompliances, Mother identified "poor eating habits" and "large amount of time eating at dinner table" as problematic behaviors. Treatment procedures involved praise for each compliance as well as "every five minutes for eating correctly." Noncompliances and poor eating habits were to be ignored.

While noncompliances other than at the dinner table dropped slightly from baseline (7.7) to treatment (5.7), a marked reduction occurred in the amount of time spent at the dinner table from a total of 7 hours, 15 minutes the first weekend of baseline to a high of 2 hours and 54 minutes during treatment. However, treatment seemed to have no effect on the amount of time spent at the table during Sunday dinners at Grandma's. There grandparents attended to undesirable behavior by arguing about James's eating and prompting him to eat. Thus the primary effect of treatment on eating time was to greatly reduce it, except in the presence of grandparents. Finally, the number of times the child tried to play and yelled so loudly as to interrupt his mother while talking on the telephone dropped from a total of 4 during baseline to 1 during treatment.

Charlotte: Subject 4. Noncompliances and complaints while complying were identified as problematic. Mother was instructed to praise Charlotte when she complied and say, "I need your help," or some similar statement when Charlotte says, "Why me?" or "Please not me again."

During baseline, prior to experimental intervention, Charlotte failed to comply an average of 9 times. When she received praise for compliances, noncompliances dropped to 3. Furthermore, complaining decreased by half from a mean frequency of 2.3 during baseline to 1 during treatment. Interestingly enough, complaining increased slightly during the third weekend, while noncompliances decreased.

Phillip: Subject 5. The frequency with which Phillip argued with his brother or sister was identified as a "disruptive" behavior by the mother. Argumentative behavior included name calling, screaming, or fighting. Mother praised Phillip for each hour no arguing occurred and used time-out procedures when arguing did occur.

Preliminary data indicated a decrease in mean frequency of argumentative behavior from baseline (5.6) to treatment period (4); however, this specific case was terminated prematurely when the mother became ill.

Allen: Subject 6. Mother initially specified target behaviors for Glenn, who was a resident at the RE-ED Center; however, the behaviors specified by the mother occurred at extremely low levels during baseline. While Glenn did not seem to be exhibiting any "problematic" behaviors, Allen, a nine-year-old son living at home, had been getting up each evening and sleeping on the couch in the den. Mother reported that Allen was "afraid" to sleep in his room and had been sleeping with Glenn until he (Glenn) moved into the center.

Treatment involved asking Allen to "lie in his bed and rest" from 9:30 p.m. to 11:30 p.m. and, if he was not asleep when Mom or Dad went to check him, he could sleep on the couch. Allen agreed to this initial procedure but could not go to sleep.

Next, it was suggested to Allen that he lie in bed until 11:00 p.m. without "yelling out to Mom or Dad." When he completed this task successfully he was allowed to stay up a half hour later the next night; if he stayed in his bed all night, he was allowed to go to the skating rink on Friday night. Allen received praise any night his performance exceeded the previous night.

The data indicate that "staying in his own bed" increased from a maximum of two hours the third night to "all night" the second night of treatment. During treatment Allen's room was rearranged, and he received an aspirin and a P.M. tablet for the first four night—but none thereafter.

The effects of the praise and contingency management procedures on Allen's behavior encouraged the parents to try these techniques with their other two children.

Sammy: Subject 7. Mother asked Sammy to read for five 15-minute blocks each weekend. Target behaviors specified by the mother were the latency, or number of minutes from the time mother asked Sammy to read to the time when reading commenced, and Sammy's asking his mother to "help him" with any word he couldn't pronounce.

The mother was instructed to praise Sammy for every two or three words he could read by himself. In addition, she was to ask Sammy to sound out each word he requested "help with." If he was able to sound out the word, he also received praise. Mother ignored words which Sammy previously vocalized but which he "requested help with," and when help was given the mother did not "sound the word out" but only pronounced it.

The data indicate an almost 80% reduction in the number of words "he requested help with" from baseline to the second weekend of treatment. Furthermore, the latency period was reduced to "zero" by the second weekend of treatment. At the same time, there was only a 20% reduction in the number of pages read, from 7.5 in baseline to 6 in treatment, indicating that the reduction in the frequency of "asking for mother's help" was not a function of a reduction in the number of pages or words read.

DISCUSSION

This study demonstrated that parents could be systematically trained to produce desirable behavior in their children. In addition, the data suggest that parents also learned to control their own behavior, which perhaps helped to maintain the levels of desirable behavior in their children. Compliant behavior of children tracked very closely the differential reinforcement contingency: when no reinforcement followed task completions during baseline, compliance was low, but, when task completions were immediately followed by reinforcement, compliance increased appreciably in all children, at a minimum, doubling. Furthermore, with Ginny (Subject 2) an added time-out for noncompliance was effective in increasing her compliance average to nearly 90%.

While the contingent reinforcement appeared to be successful in producing desirable behavior, the nature of the setting and the types of problems encountered prohibited the use of the traditional ABAB design to determine the lawful effects of experimental procedures. That design, employing a reversal technique (Baer et al., 1968) by alternating presentations of baseline and experimental conditions to a subject or group of subjects, might have decreased the probability of parents remaining in the study and would have produced undesirable effects on their children.

In the present investigation the design provided a valuable alternative to the ABAB design. In this design no reversal of conditions was required to demonstrate the efficacy of the experimental procedures. Instead, data were collected across different behaviors and across different individuals who were in different home environments.

Thus, different parents improved different child behaviors in different homes, providing independent replications of the general finding that parents could be trained with minimal contact to use praising, ignoring, contingency management, and occasional time-out to better control their children's misbehavior.

The success of this program in producing high levels of desirable behavior is probably based upon a number of factors. Generally, the willingness of subjects or clients to enter into a "personal contract" with a trainer depends in part on whether the client is in a crisis situation (Caplan, 1964). While the present program was designed as an intervention as well as a preventative program, parents must still believe that the program will benefit them. Thus, we believe that a critical component of this program involves parent commitment to participate while the children are exhibiting a high level of disruptive behavior at home. In addition, the data-logs used by the parents to collect data served to increase the level of commitment.

The effects of self-reinforcement procedures served to maintain the desirable levels of the children's behavior. It may be that parents who are successful in implementing reinforcement procedures need an additional treatment to systematically implement these procedures over a long period of time. While parents may be able to see the lawful effects of their behavior on target behaviors of their child, they may not be able to reward themselves covertly for "being a good parent." The sense of purpose and meaning is in part a function of whether individuals see their actions as under their own control. Indeed, the words

192   *Behavior Modification Approaches to Parenting*

parents use to "talk to themselves" may serve as reinforcing stimuli to maintain the desirable level of behavior. Certain words and images can be associated systematically by the individual with other words and images to add new personal meaning to one's life (Staats, 1972).

Consistent with the previous definition of self-control, three parents (Subjects 2, 5 and 7) chose to utilize the positive reinforcement procedures which had produced desirable changes in one child to control behavior of other children in the family. Certainly the generalization of these procedures to other children presents a choice situation without external constraints.

The fact that parents chose to use the same techniques with children not included in the study, with minimal external demands, constitutes one of the major aspects of self-regulation. It may be that certain aspects of choice and self-regulation possess reinforcing properties.

Indeed, by increasing the choices and response options, the treatment program served to "free" parents from their fears and anxieties which often led to punishment or avoidance of desirable behavior. Parents no longer utilized immediate external contingencies to control maladaptive behavior; rather, parents utilized positive "child-control behaviors" which were under the control of long-term consequences (eventual good child behavior). Initially, ineffective child-control behavior was more likely when maladaptive behavior occurred. Thus, parents' behavior came under the control of their own self-imposed contingencies.

REFERENCES

BANDURA, A.: *Principles of Behavior Modification.* New York: Holt, Rinehart and Winston, 1969.

CAPLAN, G.: *Principles of Preventative Psychiatry,* New York: Basic Books, 1964.

MAHONEY, M. J.: Research issues in self-management. *Behav. Ther.,* 3, 45-63, 1972.

PATTERSON, G. R.: Reprogramming the families of aggressive boys. In: C. E. Thoresen (Ed.), *Behavior Modification in Education.* Seventy-Second Yearbook of the National Society for the Study of Education, Part I. Chicago: U. of Chicago Press, 1973. Pp. 154-192.

PATTERSON, G. R., COBB, J. A., and RAY, R. S.: Direct intervention in the classroom: A set of procedures for the aggressive child. In: F. W. Clark, D. R. Evans, and L. A. Hamerlynck (Eds.), *Implementing Behavioral Programs for Schools and Clinics.* Champaign, Ill.: Research Press, 1972. Pp. 151-201.

SKINNER, B. F.: *Science and Human Behavior.* New York: Macmillan, 1953.

STAATS, A. W.: Language behavior therapy: A derivative of social behaviorism. *Behav. Ther.,* 3, 165-192, 1972.

STUART, R. B.: Situational versus self-control. In: R. D. Rubin, H. Fensterheim, J. D. Henderson, and L. P. Ullman (Eds.), *Advances in Behavior Therapy.* New York: Academic Press, 1972. Pp. 129-146.

STUART, R. B., and DAVIS, B.: *Slim Chance in a Fat World: Behavioral Control of Obesity.* Champaign, Ill.: Research Press, 1972.

THORESEN, C. E., and MAHONEY, M. J.: *Behavioral Self-Control.* New York: Holt, Rinehart and Winston, 1974.

12

Parents and Siblings as Teachers

MARGARET STEWARD
and
DAVID STEWARD

One of the most striking results on the American scene of the impact of Piaget's dynamic view of the growth of intelligence has been our increasing awareness that the ability to learn is a function of the interaction between the developing child and an environment which lends itself to the capacities the child brings (Hunt, 1961). Deutsch (1968), Blank and Solomon (1968), Nelder (1971), and others have demonstrated that it is the patterning or structuring of the environment by the teacher which makes a difference in directing early learning. Hess (1965, 1968), Bee (1969), and their colleagues have focused on maternal teaching strategies as better predictors of children's performance than such frequently invoked variables as IQ or social class. These insights have been institutionalized in many experimental school programs for young children (Maccoby and Zellner, 1970; Parker, 1972). However, the observation of and planning for the early learning environment which the home itself constitutes are less complete.

Our research in family learning (Steward and Steward, 1973, 1974b) has been an effort to map the pattern of interaction in which young children participate in the home as they "learn how to learn." In the process of our research we have collected videotape data of parent-child interactions in the home around both cognitive and motor tasks. A wide variety of family members appeared spontaneously "on camera" to "help" the learning process along. Our initial focus was on mother-son pairs. In the present study we will examine the pivotal role and function of firstborn children, who are students to their parents at the same time that they are teachers of younger brothers and sisters.

There is a paucity of clinical or experimental work based on the interaction between a firstborn and later siblings. Robert White (1972) notes that this is not so surprising for "there is a reassuring regularity in the biological circumstances that every child has a father and a mother, never more or less. On this foundation was built, for better or worse, the abstract model of the isolated three-person family; on it rested the hope that parent-child relations could be captured in systematic theory. But when it comes to siblings, the variety of patterns seems designed to defeat orderly thinking. There may be no brothers and sisters, there may be a lot of each, the number and sex distribution can fall in an almost infinite variety of patterns, and as a crowning insult to systematic thought, Nature every so often throws in a multiple birth" (p. 87).

The academic and career success of the firstborn has been a focus since 1874, when Sir Francis Galton published his famous book, *English Men of Science*, through the work of Cattell in 1906 on American men of science, and Terman in 1925 on a thousand gifted children, to the contemporary statistics on the performance of National Merit Scholars and the recent compilation of Altus (1966). Jones's pioneering research in the 1930's of ordinal position of siblings stood virtually alone until Schachter's book, *The Psychology of Affiliation* (1959), opened the floodgates of studies. However, Zigler and his colleagues (1971) have cautioned that, although the birth order variable has precipitated a great deal of research, many investigators do not appear sufficiently cognizant of the fact that birth order is not in and of itself a psychological variable.

Indeed, in their book, *The Sibling*, Sutton-Smith and Rosenberg (1970) posit the thesis that sibling status is a "silent variable" which functions to focus systematic patterns of behavior, yet with "no clear physiological signs that announce the biological character and expected actions of the person who is a firstborn, an older brother or younger sister" (p. 1). The dedication of their book "to our older siblings who will undoubtedly regard this as just another form of harassment" is a testament to the powerful process that these authors have also learned from the experiences of sibship. This introduction is in striking contrast to the literature reviewed which focuses not on process, but on resultant differential development of such things as affiliation, conformity, achievement, sex roles, and power.

The exploration of the firstborn's behavior thus must be conceptualized within a system of relationships in the family, wherein children deal not only in dyadic relationship to parents, but also deal with one another. We have chosen to delimit the multitude of roles which sibs play with each other by focusing only on the teaching role played by the firstborn. Moreover, we have selected as a variable the level of cognitive development as defined by Piaget, which is of interest psychologically and which catches up patterns generally accounted for by such demographic variables as family size, ordinal position, and age spacing of children. The focus of this report will be on the teaching maneuvers employed with preoperational children (ranging in age from about 2 to 5 years) by firstborn siblings who are either concrete operational thinkers (about 6 to 11 years), or formal operational thinkers (about 12 years and up), or by formal operational thinkers who are also their mothers. From Turiel's work (1966, 1969) it has been shown that attempts to change a child's thought mode are more successful when the model is developmentally only one stage higher than the child.

Our research methodology draws from three theoretical positions: (1) From social learning theory we have developed the concept of a "teaching loop" in which the teacher initiates and maintains the teaching-learning situation and the child responds to these teaching maneuvers. An instrument has been developed—the Parent Interaction Code—to analyze the content and function of the teaching-learning interactions. The components of the code include (a) alerting—gaining the attention of the child, (b) instructing—providing information to the child about the task to be done, (c) child's response to alert and instruction, and (d) feedback—teacher's informational and affective response to child's response. (2) From systems theory we focus our analysis on redundant, stable, observable behaviors and look for patterns of interactions and behavioral contingencies, not simply magnitude of single variables. The use of videotape increases the possibility of multiple coding of sequential data and the coding of both verbal and nonverbal behavior. (3) From ethological concerns, and mindful of Bronfenbrenner's tongue-in-cheek accusation that child psychology is the result of children's behavior in strange situations with strange adults, children were observed in environments in which they could comfortably interact.

The data reported below are from two studies. The first involves some data from a newly completed sibling study; the second is a reanalysis of some mother-child dyads reported in Steward and Steward (1973).

METHODOLOGY

Subjects

The subject population included 12 mother-child dyads (MC) and 22 same-sex sibling pairs. The children in the MC dyads were three- to four-year-old boys. The sibling pairs consisted of 10 firstborn children who were formal operational thinkers (formal with siblings, or FS) and 12 firstborn children who were concrete operational thinkers (concrete with siblings, or CS). Half of the FS and CS pairs were girls, half were boys. The average age of the FS firstborns was 12.2 years, and the average age of their younger siblings was 4.2 years. The average age of the CS firstborns was 8.3 years, and the average age of their younger siblings was 3.8 years. All of the younger children were preoperational thinkers, and there were no significant differences in the ages of the younger children from the three groups. All dyads were Anglo-American and found through contacting public and private nursery schools in northern California. The mother-child dyads were easily identified; however, an extensive search was conducted to find families with a firstborn child in elementary or high school which also had a same-sex child of three or four years. After preliminary screening, over 200 families were contacted before the search was terminated. After family constellation criteria were met, firstborns were pretested on two common Piagetian tasks—a cognitive sorting task and a hierarchy task—so that age and cognitive performance differentiated the two sibling groups.

Procedures

In all dyads, a Piagetian sorting game involving the classification of color, shape, and size of objects served as the occasion for the observation of teacher-learner interaction. In every case, the teacher was taught by the experimenter and was then asked to teach the young child to classify along the same dimensions. Teachers were free to proceed in any manner they chose and to spend as much time as they wanted on the task. The data were collected on ½-inch videotape equipment. Tapes were replayed for the families and permission granted before the data became part of the research study. In no instance did a family refuse to grant consent; in fact, the response to the procedure as well as the purpose of the study was universally positive. Research team members were trained by the authors to code both the verbal and nonverbal behavior employing the Parent Interaction Code, with interrater reliability established in excess of .85 (see Table 1 for operational definitions).

TABLE 1

Definitions for Parent Interaction Code

PROGRAMMATIC VARIABLES
  Total Time: Time spent by teacher and student to complete the task
  Loops: Number of instructional loops used to complete the task
  Pacing: The ratio of loops/total time

LOOP VARIABLES
  Alerts: Behavior by the teacher which gains the attention of the student
  Instructions: Information given by the teacher about the task to be done
    Content: Instructions given may use words used to teach the game to the teacher (original content), or instructions given may use words modified from the original instructions (embroidery).
    Form: Instructions may be given verbally and/or nonverbally; instructions may be given as questions or statements.
  Specificity:
  Level   I: Orienting instructions which designate neither actions to be done nor objects to use.
          II: Instructions which designate either action to be done or object to use, but not both.
          III: Instructions which designate both action to be done and object to use.
  Child Response: Response of student to teacher's instruction
    Accept: Student begins to act on instructions immediately
    Passive: Student remains inactive following instructions
    Demand: Student asks for help after instructions are given
    Ignore: Student continues activity in progress before instructions were given
    Refuse: Student actively rejects instructions
  Feedback: Information teacher gives student about responses to instructions
    + Information about the task accompanied by positive affect
    — Information about the task accompanied by negative affect
    I Information about the task with no accompanying affect

RESULTS

Data from the three dyad groups were analyzed by employing a one-way analysis of variance for unequal n's and, when significant differences were found, a Duncan Multiple Range Test was used as a conservative test of cell mean differences (see Table 2).

Programmatic variables. The structure of the learning environment was analyzed into three components: total time, number of teaching loops, and pacing, which is the ratio of teaching loops to total time. There were no differences found among the three groups in total time spent on the task. Within the task, however, mothers initiated a greater number of teaching loops than did sibling teachers ($F = 4.83$, $df = 2,31$, $p < .025$). Significant differences were found for the pacing of the learn-

TABLE 2

Duncan's Multiple-Range Tests On Group Means

Variables	Mothers	Formal	Siblings Concrete
Programmatic:			
Loops	53$_a$	28$_b$	25$_b$
Pacing	3.32$_a$	1.95$_b$	1.02$_c$
Total time	16$_a$	16$_a$	24$_a$
Loop:			
Alerts	.14$_a$	.18$_a$	.41$_b$
Instruction Content:			
Original	.04$_a$	.24$_b$	.19$_b$
Embroidery	.98$_a$	.92$_a$	.97$_a$
Instruction Form			
Statement	.51$_a$	.53$_a$	.60$_a$
Question	.47$_a$	.39$_a$	.46$_a$
Nonverbal	.54$_a$	.66$_a$	.72$_a$
Instruction Specificity:			
Level 1	.16$_a$	.21$_a$	.18$_a$
2	.08$_a$	.37$_b$	.43$_b$
3	.76$_a$	.42$_b$	.39$_b$
Child Response:			
A Accept	.63$_a$	.95$_b$	1.06$_b$
B Passive	.17$_a$	.04$_b$	.02$_b$
C Ignore	.05$_a$	.04$_a$	.16$_a$
D Refuse	.12$_a$	.02$_a$	.08$_a$
E Demand	.11$_a$	.12$_a$	.34$_b$
Feedback:			
Total	.51$_a$	.91$_b$	1.22$_b$
Positive	.07$_a$	.37$_b$	.37$_b$
Negative	.01$_a$	.04$_a$	.19$_b$
Information Only	.43$_a$	.35$_a$	.26$_a$

Means that share a common subscript are not significantly different.
Significance level is set at p = .05.

ing, with mothers presenting faster pacing than formal siblings, and formal siblings in turn pacing faster than concrete siblings ($F = 25.01$, $df = 2,31$, $p < .001$).

Loop variables. The teaching loop, consisting of alert, instruction, child response, and feedback, served as the basic unit of analysis. All computations reported below were based on a per loop statistic. Concrete siblings employed more alerting, using it nearly every other loop, than did formal siblings or mothers ($F = 4.06$, $df = 2,31$, $p < .05$).

Instructions were coded and analyzed in three ways. The content of the instructions used by sibling teachers included more of the instructions originally given them by the experimenter than did the mothers' instructions ($F = 4.87$, $df = 2,31$, $p < .025$); however, all teachers used words other than those given in the original instructions (embroidery) in nearly every loop ($F < 1$). All teachers employed directive statements and questioning strategies with equal frequency in giving instructions. There was a trend for nonverbal strategies to be employed most often by concrete siblings, next by formal siblings, and least frequently by the mothers ($F = 2.68$, $df = 2,31$, $p < .10$; linear trend $F = 5.03$, $df = 1,31$, $p < .05$). Instructional specificity revealed that all teachers used general orienting statements with equal frequency ($F < 1$). However, sibling teachers more frequently employed specificity which gave information about either the object or the activity of the task ($F = 10.02$, $df = 2,31$, $p < .001$), while mothers gave more instructions which specified both the object and the activity ($F = 10.80$, $df = 2,31$, $p < .001$).

The children being taught responded differentially to their teachers. Sibling teachers elicited significantly more active accepting responses and fewer passive ones from their younger sibs than mothers elicited from their sons ($F = 11.28$, $df = 2,31$, $p < .001$; and $F = 13.21$, $df = 2,31$, $p < .001$, respectively). There was a significantly higher demand for help placed on the concrete sibling teachers and a trend to ignore their instructions ($F = 4.27$, $df = 2,31$, $p < .025$; and $F = 2.66$, $df = 2,31$, $p < .10$, respectively). No differences reached significance level for refusal.

Following the child response, sibling teachers gave their brothers and sisters significantly more total feedback ($F = 8.37$, $df = 2,31$, $p < .005$), and in that total feedback, more positive reinforcement than mothers gave their sons ($F = 8.74$, $df = 2,31$, $p < .001$). Concrete sibling teachers gave more negative reinforcement than did formal sibling teachers or mothers ($F = 20.80$, $df = 2,31$, $p < .001$). All groups of teachers gave equal amounts of information, without affective components.

DISCUSSION

We have already noted that there is almost no research comparing parent and sibling teaching. Siblings could be considered peers, but the peer teaching literature is primarily reflective of sociometric research which yields general data about beliefs, values, and style of living (McCandless, 1969; McCandless and Evans, 1973).

Piaget's early work is exploratory research which attempts to chart broad issues in the development of intelligence (Ginsburg and Opper, 1969). His comments on the development of language and moral judgment provide categories which help us interpret our data.

Our data show that parents give significantly fewer original instructions than do siblings, although all groups give the same amount of embroidery. We have conceptualized this result as a sign of the developmental capacity of the teachers. Flavell (1968) observed a developing capacity of the child through adolescence to communicate depending on his skill in "role-taking"—placing himself in the shoes of another person while, simultaneously, holding on to his own point of view. Elkind (1970) calls this the move from egocentrism to sociocentrism.

Piaget's work is full of the child's movement from centeredness to flexibility. For our purpose, his early work, *The Language and Thought of the Child* (1923), will serve. There he observed that the origins of the social use of language involve movement through what he calls "collective monologue"—the use of language in groups for the instruction only of the speaker. It is our hunch that the use of embroidery across all ages of teachers indicates enough development of role-taking skills to result in sociocentric communication, but that the mastery of such communication skills is still incomplete for both formal and concrete sibling teachers. This is indicated by their frequent use of original instructions, usually in the same teaching loop as embroidery. We interpret the process to be an initial rehearsal by the siblings of the original instruction for *their own mastery purposes,* followed by their active accommodation to the younger children, through role-taking, by rephrasing the message. This same pattern was observed in behavior in a knot-tying game not presented here. Often the teaching siblings would precede their instruction by egocentrically bending over their own knot boards and tying the knot for themselves first. We suggest that this preliminary check and the verbalizing of original instructions constitute forms of "collective monologue." Mothers have internalized this rehearsal function, and therefore do not exhibit so many original instructions.

The notion of incomplete mastery, and a resulting intermediate step, may clarify our specificity data, too. We found that, while all groups provided the same frequency of orienting instructions, parents gave fewer instructions with middle-range specificity and more highly specific instructions which involve two variables simultaneously. In the methodological introduction to *The Child's Conception of the World* (1929), Piaget suggests that the tracing of development is more certain when the movement from stage to stage is through an intermediate step which advances the performance of the initial stage in the direction of a later stage. We have applied a Piagetian notion of the discrimination and conceptual holding of multiple variables to our specificity data in order to make a developmental interpretation of them. From this point of view there is a scale from general orienting instructions (e.g., "we're going to play this game") to the detailing of object and action (e.g., "put the yellow circle in this pile"), with instructions pertaining either to object (e.g., "the yellow one") or to action (e.g., "over here") as intermediary.

Orienting instructions serve, according to this interpretation, as an entrée to the task. It's a tooling up by the teacher for the task, and probably serves primarily as a self-alert. It triggers a series of thoughts which emerge in later sequences of level II and III specificity of instructions. In this function it constitutes another example of "collective monologue." It may also alert the learner and thereby serve as an effective piece of communication.

The paucity of level II specificity by the mothers and their extensive use of level III specificity suggest that they have conceptualized the task as a whole—a formal thought expression—and are instructing efficiently out of the understanding that classification requires the making of combinations through the combination of perceptual selection and active placement. While this combinatorial exercise is well within the range of both concrete and formal children (and even, with help, of preoperational children), we suggest that it is complicated enough to distract older siblings when they are immersed in the interpersonal demands of teaching younger siblings. It is our hunch that the frequency of the level II specificity among sibling teachers reflects their centering on one or another aspect of the task as there is an immediate pull for that response through the action of the learner. Since the "task as a whole" is less firm in their minds, sibling teachers may be distracted by the immediate action of the learner and respond to the part-task that needs to be solved. For example, the learner may have lifted a yellow circle and may be holding it aloft. The mother reiterates, "put the yellow circle in this pile." The sibling teacher may focus on the part-task to be completed, point to the appropriate pile, and simply say, "here." The sibling's intermediate response, according to this interpretation, will be more useful to the preoperational thinker.

In our study, young learners accepted the task presented by the mothers' instructions significantly less often than they did when their siblings were teachers. Also, learners responded to their mothers' instruc tions with passivity significantly more frequently than when their sib lings were teachers. Turiel (1966, 1969) has demonstrated that children make more advanced moral judgments, and Silverman and Geiringer (1973) have demonstrated that children can be taught to conserve more effectively by persons one stage beyond them than by persons who per form more than one stage in advance of them. Our data may be inter preted to indicate a similar point. The problem mothers have in setting the task in a way which can gain the accepting response of the child may be interpreted to be a function of secure formal thought. Piaget, in *The Moral Judgment of the Child,* discriminates between judgments based on the experience of external constraint and judgments based on the experience of cooperation. Despite the desirability of the latter, the development of moral judgment inevitably begins with constraint re sponses assumed to derive from parent-child relations in the home, and proceeds to cooperative responses after the child has had some peer experience. Piaget and his wife worked carefully to provide experiences of cooperation in their relation with their own young children, but failed. Part of the reason was the attribution by the children of absolute authority to the parent—a product of the conceptual limitation and inflexibility of children early in their development.

It is our interpretation that the conceptual distance is also a function of inflexibility on the part of the adult. Furth (1969) presents Piaget's notion of memory as a process which has state limitations. Because, for Piaget, perception and conception are bound together tightly in the construction of reality, experience becomes as much a product of the structure of the mind as it does of the shape of the external world. It is our claim that mothers conceptualize the whole task, but it is the very power of that conceptualization which makes it difficult for them to be aware of the conceptual limitations of the child. Their instructions may accommodate verbally to the children (embroidery), but the less obvious structure of their instructions (higher level of specificity and fewer non verbal instructions) remains at a level of complexity which they, but not the children, can handle consistently. The children respond, we would interpret, with less acceptance and more passivity because they are "lost." The sibling teachers succeed in maintaining contact with the learners because the formal structure is not set so firmly in their minds, and they find themselves "slipping" again and again into the thought patterns of the younger siblings. The result is a greater proportion of more simply structured instructions.

We returned to our videotaped data to reexamine the teaching behavior of the children who had pretested in the formal stage. Only
three of them, out of ten, maintained their formal behavior in the
teaching interaction. By reclassifying the three children who stayed the
same as "formal-formal" and the remaining ones who changed from
formal learners to concrete teachers as "formal-concrete," the point becomes even clearer. We now understand that the great majority of our
formal children were only *working toward formal* cognitive structures
when they were functioning as teachers.

The interpretation of the differences between mother and sibling
teachers provides a framework for interpreting the differences found between concrete sibling teachers on the one hand and formal sibling and
teaching mothers on the other hand. Concrete sibling teachers administered significantly more alerts, received significantly more demand responses, and gave significantly more negative feedback. We understand
these findings to be a function of the particularism and realism of concrete thought.

In *The Moral Judgment of the Child,* Piaget documents the inflexibility of children regarding the rules of the game. The "idea" of the
game (e.g., that classification be accomplished) is subordinated to the
details of procedure (e.g., the yellow circles go precisely in *this* spot and
nowhere else; and furthermore, shape must be sorted before size, etc.).
When this perception of arbitrary right and wrong ways to do things
is related to the property of concrete thought which makes the child
focus on the "next thing to do" rather than the task as a whole, our
data gain meaning. Concrete rigidity of rules makes possible many more
"wrong" moves by the learner; hence, negative reinforcement has more
opportunity to be expressed. The particularism of the approach to the
task segments the process, raising the probability of demands on the part
of the learner for more help and increasing the necessity to realert after
each loop. The learner is able to ask, "What do I do now?" more frequently, and the concrete sibling teacher is required to start the next
step more often.

Finally, there appears to be a cluster of teaching behaviors shared by
all teachers. The stimulus qualities of the game itself pull for a common
period of time, i.e., it only takes so long to teach a three- to four-year-old
how to play the game and, when it is completed, all teachers stop. The
game instructions given the teacher by the experimenter also probably
need to be elaborated from adult speech to make them appropriate for
young children, and all teachers have put the task "in their own words."

More interesting are the teaching maneuvers which we identify as characteristics of the Anglo-American ethnic teaching style—in contrast to teaching behaviors characteristic of Mexican-American and Chinese American teachers on the same game (Steward and Steward, 1973, 1974a). All of our teachers in this study employed a similar ratio of statement to question and a fairly high percentage of general orienting statements in the instructional format, as well as providing a large amount of affectively neutral informational feedback. Thus Anglo children teach like their Anglo mothers in some important ways.

In considering the findings of this study, we note three areas that contribute to issues which are alive in behavior modification approaches to parenting. One of the themes, raised by Patterson (1975) and echoed by researchers and practitioners alike, is the need to extend the technology of behavior modification from the consideration of reinforcement contingencies to factors which stimulate and initiate behavior. The teaching loop provides a conceptualization of teacher-learner interaction in which both antecedent and consequent conditions are related in a system. Therefore it provides easy access to a more complex sequential analysis of behavior. A second issue, raised by Horowitz (1975), is the question of the impact of development on the study of parent-child interactions. This study uses a major developmental theory as a framework for the interpretation of observed family interactions. Thirdly, the extension of behavior modification to normal families has been proposed by Risley et al. (1975) and others. The present study serves to provide base-rate data on teaching-learning behavior in normal families and suggests that systematic differences can be expected in the learning experiences and level of mastery of young children when taught by different family members.

REFERENCES

ALTUS, W. D.: Birth order and its sequelae. *Science*, 151, 44-49, 1966.
BEE, H. L., VAN EGEREN, L. R., STREISSGUTH, A. P., NYMAN, B. A., and LECKIE, M. S.: Social class differences in maternal teaching strategies and speech patterns. *Devel. Psychol.* 1, 726-734, 1969.
BLANK, M., and SOLOMON, F.: A tutorial language program to develop abstract thinking in socially disadvantaged preschool children. *Child Devel.*, 39, 379-389, 1968.
CATTELL, J. M.: Statistical study of American men of Science. *Science*, 24, 658-665, 699-707, 732-742, 1906.
DEUTSCH, P., and DEUTSCH, M.: Brief reflections on the theory of early childhood enrichment programs. In: R. D. Hess and R. M. Baer (Eds.), *Early Education*. Chicago: Aldine, 1968.

ELKIND, D.: *Children and Adolescents: Interpretive Essays on Jean Piaget.* New York: Oxford U. Press, 1970.

FLAVELL, J. H.: *The Development of Role-Taking and Communication Skills in Children.* New York: John Wiley, 1968.

FURTH, HANS G.: *Piaget and Knowledge.* Englewood Cliffs, N. J.: Prentice-Hall, 1969.

GALTON, SIR FRANCIS: *English Men of Science: Their Nature and Nurture.* London: Macmillan, 1874.

GINSBURG, H., and OPPER, S.: *Piaget's Theory of Intellectual Development: An Introduction.* Englewood Cliffs. N. J.: Prentice Hall, 1969.

HESS, R. D., and SHIPMAN, V. C.: Early education and the socialization of cognitive modes in children. *Child Devel.,* 36, 869-886, 1965.

HESS, R. D., and BAER, R. M.: *Early Education.* Chicago: Aldine, 1968.

HOROWITZ, F. D.: Directions for parenting. In: E. J. Mash, L. A. Hamerlynck, and L. C. Handy (Eds.), *Behavior Modification and Families.* New York: Brunner/ Mazel, 1975.

HUNT, J. McV.: *Intelligence and Experience.* New York: Ronald Press, 1961.

JONES, H. E.: Order of birth in relation to the development of the child. In: C. Murchison (Ed.), *A Handbook of Child Psychology.* Worcester, Mass.: Clark U. Press, 1933.

MACCOBY, E. E., and ZELLNER, M.: *Experiments in Primary Education.* New York: Harcourt, Brace and Jovanovich, 1970.

MCCANDLESS, B. R.: Childhood Socialization. In: D. A. Goslin (Ed.), *Handbook of Socialization Theory and Research.* Chicago: Rand McNally, 1969. Pp. 791-820.

MCCANDLESS, B. R., and EVANS, E. D.: *Children and Youth: Psychosocial Development* Hinsdale, Ill.: Dryden, 1973.

NELDER, S., and SEBERA, P.: Intervention strategies for Spanish-speaking preschool children. *Child Devel.,* 42, 259-268, 1971.

PARKER, R. K. (Ed.): *The Preschool in Action: Exploring Early Childhood Education Programs.* Boston: Allyn and Bacon, 1972.

PATTERSON, G. R.: The aggressive child: Victim and architect of a coercive system. In: E. J. Mash, L. A. Hamerlynck, and L. C. Handy (Eds.), *Behavior Modification and Families.* New York: Brunner/Mazel, 1975.

PIAGET, J.: *The Child's Conception of the World.* Totowa, N. J.: Littlefield, Adams, 1960. First published in 1929.

PIAGET, J.: *The Language and Thought of the Child.* New York: Meridian Books, 1955. First published in 1923.

PIAGET, J.: *The Moral Judgment of the Child.* New York: Free Press, 1965. First published in 1932.

RISLEY, T. R., CLARK, H. B., and CATALDO, M. F.: Behavioral technology for the normal middle-class family. In: E. J. Mash, L. A. Hamerlynck, and L. C. Handy (Eds.), *Behavior Modification and Families.* New York: Brunner/Mazel, 1975.

SCHACHTER, S.: *The Psychology of Affiliation.* Stanford, Cal.: Stanford U. Press, 1959.

SILVERMAN, I. W., and GEIRINGER, E.: Dyadic interaction and conservation induction: A test of Piaget's equilibration model. *Child Devel.,* 44, 815-820, 1973.

STEWARD, M. S., and STEWARD, D. C.: The observation of Anglo-, Mexican-, and Chinese-American mothers teaching their young sons. *Child Devel.,* 44, 329-337, 1973.

STEWARD, M. S., and STEWARD, D. S.: The effect of social distance on teaching strategies of Anglo and Mexican American Mothers. *Devel. Psychol.,* 10, 797-807, 1974a.

STEWARD, M. S., and STEWARD, D. S.: Early learning in the family, a report of research in progress. *Character Potential,* 6, 171-176, 1974b.

SUTTON-SMITH, B., and ROSENBERG, B. G.: *The Sibling.* New York: Holt, Rinehart and Winston, 1970.

TERMAN, L. M.: *The Mental and Physical Traits of a Thousand Gifted Children*, Vol. 1. Stanford, Cal.: Stanford U. Press, 1925.

TURIEL, E.: An experimental test of the sequentiality of developmental stages in the child's moral judgments. *J. Pers. and Soc. Psychol.*, 3, 611-618, 1966.

TURIEL, E.: Developmental processes in the child's moral thinking. In: P. H. Mussen, J. Langer, and M. Covington (Eds.), *Trends and Issues in Developmental Psychology*. New York: Holt, Rinehart and Winston, 1969.

WHITE, R.: *The Enterprise of Living*. New York: Holt, Rinehart and Winston, 1972.

ZIGLER, E., GROSSE, M., and UNRUH, S. G.: Birth order, number of siblings and social reinforcer effectiveness in children. *Child Devel.*, 42, 1153-1163, 1971.

Section IV
APPLICATIONS WITH EXCEPTIONAL
CHILDREN OR FAMILIES

13

Parental Depression: Incompatible with Effective Parenting

Peter D. McLean

There are two particularly striking features of clinical depression—the pervasiveness of its occurrence and the number of theories available to explain its development. Despite the variety of theoretical explanations, there is no single treatment intervention which has demonstrated consistent efficacy in ameliorating depression in its various forms. Originally considered to be the result of a physiological disorder (Maddison and Duncan, 1965), depression has been subject to considerable reconceptualization in the last decade. Current theories can be divided into four groups: genetic, biochemical (biochemical disturbance being triggered by either constitutional predisposition or environmental stressors), intrapsychic, and behavioral. These groups frequently overlap, as in somatic theories, which often require both genetic and biochemical factors, and cognitive theories (e.g., Beck, 1967), which combine intrapsychic and behavioral factors. Accordingly, the typology of depression theories can, in its simplest form, be categorized into biogenetic and psychosocial theories. The National Institute of Mental Health has used a similar classification; it sponsored a conference on the psychobiology of depression in 1969 and a second on the psychology of depression in 1971 (the results of these conferences were published by Williams et al., 1972, and Friedman and Katz, 1974, respectively).

The development of psychotropic drugs and the pursuit of the putative constitutional factor (e.g., Dorzab et al., 1971; Winokur, 1972) have focused major attention on biogenic theories. Psychosocial variables,

I would like to thank Joe Becker for his helpful comments in the final preparation of this paper.

TABLE 1

Reactive Depression Disorders (Rates per 100,000 Population)
in Psychiatric Institutions—1969-1970

Proportion compared to all psychiatric disorders	18.8%	(Canada)*
	24.7%	(U.S.A.)†
Proportion compared to all psychoneurotic disorders	74.2%	(Canada)
	67.2%	(U.S.A.)
Female proportion of	67.2%	(Canada)
	74.1%	(U.S.A.)

* Discharges—all institutions (Statistics Canada).
† Discharges—psychiatric services in general hospitals (National Institute of Mental Health).

however, have increasingly been recognized as critical in the etiology and maintenance of clinical depression. Interaction within one's social environment, negative life events and other environmental stressors have been identified as precursors and triggering events in the onset of depression (Brown et al., 1973). Furthermore, the prognosis of depression seems to depend on the continuing status of these antecedent events.

This paper presents material which suggests that the social environment is a potent determinant of depression.

Incidence of Depression and High-Risk Factors

Reactive or neurotic depression accounts for approximately one-fifth to one-quarter of the entire mental health population in Canada and the United States, depending on the type of mental health facility involved* (see Table 1). If all forms of depressive disorders were included, their proportion of the total mental health population would rise to 30.1% in Canada (Statistics Canada, 1970) and 33.7% in the U.S.A. (NIMH, 1969-1970).

A characteristic of depressive disorders is the apparent selectivity of their occurrence as a function of certain demographic variables. For example, there are two to three times as many women as men diagnosed as depressed in psychiatric facilities and, for some reason, the sex discrepancy is increasing over the years with proportionately more women than men becoming clinically depressed each year from 1951 to the

---

* Canadian data include institutions for long-term care disorders, such as schizophrenia, organic brain syndromes, mental retardation, etc., compared to the U.S.A. data which are descriptive only of psychiatric wards in general hospitals.

present (Statistics Canada, 1951-1973). Furthermore, while married, separated, divorced, and widowed women are most vulnerable to depression, single women of the same age are relatively exempt from depression (Porter, 1970). Finally, compared to women having any other mental disorder, depressed women in psychiatric facilities are more than twice as likely to be mothers (Statistics Canada, 1954).

In summary, the three demographic factors which appear to make for high risk in becoming clinically depressed are (1) being female, (2) being married, separated, widowed, or divorced, and (3) having children.

A Behavioral Model of Depression

A behavioral model of depression suggests that people become depressed primarily as a result of their current circumstances and secondarily as a result of earlier experiences or learning. Strong support for this position comes from the extensive literature on the relationship between life events and depression. Paykel et al. (1969) found in a study of 185 hospitalized depressed patients that, compared to a matched control group from the community, the depressed patients experienced significantly more undesirable life events than did the community control subjects in the six months immediately prior to the symptomatic onset of depression. A qualitative analysis of the life events showed that exits (losses) from the social field rather than entrances into the social field (gains) particularly distinguished depressed patients from control subjects. The most discriminative individual event was "increase in arguments with spouse," which was of high frequency only in the depressed population. Brown and his colleagues (1973) have recently reported data which show that undesirable life events experienced in concentration are a causal link in the development of depression. They found that a large proportion of depressive disorders were directly the result of undesirable life events and that the onset of depression would not have occurred when it did, or at all, without the precipitating behavioral event(s).

Most depressions develop when anticipated or real personal failure becomes generalized. Such failure may occur in the form of a life event, as in the case of divorce, job loss, or severe illness, or it may occur less dramatically in the form of prolonged marital discord, goal frustration, or when one's work is taken for granted and is not given due recognition. A task analysis of many housewife-mother positions, for example, would fall into the latter category and may explain the relatively high incidence of clinical depression in this group. A number of variations on a behavioral formulation theme have been offered to account for depression—interpersonal disturbance (Stuart, 1967), learned helplessness as the result of a punitive and unpredictable environment (Seligman and Groves, 1970), loss of reinforcer effectiveness (Costello, 1972), lack of contingent positive reinforcement (Burgess, 1969), deficient interpersonal communication modes (Lewinsohn and Shaw, 1969), and failure to control interpersonal situations (Wolpe, 1971). Implicit in such behavioral formulations is the recognition that prolonged exposure to a relatively high ratio of personal success over failure is conducive to a feeling of personal effectiveness, while a relatively low personal success/failure ratio is conducive to depression.

Since an individual's feeling of how well he or she is doing is influenced by the reflected appraisal of significant others, family members are intimately involved in the development and reversal of depression in any family member. Families which are at high risk of one or both of its senior partners becoming depressed are those whose pattern of communication, work distribution, planning, and intrafamily reinforcement is competitive. A competitive social relationship is one which maximizes personal gain, whereas in a cooperative social relationship mutual interests are maximized (Davis, 1971). In family interactions, justifying one's position without considering another individual's point of view, routinely changing other people's priorities to accommodate one's own, not investing time to inquire into the interests of individual family members, and other apathetic or self-serving interaction strategies all qualify as examples of a competitive social relationship. Competitive interaction strategies are somewhat addictive and self-maintaining inasmuch as they result in an immediate benefit to the dominant individual, but over time the cumulative effect of negative outcomes for the less successful family member often results in low self-esteem, avoidance behavior, and depression. Once depression symptomatology becomes noticeable to other family members it most frequently evokes their sympathy which, in turn, facilitates the maintenance of the depression.

In changing family interaction from a competitive to a cooperative pattern, it is necessary to identify both the desirable and undesirable behavior within the family and then to alter, if necessary, the consequences of both types of behavior. This process is made easier by first identifying both the desirable and undesirable behavior and then noting what reinforcement is currently available for each type of behavior.

Family Interactions

There are several reasons why the nature of family interactions deserves scrutiny when depression is present. First, since it is the mother who is the family member most likely to become depressed (childhood depression is relatively rare and, although adolescent depression can be acute, its term is typically very short) and since she usually has primary responsibility for child management, her depressive state represents a strategic loss from the point of view of effective parenting. Considering the development and maintenance of depression, the identification of the consequences of the depressed parent's adaptive and depressive behavior is logistically more difficult in families where there is no obvious marital discord present and where no major life events can be identified as being formative in the development of the depression. As a result, it is quite possible to negate or be unaware of the effect of many undramatic and routine family interactions. One methodological approach to collecting this information is to involve the family in home recordings, as illustrated by the following case.

Mrs. A had been clinically depressed for 11 years and had been hospitalized repeatedly for periods of two weeks to four months throughout these 11 years. She lived with her husband and two teenage sons in a rural area and was deeply committed to her family. She specified a number of goal behaviors that she wanted to be able to achieve but could not consistently because of her depression. These target behaviors, which primarily involved domestic accomplishments, were assigned points as a function of their importance to Mrs. A. Similarly, undesirable behaviors, such as excessive weeping, periods of suicidal preoccupation, and social avoidance behavior, were assigned negative points. As a result, a total daily score of self-recorded points would indicate her level of productivity and her mood. Her husband and sons individually recorded their interactions with Mrs. A such that they received points for defined periods of interaction with her (e.g., watching television together, dinner conversation, going places together). Figure 1 shows the interaction of these daily scores and indicates a significant inverse relationship ($r = -.43$, $p < .05$). When Mrs. A was productive she received relatively little attention from her family, but when she behaved in a grossly depressed manner she received more attention than at any other time. This descriptive finding shows that Mrs. A's depressive behavior is more adaptive than domestic competence if she values family interaction. Separate analysis of the husband and two sons showed that

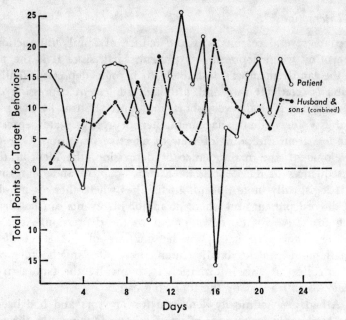

FIGURE 1. Relationship between a depressed mother's target behavior and her family's social interaction with her.

the attention Mr. A. gave his wife was indiscriminate in terms of her condition $(r = -.05)$. Both sons, however, tended to interact with their mother primarily when she was depressed $(r = -.54, p < .01; r = -.42, p < .05)$ and tended to ignore her when she was engaged in behavior that she considered to be important. This type of analysis is not only helpful in determining the relative amount of reinforcement awarded specific classes of behavior by family members, but it provides a contingency measure for each source of reinforcement.

The second reason why family interactions are of interest in depression is that such a large number of depression cases, particularly those resulting from marital discord, are characterized by relatively infrequent communication. In a previous study (McLean et al., 1973), we found that 20 out of 20 depressed patients claimed they did not communicate with their spouse. Home tape-recordings of verbal interactions between patient and spouse showed that these couples used a high proportion of negative, as compared to positive, verbal interchanges to justify their polarized position or to coerce one another into complying with their expectancies. After conjoint treatment, which consisted of (1) training in social learning principles, (2) home discussion sessions with feedback on the perception of one another's verbal communication, and (3) training in the construction and use of reciprocal behavioral contracts, there was a significant improvement in behavioral and mood measures and in the quality of verbal interchanges (i.e., proportionately fewer negative interchanges) in the behavior therapy group compared to a comparison treatment group. (Treatment for the comparison group varied as a function of the treatment agency, e.g., psychiatrist, general practitioner, social work agency, etc., but usually involved either medication, group therapy, individual psychotherapy, or some combination of these.) Subsequent analysis of the family verbal recordings in both treatment groups shows that, when responses to verbal interchanges were unpleasant (e.g., being ignored, receiving sarcasm or criticism, changing the topic), individual parents responded negatively 75.7% of the time. After treatment the behavior therapy group used relatively fewer negative interchanges compared to the comparison group ($F = 4.8$, $df = 1.32$, $p < .025$) for the same time period.

One interesting finding in these home-tape analyses has been the pervasive use of personal criticism in domestic conversations as a means to motivate other family members and to justify one's own position. Two responses appear highly predictable as a consequence of such personal criticism: (1) either conversation stops or the criticism is returned, and (2) any ongoing problem-solving is deterred or sidetracked. In not one of 40 home tape-recordings could a single case of personal criticism be identified as having been received as constructive. The familiar complaint "we don't talk any more" is a likely consequence of such aversive interchanges. The finding that depressed patients are more sensitive and show a significantly greater autonomic response to aversive stimuli than other people do (Lewinsohn et al., 1973) may account for the avoidance of anticipated negative verbal exchanges.

Another noteworthy feature of the taped verbal interactions is that appropriate behavior tended to be taken for granted, while criticism was reserved for unappreciated behaviors. The resultant tendency to avoid certain content areas (e.g., preferences in sexual practice, in-laws) seemed to preclude the possibility of successful resolution.

Influence of Parental Depression on Children

A critical question is: What effect, if any, does parental depression have on effective parenting? There are no empirical studies in the literature on this topic, but information from three sources provides indications that effective parenting and the absence of depression are related.

The first source involves *self-reports from depressed parents*. When patients from our previous study (McLean et al., 1973) were asked how they knew they were depressed, 68% of the depressed parents (19 out of 20 patients were parents) volunteered that they were no longer as effective in child management as they had been prior to the onset of depression. After treatment, the behavior therapy group patients indicated significant improvement in this area (scaled self-report) compared to the comparison treatment group (Mann-Whitney $U = 5$, $N1 = 6$, $N2 = 7$, $p <$ .01). A major factor, which can be attributed to the increased competence experienced by the behavior therapy patients as a function of treatment, is that treatment was conjoint, thereby ensuring spouse involvement in child management. Similar indications of concern over parenting abilities on the part of clinically depressed parents come from Weissman and Klerman (1973), who analyzed the content of 774 individual patient interviews and found that the topic of children was brought up and discussed by patients for periods ranging from 6 to over 15 minutes in 58% of all patient interviews.

A second source of information which indicates that poor parenting practices are concurrent with parental depression is the *effect of parental modeling*. A widely held belief in the depression literature is that endogenous depression has a genetic component which is manifested in a biochemical imbalance. To substantiate this hypothesis, frequent reference is made to family studies which note the incidence of depressive disorders within intact families over two generations. An alternative and more likely hypothesis, from the social learning point of view, is that depressed parents establish many of the necessary antecedent conditions for the subsequent development of depression in their own child. That is, if hopelessness, lack of assertiveness, fear of failure, indecisiveness, self-depreciation, and social withdrawal are modeled by one or both parents during the formative years when early social skills are acquired, it would be expected that their children would be more likely to develop depressive disorders in the future.

The third line of evidence that suggests parental depression reduces parenting effectiveness derives from studies in *self-esteem in preadolescents* by Coopersmith (1967). His approach was to contrast low- and high-self-esteem preadolescents (ages 10 to 12) and then to identify differential characteristics of both the youths and their parents' parenting policies. This evidence is oblique inasmuch as most parents of low-

TABLE 2

Characteristics Which Discriminate between Levels of
Self-Esteem in Preadolescent Youths
(from Coopersmith, 1967)

Low Self-Esteem	*High Self-Esteem*
—more sensitive to criticism.	—mother satisfied with father's involvement in child rearing.
—less willing to express contrary views.	
—mother has more frequent problems and anxieties.	—mother employed longer.
	—parents provide training in independence.
—mother limits youth's social relationships.	
—protected and indulged by parents.	—parents stress democratic parent/child relationships.

esteem youths are probably not depressed. It does indicate, however, the
kind of parenting required to avoid the development of low self-esteem
in children, which is a likely precursor of depression in adults. Among
the more important differences between these two groups in relation to
depression is the finding that the low-self-esteem youths were significantly more sensitive to criticism and less willing to take risks than
were the high-self-esteem youths (see Table 2). Since developing a strong
sense of self-esteem during the stage of youth is generally considered to
be advantageous, it would seem that a family with a depressed parent
is at a considerable disadvantage in its ability to develop high-self-
esteem characteristics in its children.

Taken together, the evidence available suggests two hypotheses regarding the presence of parental depression: (1) it renders parents markedly
less capable of effective parenting, and (2) it provides an opportunity
for children to acquire ineffective interpersonal coping strategies through
parental modeling.

CONCLUSIONS

Depression has been defined as a generalized feeling of anticipatory,
or real, personal failure. Rather than being an individual phenomenon,
parental depression inextricably involves other members of the family.
The nature of the events which are most often antecedent to depression
(e.g., poor marital communication, competitive interpersonal interchanges within the family, no viable means of earning personal recognition), as well as the limitations in personal competence imposed by the
depression disorder itself, diminishes the possibility of effective parent-

ing. Behaviorally oriented therapy programs can be effective in reversing the clinical state of depression in parents and reinstating their feeling of competence in parenting. Some of the essential features of a family treatment program for a depressed parent (this would have to be adjusted for a single-parent-family unit) are:

General

Family Involvement (1) The participation of the spouse is particularly crucial.

Positive Control (2) The family members must attempt to monitor their own daily interactions with one another to ensure that these interactions are *positive* in nature (e.g., showing appreciation, agreeing with one another, accepting responsibility, compromising difficulties, being affectionate). It is better to change behavior by consistently demonstrating appreciation when the other person does those things considered to be desirable.

Negative Control (3) Families must be consistently reminded that criticism as a form of punishment serves to inspire retaliation and promote psychopathology. Interactions must not be *negative* (e.g., complaining, making excuses, blaming, shouting).

Independence Training (4) All members of the family, particularly the depressed parent and the children, must have an opportunity to gain personal recognition for pursuing their goals and interests. Efforts must be invested to assist other family members in these pursuits until the events become self-supporting.

Specific

Contract (5) The family should negotiate or plan the different agendas and preferences of each member of the family in the form of a "contract" where a small number of specific expectancies of each other are written down in a manner that will make it clear whether the desired behavior was forthcoming. If doing something proves too difficult, it must be broken down into as small units as are necessary to guarantee that the person can complete them. Contracts should be reciprocal.

Conversation (6) Ensure daily 20-minute periods of home conversation during which the family can solve problems, discuss issues, etc., but members must do so only in a constructive and positive manner.

In our experience, such depression intervention programs require client supervision at the minimum rate of twice per week for the first few weeks and must emphasize change in small, tangible, and frequently occurring events at first.

The relationships between parental depression and parent effectiveness remain correlational in nature. Microanalysis of family interaction contingencies, however, provides a method of securing both assessment and treatment information from which causal relationships can be investigated.

REFERENCES

BECK, A. T.: *Depression.* New York: Harper and Row, 1967.

BROWN, G. W., HARRIS, T. O., and PETO, J.: Life events and psychiatric disorders. Part 2: Nature of causal link. *Psychol. Med., 3,* 159-176, 1973.

BURGESS, E. P.: The modification of depressive behaviors. In: R. O. Rubin and C. M. Franks (Eds.), *Advances in Behavior Therapy.* New York: Academic Press, 1969. Pp. 193-199.

COOPERSMITH, S.: *The Antecedents of Self-Esteem.* San Francisco: W. H. Freeman, 1967.

COSTELLO, C. G.: Depression: Loss of reinforcers or loss of reinforcer effectiveness? *Behav. Ther., 3,* 240-247, 1972.

DAVIS, J. D.: *The Interview as Arena.* Stanford, Cal.: Stanford U. Press, 1971.

DORZAB, J., BAKER, M., CADORET, R. J., and WINOKUR, G.: Depressive disease: Familal psychiatric illness. *Amer. J. Psychiat., 127,* 1128-1133, 1971.

FRIEDMAN, R. J., and KATZ, M. M. (Eds.): *The Psychology of Depression: Contemporary Theory and Research.* New York: Wiley, 1974.

LEWINSOHN, P. M., LOBITZ, C. W., and WILSON, S.: "Sensitivity" of depressed individuals to aversive stimuli. *J. Abnorm. Psychol., 81,* 259-263, 1973.

LEWINSOHN, P. M., and SHAW, D. A.: Feedback about interpersonal behavior as an agent of behavior change. *Psychotherapy and Psychosomatics, 17,* 82-88, 1969.

McLEAN, P. D., OGSTON, K., and GRAUER, L.: A behavioral approach to the treatment of depression. *J. Behav. Ther. and Exper. Psychiat., 4,* 323-330, 1973.

MADDISON, D., and DUNCAN, G. M.: *Aspects of Depressive Illness.* Edinburgh: Livingston, 1965.

National Institute of Mental Health, Psychiatric Services in General Hospitals 1969-1970, Rockville, Md.

PAYKEL, E. S., MYERS, J. K., DIENELT, M. N., KLERMAN, G. L., LINDENTHAL, J. J., and PEPPER, M. P.: Life events and depression. *Arch. Gen. Psychiat., 21,* 753-760, 1969.

PORTER, A. M. W.: Depressive illness in general practice. *Brit. Med. J., 1,* 773-778, 1970.

SELIGMAN, M. E., and GROVES, D.: Non-transient learned helplessness. *Psychosomatic Science, 19,* 191-192, 1970.

Statistics Canada, Mental Health Statistics, Ottawa, Ontario, 1951 . . . 1973.

STUART, R. B.: Casework treatment of depression viewed as an interpersonal disturbance. *Social Work, 12,* 27-36, 1967.

WEISSMAN, M. M., and KLERMAN, G. L.: Psychotherapy with depressed women: An empirical study of content themes and reflection. *Brit. J. Psychiat., 123,* 55-61, 1973.

WILLIAMS, T. A., KATZ, M. M., and SHIELD, J. A., JR. (Eds.): *Recent Advances in the Psychobiology of the Depressive Illnesses.* Washington, D. C.: U.S. Government Printing Office, 1972.

WINOKUR, G.: Depression spectrum disease: Description and family study. *Comprehensive Psychiat.,* 13, 3-8, 1972.

WOLPE, J.: Neurotic depression: Experimental analog, clinical syndromes and treatment. *Amer. J. Psychother.,* 25, 362-368, 1971.

14

Parents as Modifiers of Somatic Disorders

W. DOYLE GENTRY

Recent years have witnessed an increased use of psychological principles in the area of learning theory, not only for modifying behaviors traditionally covered under the rubric of mental health (Franks, 1969; Krasner, 1971), e.g., disorders such as depression, schizophrenia, and mental retardation, but also for modifying somatic disorders or problems related to physical health. The pioneering work of Miller (1969) and DiCara (1970) with respect to learning in the visceral or autonomic nervous system of animals provided a scientific basis from which to apply therapeutic techniques collectively labeled behavior modification and/or behavior therapy to a wide variety of somatic disorders, including: problems related to the heart, such as premature ventricular contractions (Weiss and Engel, 1971), cardiac arrhythmias (Engel and Melmon, 1968), and chronic atrial fibrillation (Bleecker and Engel, 1973); hypertension (Benson et al., 1971); asthma (Alexander et al., 1972; Alexander et al., 1973; Creer, 1970; Davis et al., 1973; Gardner, 1968; Moore, 1965; Neisworth and Moore, 1972); chronic pain (Fordyce, Fowler, Lehmann, and DeLateur, 1968; Fordyce, Fowler, and DeLateur, 1968; Fordyce et al., 1971); headaches (Budzynski et al., 1970; Budzynski et al., 1973; Lutker, 1971; Mitchell and Mitchell, 1971; Sargent et al., 1973; Yen and McIntire, 1971); spasms associated with cerebral palsy (Sachs, 1972; Sachs and Mayhall, 1971); spasmodic torticollis or wry neck (Agras and Marshall, 1965; Bernhardt et al., 1972; Brierley, 1967); neurodermatitis (Allen and Harris, 1966; Ratliff and Stein, 1968; Walton, 1960); epilepsy (Sterman and Friar, 1972; Sterman et al., 1974); diarrhea (Hedberg, 1973); and benign vocal nodules (Gray et al., 1965).

Most of the reports of behavior modification of somatic disorders have been case studies, and the majority of such attempts have been with adult patients. A sufficient number, however, have described work with children or adolescents and, in addition, have involved a parent as the therapist or modifier of the disorder in question; these warrant discussion. Specifically, the present paper (1) summarizes the application of two different psychological treatment models, i.e., the *operant* and the *respondent,* for effecting change(s) in somatic behavior, (2) reviews the various behaviors treated to date under each model and, most importantly, (3) focuses on the parent both as a potential cause of certain somatic disorders and as a change agent in modifying these disorders.

TREATMENT MODELS

The universal model for understanding and treating somatic disorders has been a *medical* or disease one. In this model, all overt, maladaptive physical behavior, e.g., a cough, a painful grimace, or the statement, "I have a headache!" merely represents symptoms or signs of some underlying pathological process or disease. The disease or underlying cause of the visible symptoms (behavior) is always inferred, whether or not it can be identified, and is essentially seen as organic or physiological in nature, e.g., germs, lesions, or viral infections. Consequently, the primary focus of treatment is aimed at chemically or surgically correcting the diseased state of the patient. Attention to the external somatic behavior is of only secondary importance and usually describes attempts at "symptom relief" or "symptom management."

A second model for understanding and treating somatic disorders is what might be called a *respondent* model in psychological terms. In many ways, it is very similar to the approach taken with the medical model just described. The observable somatic behavior in this model is a response to an underlying state of tension or anxiety characterized by both subjective and physiological properties. In some instances, the stimulus-response relationship between anxiety and the disorder in question is clearly identified, e.g., Budzynski et al. (1970) noted a close correspondence between electromyographic (EMG) activity in scalp and neck muscles and reported intensity of headaches in parents suffering from tension headaches. In other instances, this relationship is simply inferred. In either event, the focus of treatment is internal and is aimed at eliminating or reducing the anxiety/tension state of the patient. The therapeutic techniques employed include systematic desensitization, relaxation training, and corrective biofeedback.

Another psychological model for treating somatic disorders is the *operant* one. Here the emphasis is on the relationship between the overt somatic behavior and its consequences in the external environment. The behavior per se is defined as the operant and the derived consequences, positive or negative, as reinforcement. Thus, the motivating force or cause for the illness is seen as coming from outside the patient, rather than from inside, and as being social or interpersonal in nature, rather than organic or physiological. Treatment techniques include a variety of experimentally derived methods of delivering or withholding reinforcement, collectively termed operant conditioning or behavior modification, such as positive reinforcement, negative reinforcement, punishment, and extinction.

REVIEW OF THE LITERATURE

To date, ten studies have been published that describe the modification of somatic disorders in children or adolescents via either of the two psychological models noted above. These studies, along with a summary of the disorders dealt with, the ages of the patients, and the particular techniques employed, are presented in Table 1. As is evident from the table, the major effort in this area has been in the treatment of asthma, accounting for seven of the ten studies. The remaining three reports include the treatment of headaches, excessive scratching, and spasms associated with cerebral palsy. The patients ranged in age from 5 through 20 years, with many being below the age of 10. For the most part, i.e., in seven of the ten studies, the operant model of treatment was used to modify the somatic disorder.

In four separate studies, Alexander and co-workers (Alexander et al., 1972; Alexander et al., 1973; Creer, 1970; Davis et al., 1973) at the Children's Asthma Research Institute and Hospital were successful in reducing coughing behavior in severely asthmatic children by means of a Sidman avoidance procedure (i.e., avoiding electric shock through cough suppression), time-out from positive reinforcement (i.e., removal of positive consequences of hospitalization such as avoidance of schoolwork, socializing with other children, television, and T.L.C. from the nursing staff), relaxation training, and relaxation training augmented by biofeedback. In one study (Creer, 1970), the operant approach was instrumental in drastically reducing both the frequency and duration of hospitalizations; in two others (Alexander et al., 1972; Davis et al., 1973), it led to a noticeable change in the youngster's respiratory behavior, specifically the peak expiratory flow rate.

TABLE 1

Summary of Studies Involving the Modification of
Somatic Disorders

Studies	Year	Disorder	Age	Treatment
Alexander et al.	1973	Asthma	15	punsihment/shock Sidman avoidance
Alexander et al.	1972	Asthma	10-15	relaxation
Allen and Harris	1966	Scratching	5	extinction positive reinforcement (primary, tokens)
Creer	1970	Asthma	10	time-out from positive reinforcement
Davis et al.	1973	Asthma	6-10 11-15	relaxation biofeedback
Gardner	1968	Asthma	6	extinction positive reinforcement (toys, tokens)
Moore	1965	Asthma	—	relaxation suggestion reciprocal inhibition
Neisworth and Moore	1972	Asthma	7	extinction positive reinforcement (money)
Sachs and Mayhall	1971	Spasms	20	punishment/shock
Yen and McIntire	1971	Headaches	14	response cost

Neisworth and Moore (1972) and Gardner (1968) noted that a combination of extinction for coughing behavior and positive reinforcement for incompatible noncoughing behavior led to a reduction in asthmatic behavior in very young children. Extinction involved the termination of parental attention and/or medication following actual or threatened asthmatic attacks. Positive reinforcement involved giving the children money or tokens, exchangeable for toys, either for "settling down and relaxing" or for coughing less over a period of time. Using an ABAB reversal design, these procedures were shown to be quite effective in reducing asthmatic behavior.

Allen and Harris (1966) utilized a similar approach with a five-year-old child whose excess scratching behavior resulted in bleeding and large sores and scabs over the top part of her body. The child was ignored whenever she scratched herself, no matter how bloody the results, and rewarded with parental approval and attention whenever she engaged herself in constructive play activities and was not scratching. The child was also given gold stars and primary reinforcement (e.g., cookies, candy, beverage) for nonscratching behavior. At the end of six weeks of such treatment, the child was free from the destructive scratching behavior, and her scars had begun to heal. At a four-month follow-up, the successful outcome had been maintained.

Sachs and Mayhall (1971) demonstrated successful treatment of spastic behavior in a 20-year-old cerebral palsied male via punishment with painful electric shocks. The young man received a 0.75-second, 2.5-ma dc shock to his hand immediately following each gross head movement or spasm (i.e., irrelevant movement of arms, legs, or body) during daily 30-minute treatment sessions. Spastic behavior decreased from an average of between 54 and 82 responses per session during baseline (prior to punishment) to only 3 responses per session at the end of eight therapy sessions.

Yen and McIntire (1971) reported a case of a 14-year-old girl who initially complained of from two to seven headaches daily, and who experienced a rapid reduction in the frequency of such complaints as a consequence of a response-cost procedure. That is, the girl was required to compulsively report in writing each headache episode—its time of occurrence, its probable cause, and what she did about it—before she could complain verbally or receive any type of medication. The aim of the procedure was to disrupt the usual relationship between reporting the disorder verbally and receiving immediate positive social reinforcement (attention), rest, and medication. From the onset of treatment, the frequency of headache complaints was reduced to one per day and, by the end of five weeks, almost no complaints were reported. Follow-up revealed a continued absence of headaches.

Finally, Moore (1965) noted that relaxation alone, relaxation with suggestion, and reciprocal inhibition were all effective in altering the subjective experience of children suffering from asthma, i.e., they felt better and reported fewer attacks. However, only those patients treated with reciprocal inhibition evidenced objective improvement, i.e., their respiratory functioning improved.

The Role of the Parent

With regard to somatic disorders in children, parents are potentially causes of such disorders and in turn can serve as change agents for modifying them.

The idea that parents could cause somatic disorders was suggested in the writings of Miller (1969) and DiCara (1970) wherein they hypothesized that children could learn different patterns of somatic responses (e.g., gastric distress versus cardiovascular symptoms such as pallor and faintness) to anxiety-evoking situations (e.g., going to school for an important examination) depending on the reaction of the mother who may be differentially responsive to one or the other type behavior. It was made even more evident by comments such as the following by Alexander et al. (1973) regarding the treatment of an asthmatic boy:

> Briefly, it was noted that Marvin had a prior history of commanding attention within the family through a variety of aches and pains which his mother apparently reinforced with sympathy and support, while the other family members offered only minimal reinforcement. Shortly after Marvin's coughing began, it seemed to have become conditioned to a variety of stimuli: the odors of beef grease, shampoo, hair spray and bath soap. He voiced no other physical complaints. Unlike his previous complaints, however, the coughing was consistently reinforced by deep concern and attention from all members of the family. Eventually, a point was reached where the family's entire life pattern began to revolve around Marvin's coughing.
>
> The cough seemed to serve several functions for Marvin and his family: (1) it gained attention and leverage within the family for Marvin; (2) its management appeared to be the major mode through which Marvin and his mother related; (3) her concern and attention to the cough, in turn, seemed to be the primary way in which his mother attained feelings of self-esteem; and (4) it seemed to hold the family together by offering a focus which deflected the parents from facing major marital problems or dealing with other tensions in the family (p. 76).

The negative effects of this type of parental concern are also demonstrated in the case of the scratching child (Allen and Harris, 1966), where the mother was basically inattentive to her daughter except to criticize and berate her for scratching behavior, and in the Creer (1970) study, where the asthmatic youngsters were initially considered to be the "darlings of the nursing staff" (parent-surrogates) and received undue attention as a consequence of being sick and in the hospital.

Parents can also serve to modify these maladaptive somatic behaviors, however. In three of the studies covered, one or both parents were utilized as the primary change agent in reducing asthmatic wheezing and coughing (Neisworth and Moore, 1972), self-scratching (Allen and Harris, 1966), and headaches (Yen and McIntire, 1971). In yet another study, parents were used to maintain a successful program of treatment initiated in the hospital (Alexander et al., 1973), i.e., they kept records of the child's disruptive somatic behavior and learned to respond in ways which would not reinforce it. In two other studies (Creer, 1970; Gardner, 1968), techniques were used, such as extinction and time-out from positive reinforcement, which could easily be employed by parents either initially or as a follow-up to a nonparent therapist.

In fact, with the exception of punishment procedures involving electric shock (Sachs and Mayhall, 1971) and the Sidman avoidance procedure (Alexander et al., 1973), the operant techniques used were actually or potentially available for parental utilization in modifying disruptive somatic behaviors. The respondent techniques of relaxation, biofeedback, and reciprocal inhibition would seem less appropriate for use by parents from both a practical and economic standpoint.

PROBLEMS

Lest one get the idea that psychological techniques are entirely successful in treating all patients, child or adult, who manifest somatic disorders, a number of general problems are presented for consideration. These include: (1) the fact that this is a relatively new area of application and one without either sufficient scientific underpinning or clinical trials; (2) the problem that, of all the known physical illnesses, only a handful (12 in fact) have been treated via the techniques under discussion; (3) the fact that some critics may suggest that the initial success achieved in this area results from selecting patients with "hysterical" or "functional" disorders, as opposed to real or organic ones; (4) the fact that one may have to take into account minimal constitutional requirements before such techniques can be successful, especially with regard to changes in the autonomic nervous system; (5) the ever-present problem of competing reinforcement contingencies, i.e., the patient may be motivated by things other than parental attention, money, or even survival; and (6) the lack of knowledge as to which techniques or reinforcement strategies are the most effective or whether or not they are differentially effective across the various disorders.

In addition, there are specific considerations for utilization of parents in treating somatic disorders. First, the parents must be both willing and able to understand the potent effect their behavior can have in causing or maintaining maladaptive somatic behavior. If they are not attending to the child, they must attend; if their attention is entirely negative (criticism, physical punishment), they must change to a more positive approach; and, if they only focus on the problem behavior, they must learn to pay attention to other incompatible behavior manifested by their child. Second, they must not regard the child's somatic disorder as though it were "all in the head," but rather appreciate the fact that asthmatic behavior caused by social consequences or anxiety can be just as incapacitating and dangerous as that derived from a purely organic basis. The cases presented by Alexander et al. (1973) and Creer (1970), for example, described children whose asthmatic behavior led to loss of consciousness, numerous hospitalizations, and eventual institutionalization. Finally, of course, the parent must be systematic in both recording manifestations of the child's maladaptive somatic behavior and in reinforcing the behavior according to the treatment plan; an inconsistent or unsystematic parent (therapist) will not only fail to change the behavior in question, but in fact stands a good chance of making it worse.

FUTURE CONSIDERATIONS

One can only be optimistic about an increased use of behavioral techniques, both operant and respondent, in modifying somatic disorders in the future. In less than a decade, a wide variety of behaviors have been successfully treated by this approach, albeit in a relatively small number of individuals. Hopefully, as the interest in the area grows, the number and variety of cases and disorders will increase. Many of the disorders treated to date in adults, e.g., diarrhea and epilepsy, may also be treated in children. All of this will certainly include an important role for parents as primary or secondary modifiers of maladaptive somatic behavior.

REFERENCES

AGRAS, A., and MARSHALL, C.: The application of negative practice to spasmodic torticollis. *Amer. J. Psychiat.*, 122, 579-582, 1965.

ALEXANDER, A. B., MIKLICH, D. R., and HERSHKOFF, H.: The immediate effects of systematic relaxation training on peak expiratory flow rates in asthmatic children. *Psychosom. Med.*, 34, 388-394, 1972.

ALEXANDER, A. B., CHAI, H., CREER, T. L., MIKLICH, D. R., RENNE, C. M., and CORDOSO, R. R.: The elimination of chronic cough by response suppression shaping. *J. Behav. Ther. and Exper. Psychiat.*, 4, 75-80, 1973.

ALLEN, K. E., and HARRIS, F. R.: Elimination of a child's excessive scratching by training the mother in reinforcement procedures. *Behav. Res. and Ther.*, 4, 79-84, 1966.

BENSON, H., SHAPIRO, D., TURSKY, B., and SCHWARTZ, G.: Decreased systolic blood pressure through operant conditioning techniques in patients with essential hypertension. *Science*, 173, 740-742, 1971.

BERNHARDT, A. J., HERSEN, M., and BARLOW, D. H.: Measurement and modification of spasmodic torticollis: An experimental analysis. *Behav. Ther.*, 3, 294-297, 1972.

BLEECKER, E. R., and ENGEL, B. T.: Learned control of ventricular rate in patients with atrial fibrillation. *Psychosom. Med.*, 35, 161-175, 1973.

BRIERLEY, D.: The treatment of hysterical spasmodic torticollis by behavior therapy. *Behav. Res. and Ther.*, 5, 139-142, 1967.

BUDZYNSKI, T., STOYVA, J., and ADLER, C.: Feedback-induced muscle relaxation: Application to tension headaches. *J. Behav. Ther. and Exper. Psychiat.*, 1, 205-211, 1970.

BUDZYNSKI, T., STOYVA, J., ADLER, C., and MULLANEY, D.: EMG biofeedback and tension headache: A controlled outcome study. *Psychosomatic Medicine*, 35, 484-496, 1973.

CREER, T.: The use of time-out from positive reinforcement procedure with asthmatic children. *J. Psychosom. Res.*, 14, 117-120, 1970.

DAVIS, M. H., SAUNDERS, D., CREER, T., and CHAI, H.: Relaxation training facilitated by biofeedback apparatus as a supplemental treatment in bronchial asthma. *J. Psychosom. Res.*, 17, 121-128, 1973.

DiCARA, L. V.: Learning in the autonomic nervous system. *Scientific American*, 14, 117-120, 1970.

ENGEL, B. T., and MELMON, L.: Operant conditioning of heart rate in patients with cardiac arrhythmias. *Conditional Reflex*, 3, 130, 1968.

FORDYCE, W. E., FOWLER, R. S., and DeLATEUR, B.: An application of behavior modification technique to a problem of chronic pain. *Behav. Res. and Ther.*, 6, 105-107, 1968.

FORDYCE, W., FOWLER, R., LEHMANN, J., and DeLATEUR, B.: Some implications of learning in problems of chronic pain. *J. Chronic Diseases*, 21, 179-190, 1968.

FORDYCE, W., SAND, P., TRIESCHMAN, R., and FOWLER, R.: Behavioral systems analyzed. *J. Rehabilitation*, March-April, 29-33, 1971.

FRANKS, C. M.: *Behavior Therapy: Appraisal and Status*. New York: McGraw-Hill, 1969.

GARDNER, J. E.: A blending of behavior therapy techniques in an approach to an asthmatic child. *Psychotherapy: Theory, Research, and Practice*. 5, 46-49, 1968.

GRAY, B. B., ENGLAND, G., and MOHONEY, J. L.: Treatment of benign vocal nodules by reciprocal inhibition. *Behav. Res. and Ther.*, 3, 187-193, 1965.

HEDBERG, A. G.: The treatment of chronic diarrhea by systematic desensitization: A case report. *J. Behav. Ther. and Exper. Psychiat.*, 4, 67-68, 1973.

KRASNER, L.: Behavior therapy. *Annual Rev. Psychol.*, 22, 483-532, 1973.

LUTKER, E. R.: Treatment of migraine headache by conditioned relaxation: A case study. *Behav. Ther.*, 2, 592-593, 1971.

MILLER, N. E.: Learning of visceral and glandular responses. *Science*, 163, 434-445, 1969.

MITCHELL, K. R., and MITCHELL, D. M.: Migraine: An exploratory treatment application of programmed behavior therapy techniques. *J. Psychosom. Res.*, 15, 137-157, 1971.

MOORE, N.: Behavior therapy in bronchial asthma: A controlled study. *J. Psychosom. Res.*, 9, 257-276, 1965.

NEISWORTH, J. T., and MOORE, F.: Operant treatment of asthmatic responding with the parent as therapist. *Behav. Ther.*, 3, 95-99, 1972.

RATLIFF, R. G., and STEIN, N. H.: Treatment of neurodermatitis by behavior therapy: A case study. *Behav. Res. and Ther.*, 6, 397-399, 1968.

SACHS, D. A.: Behavioral analysis techniques and their application to cerebral palsy. Paper presented at American Psychological Association, Hawaii, 1972.

SACHS, D. A., and MAYHALL, B.: Behavioral control of spasms using aversive conditioning with a cerebral palsied adult. *J. Nerv. and Ment. Disease*, 152, 362-363, 1971.

SARGENT, J. D., GREEN, E. E., and WALTERS, E. D.: Preliminary report on the use of autogenic feedback training in the treatment of migraine and tension headaches. *Psychosom. Med.*, 35, 129-135, 1973.

STERMAN, M. B., and FRIAR, L.: Suppression of seizures in an epileptic following sensorimotor EEG feedback training. *Electroenceph. Clin. Neurophysiol.*, 33, 89-95, 1972.

STERMAN, M. B., MacDONALD, L. R., and STONE, R. K.: Biofeedback training of the sensorimotor EEG rhythm in man: Effects on epilepsy. *Epilepsia*, 15, 395-416, 1974.

WALTON, D.: The application of learning theory to the treatment of a case of neurodermatitis. In: H. Eysenck (Ed.), *Behaviour Therapy and the Neuroses*. Oxford: Pergamon Press, 1960. Pp. 272-274.

WEISS, T., and ENGEL, B. T.: Operant conditioning of heart rate in patients with premature ventricular contractions. *Psychosom. Med.*, 33, 301-322, 1971.

YEN, S., and McINTIRE, R. W.: Operant therapy for constant headache complaints: A simple response-cost approach. *Psychol. Reports*, 28, 267-270, 1971.

15

The Development of Discriminative Stimulus Materials to Increase Communication Between Parents and Deaf Children

ALLISON ROSSETT

and

TODD EACHUS

A recurring issue in the application of principles of behavior to social problems is that of "who shall select and who shall decide." Whenever the efficacy of behavior modification procedures is demonstrated, critics imbued with nonempiricist values raise issues concerned with the selection of target behaviors, consequences, and reinforcers. A systematic prompting of individual parents' communication strengths and weaknesses, and the transition from statements of individual problems to the application of behavioral procedures are presented in this paper. Based on individual response to visual prompts within a group setting, parents and leaders make joint decisions as to target behaviors, consequences, and reinforcers.

When behavior analysts concern themselves with areas of human functioning which are emotionally toned or closely tied to basic human functions, the problems of ethics and morality are compounded. The analysis of those behaviors involved in parenting is particularly subject to emotionally stated arguments concerning the selection of target behaviors, the use of extrinsic reinforcers, and the manipulation of behavior. Parenting is certainly one of the most complex and critical of human functions. The likelihood of greater resistance to behavior modification procedures than that which is ordinarily voiced is increased when analyzing parent-child relationships.

With the increased success of behavior modifiers in generating effective programs in schools, clinics, residential institutions, penal facilities, and with individuals, the press for reliable and efficient methods for generating substance and structure for programs has also increased. Ordinarily, individual behavior modifiers generate training programs for specific audiences. That is, little attention has been paid to the process of identifying the ways in which such people as teachers, counselors, and ward attendants select particular student or patient behaviors which *should* be increased or decreased in frequency. Undoubtedly, a few catastrophic errors have been made in the selection of target or terminal behaviors.

Further, most behavior modification programs depend for their effectiveness on the capabilities of the individuals running the program to evoke, consequate, and develop generalized behaviors in the other individuals concerned. With the increased frequency and number of programs involving behavior modification, *there is an increasing requirement for procedures to generate certain behaviors among given audiences*. Two ends can be achieved through such procedures. The target audience for a program can (1) identify the specific terminal behaviors for the program and (2) generate those stimulus conditions which are most likely to produce the behaviors desired by program participants.

Of particular importance in the development of behavior modification programs is the generation of terminal behaviors which are suitable for a widespread audience of clients. That is, classroom teachers are faced with problems in common, and parents learn to cope with the manifold problems of child rearing regardless of circumstances or location. Teaching and parenting can be identified as coherent, consistent repertoires of human functioning. By turning to the verbal communities of teachers, parents, and program developers, one can obtain reliable data with which to generate materials and procedures for widespread application to those verbal communities in general.

The process reported here for the development of discriminative stimuli to change certain verbal behaviors can be briefly described as an extension of the statement, "If you need to know what they want, go ask them." Simply put, the concern is with utilizing the information available in a verbal community to frame and structure the widespread application of behavior procedures. The dangers inherent in selection of terminal behaviors by an individual can be avoided through utilization of a systematic process to obtain such information from the verbal community concerned. Also, processes can be utilized to insure that programs are built which result in the generation of appropriate behavior from participants by developing discriminative stimuli based on the operationalization of goal statements from members of that particular verbal community.

The application reported here of such developmental procedures is directed at the special problems related to parenting of deaf children by hearing adults.

THE NEED FOR THE PROGRAM

Young deaf children rely more on their parents than do their hearing peers. They turn to these parents for help with all of the unknowns that are easily inferred by a hearing child through supplementary contacts. They turn to these parents for the fun and games and language that other children receive from constant interaction with varying people. They will turn to their parents for the experiences that their youth and deafness make difficult. Sesame Street, the soap operas, and the neighborhood kids cannot provide deaf children with the essential stimulation that some parents fail to provide.

Deafness makes a tremendous impact on communication between parent and child. Schlesinger and Meadow (1972) state that ". . . the primary handicap imposed by early childhood deafness is that it jams and weakens communication between the child and others in his environment."

Mindel and Vernon (1971) and Rainer and Altshuler (1967) provide a basic picture of the *angst* involved in communication between hearing parents and deaf children. Goss (1970), Altman (1973), Simmons-Martin (1972), and Schlesinger and Meadow (1972) have provided specific research describing the interactions which occur in a home with a deaf child. Their work sheds additional light on the shape and strength of the intrusion that deafness makes within a home. Goss (1970) compared the language used by mothers of hearing children with the language used by mothers of deaf children. He found that the mothers of hearing children were more likely to ask questions, to ask for opinions, and to use language showing solidarity and agreement. On the other hand, he found that mothers of deaf children were more likely to show disagreement, to appear tense, and to make suggestions. These mothers of the deaf were not as likely as the mothers of hearing children to use verbal praise. Considering the impact of parents in stimulating language growth through their own verbal language (Levenstein and Sunley,

1967), there is an obvious importance in these major differences in parental communication with deaf and hearing children.

Simmons-Martin (1972) observed mother-infant interactions in homes of hearing children and listed the frequency of their occurrence. From the most frequently occurring to the least frequently occurring she listed the following activities: holding, talking, talking to infant, feeding, and looking at face. Simmons-Martin finds that, in a home with a deaf infant, the talking and the talking to the infant are likely to be extinguished. The deaf child fails to provide the pivotal reinforcement for that important form of parent-child communication.

Schlesinger and Meadow (1972) describe their observation of communication between hearing parents and deaf children in *Sound and Sign*. From counseling sessions with parents and home observations, they observe that hearing parents of deaf children using total communication rely on an abundance of tactile stimuli and frequently run toys and fingers over the deaf child's face and head. They have often observed parents making signs right on the infant's or child's body. In a comparison study of maternal interaction with hearing parents of deaf children and hearing children, Schlesinger and Meadow found highly significant differences in interaction behaviors. Mothers of deaf children were rated as significantly less flexible, permissive, encouraging, and imaginative. The mothers of deaf children were also rated as significantly more intrusive and didactive. These blatant and major differences in communication and child-rearing patterns were definitely related to the deaf child's communication deficit. When backgrounds of the 60 mothers were screened for significant personality characteristics and education or ethnic variables, the analyses still pointed to deafness as the distinguishing variable.

A study by Altman (1973) focused on ten deaf children. She used professionals to rate the children on their communicative competence. These children were distinguished by their one- or two-word utterances and it was found that their mothers gave out more facts and information than did the mothers of the children rated as more competent communicators. Mothers with children rated as more competent tended to speak more frequently and had more to say when they did speak.

From an oralist's perspective, the Altman study described the characteristics of mothers of deaf children rated as being highly competent communicators. She found that mothers of the more competent children corrected their children more often. They also demanded more frequent repetitions of sentences and words from the deaf four- to seven-year-olds in the study. These same mothers asked more questions of their children, and the children responded more often to their mothers' queries. In general, Altman found that the mothers of the more competent communicators offered more feedback to the children, placed more pressure to excel on the children, used more positive reinforcers, manifested more positive affection and warmth, and introspected more frequently on their performance as mothers of deaf children. Based on her observations, a program, even a total communication program, should be aimed at evoking or increasing the frequency of the described parental behaviors.

The work of Stuckless and Birch (1966), Quigley and Frisina (1961), Stevenson (1964), Schlesinger and Meadow (1972), Vernon and Koh (1970), Howse and Fitch (1972), and Brill (1960, 1969) supports the utilization of sign language and finger-spelling by parents with their infant and very young deaf children. Reacting to the ancient contention that the early use of signs is harmful to the speech development of the deaf person, Stuckless and Birch (1966) found that there was no significant difference in the speech intelligibility of deaf children between those educated in early manual communication (sign language and finger-spelling) classes and those educated in early oral education programs. While the speech intelligibility figures offered no significant differences, significant differences in reading, speech reading (lip reading), and written language were found in the early manual communication groups over the early oral group. Vernon and Koh (1970) concur in the findings which show higher educational achievement in children educated through early manual communication. Howse and Fitch (1972) studied the effects of a sign language orientation course for parents on the expressive language of deaf children and their hearing parents. They found a significant increase in the desired expressive language after the parents' exposure to sign language. Schlesinger and Meadow (1972), looking at deaf parents with their deaf children, attributed the significant educational differences to the early parental input of language via total communication and the resulting relative ease of childrearing. They reiterate the Howse and Fitch finding of improved parent-child communication based on the introduction of sign language into the interaction.

The requirement for improved means for assessing parents of deaf children is evident in the studies described. The aspects of parent-child interaction which seem detrimental to the development of deaf children as well as those which seem supportive of it are apparent. The development of the mediated program described here relies on those data reported by others in which they guided the refinement of information obtained from parents and children.

THE DEVELOPMENTAL PROCESS

In the fall of 1971, the Northeast Regional Media Center for the Deaf, a federally funded Office of Education, Bureau for the Education of the Handicapped project, gathered 14 deaf adolescents and asked them for assistance in program development. The youths were very explicit about their needs and the direction project efforts should take in response to these needs. Clearly and directly, they made these statements:

"My parents don't know how to communicate with me."

"My parents are overprotective."

"My parents are ashamed of me. They send me to spend weekends with my friends who have deaf parents."

"My parents don't understand me."

"I can't understand my parents."

"My parents should show more love."

"If we can learn to communicate better, then everything will be O.K."

The deaf adolescents wrote, signed, and/or spoke a message which left little room for confusion. They urged the development of a program to improve communication between hearing parents and their deaf children. Consultation with parents, teachers, and administrators helped to more clearly define the problem suggested by the adolescents. Parents and adolescents, when asked for further information, provided the feedback necessary to the development of the program. Visits to parent groups were made; ideas obtained there generated visual materials; visuals and written accompaniment were then presented to the deaf adolescents and to parents, educators, and counselors of the deaf. This process was repeated throughout the course of the 18-month developmental period.

These steps revealed an almost universal progression of experiences and concerns faced by parents of deaf children. These experiences and concerns were reiterated by the educators of the deaf, the deaf adolescents, and the parents who served as resources in the development of the program. Visits to parent groups yielded graphic descriptions and poignant discussions of key moments and interactions in the parenting of a deaf child. These moments and interactions were translated into the discussion-stimulating visuals which serve as the basis for the program.

A visit with a parent group at the Robbin's Speech and Hearing Clinic, in Boston, Massachusetts, was typical of the way the ideas for the open-ended visuals were generated. Parents talked about restaurants and their children's temper tantrums in these restaurants. Parental concern about people associating the annoying tantrum behavior with deafness was evident. The parents' task of deciding whether or not to put the hearing aid on the child in public caused them considerable pain and evoked discussion of discipline, public reaction to deafness, necessity for amplification, and the self-concept of the deaf child. Another similar and meaty discussion centered around blindness and deafness. The six mothers in the room were evenly split on the subject of which was the most debilitating handicap on the cihld? What are the functions of a child's hearing? What is the likely impact of congenital deafness as compared to adventitious deafness? What do individual parents feel about deafness, and how do they communicate these feelings to their child? Another area highlighted by the Robbins group was responding to strangers' questions about deafness generated by the young child's hearing aid. The parents described incidents in supermarkets, trains, and playgrounds, and they asked important questions: What should I say? Why do people ask these questions? What is the germane information that I should impart? Why do I feel anger at these people? Should I tell my child about the questioning? Should I invite the child to respond if she/he is capable of responding?

These are three examples of parent discussion and description of incidents; visits with many other parent groups provided additional material. The incidents they all described resulted in ideas about parent concerns and the generation of visuals which depict these concerns. Once in systematized visual form, they stimulated parent verbal behavior or behavior rehearsal related to improved interaction with their deaf child.

Deaf adolescents were another source of ideas for the discriminative stimuli. Their suggestions for this project were elicited in a structured fashion. They were asked to respond to these open-ended questions: (1) I am happiest with my parents when we . . .; (2) I am saddest with my parents when we . . .; (3) A happy time that I can remember was when we . . .; (4) A sad time that I can remember was when we. . . . Their responses suggested many important moments and incidents in interaction with their parents. They wrote about mealtime, telephone conversations with distant relatives, family parties, sibling privileges in which they could not participate, curiosity over television newscasts, and social relationships with hearing peers. Their descriptions of parent-child interactions surrounding key issues provided the impetus for many other visuals.

The needs and concerns of parents of deaf children serve as the themes for the visuals. These visuals elicit the interparent behavior likely to bring about change in the parents' communication with their deaf children. The focus is on process; the focus is on parents serving as behavior modifiers in an effort to increase the quality of their interactions with their deaf children. This improvement comes out of the discussion stimulated by the visuals and the direction provided to the leader by the facilitator's manual.

<hr />

FORM AND CONTENT OF THE PROGRAM

There is ample support for the contention that *effective parent education—education which will yield an increase in the selected parent and/or child behaviors—can be brought about through a focus on parent and child behaviors and parent education in behavior modification.* The program described in this paper creates an environment to bring about this parent behavior change.

Work on the application of operant theory to child rearing has been carried out by Allen and Harris (1966) and Hall and Broden (1967). Their suggestions have been utilized in seeking to demonstrate the effectiveness of parents in changing their children's behaviors (Wahler and Erikson, 1969). Additional applications of behavioral principles to home settings yield plentiful data supporting their use in decreasing children's maladaptive behaviors (Knight et al., 1971; O'Leary and Becker, 1967). The needs of exceptional children and parents of these children have also been met with these procedures.

Mira (1967) details the effectiveness of these operant procedures with deaf children and their parents. When several parents of deaf children described the marked negativism of their children, Mira trained them to institute time-out procedures when the child demonstrated the described negativism. The parent indicates (through signs or a combination of signs and vocal language, "When you do that, you can't stay in the room with us.") that this negativism was unacceptable behavior. Mira designed similar applications of operant procedures for children who refused to wear hearing aids and for some who were foot stompers. In all cases, there was a decrease in the target behavior(s). Mira suggests that the special potency of behavior modification over traditional psychoanalytic treatment for children with communication disorders is based on its freedom from reliance on verbal instruction as reinforcements. The Carpenter and Augustine (1973) study of four parents with children with communication disorders yielded almost as striking results. In three out of the four homes, the parents trained in behavior change techniques related significant improvement in their child management and communication skills.

While not yet carried out with deaf children, two studies—Herbert and Baer (1972) and Kogan et al. (1972)—have obvious applications to children with communication limitations. Herbert and Baer demonstrate how uncomplicated parent education procedures can bring about desired increases in the parents' and children's behaviors. In this study, parents were given wrist counters and told to attend more frequently to selected desired behaviors. This instruction and the counter yielded large increases in the parents' attention and the children's demonstration of the desired behavior. The Kogan et al. study shows similar promise, but with a far larger and more comprehensive approach. Computer diagnosis of videotaped mother-child interactions was used to prescribe remediation. The computer quantified the frequencies of specific behaviors within general classes of interaction like warmth overtures, child's solicitation of guidance, and physical demonstration of affection. The trainers then worked with parents to increase and decrease selected interaction behaviors.

These studies support and detail the application of operant procedures to parent-child interactions. The effectiveness of these procedures is assured; what is not always assured is the method of getting at individual needs and of selecting consequences to structure programs. Questions obviously remain concerning the creation and utilization of an environment aimed at the evocation of deficits in communication behaviors and the structuring of programs to respond to these deficits. The NRMCD program, a program designed to provide this environment, is composed of the following major components:

1. *Stimulus, open-ended visuals.* Stimulus visuals are materials which precipitate rather than complete the educational process. They are important not for what they are, but for what they begin in the group which views them. The visuals provide no answers; rather they provide the impetus for individual answer-finding or additional question-posing. The open-ended, unresolved format utilizes the basic communication situations universal to families with a deaf child while encouraging individual suggestions for parent communication behaviors. The open format stimulates parents to observe the strengths and weaknesses in

their communication behaviors. Procedures based on these statements can then be developed in concert with parents. The focus of these materials and the concomitant procedures is the systematizing and structuring of an environment to bring about change in parent behavior with deaf children.

2. *A facilitator's manual.* The facilitator's manual enables someone who is unfamiliar with the visuals but who knows something about deafness and/or parent education and/or being the parent of a deaf child to lead a group of parents towards an increase in selected communication behaviors. The manual discusses each visual in light of the basic visual content, the questions facilitators should raise (both affective and cognitive), the parent concerns and reactions touched on in the visual, and the parent communication behaviors applicable to the situation. The written treatment of the visuals is based on the operationalization by many parents and educators of the deaf of "effective parent-child communication." The listing of specific behaviors which would be observed in a home with such effective communication provides the suggested parent behaviors in response to each visual. Decisions about optimal behavior and additions to the listing would be made by individual parents in consultation with professionals. Appropriate leadership behaviors, those actions likely to bring the parents of the deaf to an increase in communication behaviors, are detailed in this manual.

3. *Parent groups.* The utilization of these materials (visuals and manual) relies on the direction and maintenance of a parent group. This form of learning opportunity is based on a strong belief in the ability of parents to educate other parents and in the importance of parents and leaders becoming an information resource for each other.

4. *Parent self-evaluation via parent checklisting of communication behaviors.* Because the visuals are designed to change what parents actually do in their homes with their deaf children, there are accompanying checklists. These checklists ask the parent to indicate the frequency of certain communication (vocal and nonvocal) behaviors. They enable the parent to look at himself/herself at the beginning of, during, and at the termination of the program. This consistent self-evaluation increases transfer of learning between parent group sessions and home communication behaviors.

5. *Bibliographies and Northeast resource listing.* Parents need to know where to go for information about deafness. Parents need to know *how* to become more knowledgeable about deafness so that they can begin making informed decisions for their young deaf child. The facilitator's manual answers these questions. Parents are provided with annotated

information on print, place and people resources on exceptionality, parent education, and deafness. A geographical listing of parent education programs for parents of deaf children is also provided.

The open-ended visuals depict hearing parents and deaf children in likely interaction situations. They freeze the depicted individuals at decision and interaction points, and stimulate behavior rehearsal from the parents who view them. The following visuals and written treatment provide examples of this utilization of visuals as discriminative stimuli for parents of the deaf. Operant procedures, based on needs and concerns evoked by the visuals, are then structured and instituted to bring about the increase in parent-child interaction.

In addition to including a presentation of suggested questions and activities to accompany the visuals, sample themes for discussion, and reactions by parents who have already viewed the visuals, the facilitator's manual provides a listing of suggested parent behaviors evoked by the situation portrayed in the visuals.

THE RESPONSE TO THE PROGRAM

In addition to the frequent presentation of the partially developed program to parent and educator groups, a more complete version of the program was placed in three field sites in the northeastern United States. The results from formative evaluation have been used in the improvement of the mediated program.

The major goals of the formative evaluation were to measure the impact of one program in light of its ability to bring about an increase in parent-selected communication behaviors and to solicit verbal statements from parents on necessary changes in and additions to the program.

Parents in the field test sites were asked to select from one to four questions dealing with differing communication behaviors. After the selection of these questions for the Communication Behaviors Checklist, they were asked to self-record the number of times each day that they performed the behavior asked about in the question. Parents were provided with instructions on how to accomplish the self-recording and were given forms for this self-measurement.

The Communication Behaviors Checklist instrument provided data which enabled us to look at the impact of the NRMCD program over time, i.e., at the end of each week and at the end of the six-week exposure. It also provided data for looking at group change in average behaviors per selected question. Most importantly, this instrument

FIGURE 1

Suggested Parent Behaviors for Figure 1:

(1) Parents discuss the child's safety and methods to assure it;

(2) Parents seek out help in finding the best way to arrange their home and immediate environment to protect the child;

(3) Parents discuss special dangers caused by the child's deafness and how to alleviate these dangers;

(4) Parents tell the child about danger spots in home and community;

(5) Parents tell the child how to avoid dangerous situations by setting down clearly defined and explained rules;

(6) Parents communicate these danger spots and protective rules in various ways—talking, drawing, signing, pantomiming possible situations;

(7) Parents set up a situation to make sure that the child understands and follows protective limits.

FIGURE 2

Suggested Parent Behaviors for Figure 2:

(1) Parents discuss the likelihood of their hurried and sometimes emotional interchanges being misunderstood by the deaf child;

(2) Parents try to avoid rapid and hostile exchanges in front of the deaf child;

(3) Parents take time to explain to the child that they are not angry at the child and that she/he is not directly involved in the dispute;

(4) Parents ask the deaf child to question them about the argument she/he has observed;

(5) Parents answer the questions asked by the child which they judge to be appropriate;

(6) When disputes which involve emotional responses are encountered on TV and in films, parents communicate with their child about these emotions;

(7) Parents draw parallels for the child between emotions portrayed in the media and the child's observations of interactions in the home.

FIGURE 3

Suggested Parent Behaviors for Figure 3:

(1) Parents discuss the difficulties of rapid, emotional communication with their deaf child;

(2) Parents discuss the deaf child's feelings about seeing communication going on all around him/her at a place like the dinner table;

(3) Parents discuss the importance of including the deaf child with the hearing children and plan for a rotating individual to take responsibility for interpreting or repeating;

(4) Parents draw, sign, or talk to the child about what is going on at the dinner table;

(5) Parents ask the deaf child's opinion during conversation;

(6) Parents encourage the hearing siblings to ask the deaf child's opinion;

(7) Parents ask the deaf child to relate a story or incident in her/his day.

FIGURE 4

Suggested Parent Behaviors for Figure 4:

(1) Parents talk to each other about what the child does well and likes to do;

(2) Parents talk to deaf adults and parents of deaf children about the jobs which do not depend on hearing;

(3) Parents talk to their child about his/her likes and abilities and what he/she sees for the future;

(4) Parents discuss their child and his/her abilities with the teachers and administration at the child's school;

(5) Parents discuss their work with the child and answer questions about it;

(6) Parents take the child to observe varying jobs which are related to his/her interests and abilities;

(7) Parents invite deaf adults with varying occupations to their home;

(8) Parents encourage the deaf child to talk with deaf adults and vocational placement persons about options for careers.

offered information on individual parents and their self-perceptions of selected communication behaviors with their deaf children during the course of the NRMCD.

Before concentrating on changes in individuals' totals, it is useful to examine the group averages. Numbers were arrived at by taking an individual parent's total behaviors per week and dividing by the number of questions selected by that parent; the results of these computations were then averaged by group. This process yielded weekly group means for behaviors per selected questions.

The oral group in Longmeadow, Massachusetts, showed the most steady increase in average frequency/question. The means for this group also show that parents reporting generally lower frequencies of communication behavior at the onset of the program made the greatest gains during and after exposure to the program. The oral communication group in Hartford, Connecticut, made slight gains in frequency of communication behaviors. Interestingly, several parents in the oral groups stated that they felt the behavior checklisting was a strong positive part of the program, and/or they intended to continue doing the behavior checklisting. The positive results of these first two group averages reflect this enthusiasm for the process of checklisting, an intrinsic part of the program.

The total communication group's averages show less change over time. The five weekly averages show a range of slightly less than 4. The difference between the week-one average and the week-five average is 1.4, a small decrease in average frequency per question. At the onset of the program, the average of the total parent group, the group which failed to show marked increases, was considerably higher than the week-one average of 11.7 behaviors per question.

Individual parent averages reflect group trends. Most of the parents who continuously and consistently participated in the behavior checklisting showed increases in frequencies of communication behaviors with their deaf children. Better than 63% of the responding parents self-reported a higher frequency of selected communication behaviors at the end of the six-week NRMCD program than they did at the beginning. The remaining 37% reported sharp (a drop of 20 or more) decreases in only 3 of the 22 cases. Within the 63% who reported an increase from week one to week five, 7 of the 14, or 50%, were sharp (increase of 20 or more) gains. Only 3 of the parents reported virtually unchanged frequency scores over the course of the six weeks. These 16% of the parents reported frequencies which fluctuated only slightly (5 or less) from earlier or later scores.

TABLE 1

Mean Quantity and Type of Interactions..

Group	N	M Parent-Facilitator	M Parent-Parent	M Individual
oral	7	12.29	19.29	31.57
oral	14	6.07	8.0	14.07
total	9	15.11	22.33	37.66

In addition to effecting an increase in parent communication behaviors with deaf children, the materials evoked parent-facilitator and parent-parent interchanges. Table 1 lists the mean number of interchanges and the direction of these interchanges.

It is interesting to note the greater mean of parent-parent interactions than parent-facilitator interactions in all three groups. Also, the oral group from Hartford, the group with the largest *n,* did not show the same pronounced gap in the quantity of the different types of interactions. A substantiation for the recommendation to diminish size of groups implementing the NRMCD program should be pointed out here. The individual number of interactions in this oral Hartford group was significantly less than in the other groups. Certainly, it is plausible to attribute this difference to the size of the group.

Verbal feedback from parents included specific suggestions for changes in the program. A list of suggestions which have been incorporated into the program follows.

1. The facilitator should present options and encourage parents to make decisions. Facilitators should not tell parents what to do.

2. Parents should be given more suggestions for possible answers to their children's questions.

3. Group should focus more on "how to handle certain situations rather than so much free discussion."

4. More visuals should be focused on the experiences of parents and their 7-14 year olds.

5. There is a need for the inclusion of more parents of deaf teenagers.

6. Expand the program so that mothers and fathers can attend.

7. Limit discussion of visuals to no more than 15 minutes.

8. Increase the attendance of parents.

9. Include deaf adolescents and their parents in the groups.

10. Questions following the visuals should not be repetitious.

11. The parent education sessions should be longer (in weeks?) and have more continuity.

12. Deaf adults should be included in the program.

The suggestions of parents, their behavior change, and the analysis of interactions evoked by the program have resulted in changes in the form and content of the program. Additional visuals, specific directions for deaf adolescents' and adults' involvement, ideas for increased parent attendance, and an operant resource listing are the major additions made in response to the formative evaluation.

CONCLUSION

The development of the program for improving parent-child communication rested on a continuous process of determining the needs of parents and deaf children through direct participation. By basing the content and format of the program on the actual difficulties and problems of parents of deaf children, we have identified behaviors which are consistently seen as desirable for and essential to the parenting of a deaf child. By refining visual materials through feedback from parent groups, we have assured that the nature and sequence of the program address common requirements and evoke verbal behavior which can be easily shaped to improve parent-child communication.

The developmental process which has been used was not intended to provide a complete program. No specific program elements have been included which are concerned with the competence of the individual program managers or precise recording procedures for use in homes by parents of deaf children. Instead, we have focused on the process of identifying behaviors which will measurably improve communication between parents and children.

Through directly involving the verbal community in the identification and selection of target behaviors, we have systematized the determination of what behaviors should be acquired. The difficult issues surrounding change in complex areas of human functioning have been addressed directly by the straightforward procedure of analyzing and relying upon the individuals needing change.

Obviously, not all of the areas of application for which behavior modification procedures are useful can utilize the strategies of this program. Such clients as institutionalized retardates cannot clearly voice the terminal objectives of greatest concern for their welfare. Teachers, parents, businesses, and others, however, can describe accurately their goals and objectives in precise, operational terms. This paper has presented a program for prompting such statements as exemplified by the concomitant planning from parents of the deaf.

REFERENCES

ALLEN, E. K., and HARRIS, R.: Elimination of a child's excessive scratching by training the mother in reinforcement procedures. *Behav. Res. and Ther.*, 5, 79-84, 1966.

ALTMAN, E. D.: Some Factors in Mother-Child Interaction Related to Language Competence in Children with Severe Congenital Deafness. Paper presented at the 44th Annual Eastern Psychological Association, Washington, D. C., May 1973.

BRILL, R. S.: A study in the adjustment of three groups of deaf children. *Exceptional Children*, 26, 464-466, 1960.

BRILL, R. S.: The superior IQ of deaf children of deaf parents. *The California Palms*, 1-4, 1969.

CARPENTER, R. L., and AUGUSTINE, E. L.: A pilot program for parent-clinicians. *J. Speech and Hearing Disorders*, 38, 48-57, Feb. 1973.

GOSS, R. N.: Language used by mothers of deaf children and mothers of hearing children. *Amer. Annals of the Deaf*, March 1970.

HALL, R. V., and BRODEN, M.: Behavior change of brain-injured children through social reinforcement. *J. Exper. Child Psychol.*, 5, 463-479, 1967.

HERBERT, E. W., and BAER, D. M.: Training parents as behavior modifiers: Self-recording of contingent attention. *J. Appl. Behav. Anal.*, 5, 139-149, 1972.

HOWSE, J. M. DeSALLE, and FITCH, J. L. Effects of parent orientation in sign language on communication skills of pre-school children. *Amer. Annals of the Deaf*, Aug. 1972.

KNIGHT, M., HASAZI, S., and McNEIL, M.: A home based program for the development of reading skills for pre-schoolers. In: E. Ramp and B. Hopkins (Eds.), *A New Direction for Education: Behavior Analysis*. Lawrence, Kansas: U. of Kansas, Department of Human Development, 1971.

KOGAN, K. L., GORDON, B. N., and WINBERGER, H.: Teaching mothers to alter interactions with their children: Implications for those who work with children and parents. *Childhood Ed.*, 107-110, 1972.

LEVENSTEIN, P., and SUNLEY, P.: An effect of stimulating verbal interaction between mothers and children around play materials. *Amer. J. Orthopsychiat.*, 37, 334-335, 1967.

MINDEL, E., and VERNON, M.: *They Grow in Silence*. Silver Spring, Md.: National Association for the Deaf, 1971.

MIRA, M.: Results of a behavior modification training program for parents and teachers. *Behav. Res. and Ther.*, 5, 1967.

O'LEARY, K. D., O'LEARY, S., and BECKER, W. C.: Modification of a deviant sibling interaction pattern in the home. *Behav. Res. and Ther.*, 5, 113-120, 1967.

QUIGLEY, S. P., and FRISINA, R.: *Institutionalization and Psycho-Educational Development of Deaf Children*. Council for Exceptional Children Research Monograph, Series A, Number 3, 1961.

RAINER, J. D., and ALTSHULER, K. Z. (Eds.): *Psychiatry and the Deaf*. Social and Rehabilitation Service, Health, Education and Welfare, Washington, D. C., 1967.

SCHLESINGER, H., and MEADOW, K.: *Sound and Sign: Childhood Deafness and Mental Health*. Berkeley, Cal.: U. of California Press, 1972.

SIMMONS-MARTIN, A.: Facilitating parent-child interactions. In: David Lillie (Ed.), *Parent Programs*. Chapel Hill, N. C.: First Chance Network, 1972.

STEVENSON, E. A.: A study of the educational achievement of deaf children of deaf parents. *California News*, 80, 1964.

STUCKLESS, E. R., and BIRCH, J. W.: The influence of early manual communication on the linguistic development of deaf children. *Amer. Annals of the Deaf*, III, 452-460; 499-504, 1966.

VERNON, M., and KOH, S. D.: Early manual communication and the deaf children's achievement. *Amer. Annals of the Deaf*, 115, 527-536, 1970.

WAHLER, R. G., and ERIKSON, M.: Child behavior therapy: A community program in Appalachia. *Behav. Res. and Ther.*, 7, 71-78, 1969.

INDEX